Yesterday's Deterrent

Rear-Admiral Alfred von Tirpitz (1849–1930) in 1900

YESTERDAY'S *DETERRENT*

Tirpitz and the Birth of the German Battle Fleet

---

by *JONATHAN STEINBERG*

Fellow of Christ's College, Cambridge

Foreword by COMMANDER SAUNDERS

THE MACMILLAN COMPANY : NEW YORK

Library of Congress Catalog Card Number: 66-27011

The Macmillan Company, New York

Printed in the United States of America

Foreword

By Commander M. G. SAUNDERS, R.N.

When Mr. Jonathan Steinberg asked me to write a foreword to his study of the origins of German sea power, I felt that the reader would like to know something of the history of the naval archives that have provided the author with so many valuable sources.

The Anglo-American haul of captured German documents brought to England at the end of the Second World War included the comprehensive archives of the German Navy, covering a period from before the Franco-Prussian War up to the end of the Hitler era. As a member of the British Admiralty's Historical Section it fell to me to supervise the exploitation of the documents relating to the Third Reich, and I also became familiar with the earlier archives covering the development of the Imperial Navy under Kaiser Wilhelm II. By virtue of their range and completeness these earlier records constituted a unique primary historical source, for it was evident that they had never been fully explored—not even by the handful of German historians who in the past had gained limited access to them.

In 1959 these older documents were returned to the Federal German authorities, but not until they had been selectively microfilmed in the Admiralty on behalf of Cambridge University and the University of Michigan. While Mr. Steinberg has drawn on many other published and unpublished German sources, he is, I believe, the first scholar to have systematically explored these valuable microfilms for his penetrating analysis of Tirpitz's part in creating the German battle fleet.

That the German naval archives ever survived the Second World War is little short of miraculous. On two occasions they narrowly escaped complete destruction. By November 1943, it was considered too risky to leave them in their normal stowage on the top floor of the Admiralty building in the Bülow Strasse in Berlin. The entire collection, weighing hundreds of tons, was loaded into a number of road trucks destined for a castle in Bavaria. On the very next night—22nd November—the building which had housed them was completely gutted during the first major incendiary bomber raid on the German capital, while the trucks containing the archives were still parked under the trees in the Grünewald. The convoy of vehicles duly proceeded south and arrived safely at Schloss Tambach, a large seventeenth century castle near Coburg. The archives were set up in the cellars of the castle, while the retired admirals continued their historical labours in its spacious rooms, far from the turmoil of war.

When the advance of the American forces threatened Coburg in April 1945, plans had already been made to destroy the archives to prevent their capture. The rapid elimination of a vast quantity of documents is no easy task, and the preparations for this eventuality were made with true German thoroughness. The grounds of the castle contained a large swimming-pool, which was kept dry. Should the military situation become desperate, the archives would be thrown into the pool, liberally interspersed with logs and long spars, and the whole would be drenched in petrol and set alight. Meanwhile, however, normal work continued, and the logs and petrol intended for the conflagration were kept in the vaults of the castle, ready for any emergency.

These arrangements were made in the autumn of 1944. But the depressing final winter of the war proved a severe trial to the elderly historians in their poorly heated rooms. Needing warmth and some relaxation, they gradually used up the logs to keep the fires going, and the petrol to supplement the meagre ration for motor transport. Why, for that matter, should the historians be a party to the destruction of documents that were essential to their own livelihood? By the time the Allied Forces reached Tambach, the fuel intended for the great blaze had been expended on more human needs, and most of the occupants had withdrawn to safer localities. Once again the Tambach archives—as they were now called—had escaped. Again they were loaded into trucks, but this time the transport was

American and the destination London. This was one of the few valuable prizes in a war that ultimately left the victors almost as empty-handed as the vanquished.

Finally the reader will perhaps bear with me if I mention a second and more personal reason for welcoming Mr. Steinberg's book. My father, who died in 1922, had been Berlin Correspondent of *The Times* from 1897 until 1908, and his dispatches, as printed in that newspaper, often reminded its readers of the motives underlying German naval ambitions, and of the Anglophobia that pervaded the German Press, particularly at the time of the first Fleet Law. These early warnings were not always well received in England, where the government of the day, being anxious to maintain friendly relations with Germany because of the supposedly greater threat from Russia, preferred to dismiss the evidence of German equivocation. Nor did the dispatches from Berlin endear their author to the Kaiser and his entourage.[1]

Shortly after the Second World War, while delving among the archives of the German Imperial Naval Cabinet (then housed in the basement of the Admiralty in London), I discovered a file of old press cuttings from *The Times*. These were the very reports that my father had sent from Berlin. Several cuttings had pencilled marginalia in the form of epigrammatic comments, some in English, others in German, but all in the unmistakable hand of the All-Highest himself. The wheel had come full circle! And for me it is both gratifying and illuminating to find in Mr. Steinberg's work such convincing corroboration of those parental forebodings in the fateful years when Imperial Germany first aspired to rank as a sea power.

[1] Fuller details will be found in *The History of the Times*, Vol. 3, Chapters XI and XII (London, 1947).

Preface

Mr. F. H. Hinsley of St. John's College, Cambridge, first became my supervisor during a year which I spent in Cambridge as a visiting American nearly eight years ago. When I returned to academic life in 1961, he became my supervisor again. His guidance, criticism and generosity with his time went well beyond the call of duty, and I am happy to be able to thank him now. I am grateful to the directors of the J. M. Kaplan Fund, Inc., New York City, for their grant to St. John's College during the first two years of research on this project, and for their subsequent grant to Christ's College, Cambridge, for the continuance of the work.

My debt to Commander M. G. Saunders, R.N., until recently Head of the Foreign Documents Section in the Naval Historical Branch of the Ministry of Defence (formerly the Historical Section of the Admiralty), is two-fold. Without his imagination and devotion to scholarship there would have been no naval archive for me to study, and without his criticism of the manuscript this book would have been poorer. I am very grateful to the Master and Fellows of Christ's College, Cambridge, for electing me to a Research Fellowship. Their kindness made the final year of work on this book extremely pleasant. Mr. W. J. Taylor-Whitehead of Macdonald & Co., Ltd., has been the ideal publisher and also a good friend. I am extremely grateful to him for his patience and his readiness to help me in every way possible. Mr. J. C. G. Röhl of the University of Sussex has given me much valuable material and that special encouragement which can only come from a colleague in the same field. Herr Kurt Bertram of the *Bundesarchiv*, Koblenz, made my visit to the institution a useful and exciting experience. I am grateful to him and to the Director and Staff of the Military Archive Department of the *Bundesarchiv* for their assistance and kind permission to reproduce several of the illustrations in this book. I want to thank Mr. E. J. Gillingham, Sub-Librarian of the Seeley Historical Library, Cambridge, for his patience and consideration during my long months in the microfilm room. I am glad to acknowledge the kind permission of the Ministry of Defence to make free use of the documents in the captured German Naval Archive. The head of the Documentary Section of the *Militärgeschlichtliches Forschungsamt* in Freiburg im Breisgau and his staff were very helpful, and I am especially grateful to Dr. Hansjoseph Maierhöfer, the *Marinereferent*, for his thoughtful and practical assistance. I want to thank the following publishers for permission to quote passages from the following books: Droste Verlag, for permission to quote from "Friedrich Naumann—Grundlagen und Ansatz seiner Politik in der nationalsozialen Zeit", an article by Werner Conze in *Schicksalswege deutscher Vergangenheit* (1950); Deutsche Verlagsanstalt, for permission to quote from *Denkwürdigkeiten der Reichskanzlerzeit* by Chlodwig Fürst zu Hohenlohe-Schillingsfürst, edited by K. A. von Müller (1931); Matthiesen Verlag, for permission to quote from "Schlachtflottenbau und Parteipolitik" by Eckart Kehr, from *Historische Studien*, cxcvii (1930); Eugen Rentsch Verlag, for permission to quote from *Das persönliche Regiment Wilhelms II* by Erich Eyck (1948); W. Kohlhammer Verlag, for permission to quote from *Der Weg zum deutschen Schlachtflottenbau* by Hans Hallmann (1933); K. F. Koehler Verlag, for permission to quote from *Erinnerungen* by Alfred von Tirpitz (1920); and Cambridge University Press, for permission to quote from *The Holstein Papers, The Memoirs, Diaries and Correspondence of Friedrich von Holstein*, edited in four volumes by Norman Rich and M. H. Fisher (1955–1963).

Note On Documentary Sources and Abbreviations

Three collections of documents provided most of the primary source material for this study. The main collection consisted of microfilms of certain sections of the official German Naval Archives, which were taken in custody by the Admiralty in London after the end of the Second World War. At the suggestion of Commander M. G. Saunders, R.N., and by permission of the Admiralty, the University of Cambridge and the University of Michigan undertook to microfilm some of the original documents. Filming began in 1956 under the direction of F. H. Hinsley of Cambridge and H. M. Ehrmann of Michigan. 111 reels of microfilm have been made, covering documents from the files of the Imperial Naval Cabinet, 1888 to 1918, the Admiralty Staff of the Navy, Sections A and B, and the Imperial Naval Office. An additional project, consisting of twenty-two reels of microfilm, was carried out by the University of Michigan and covers documents relating to a later period of German history. Filming was completed in July 1959, and copies of all 133 reels were given to the Public Record Office in London. Cambridge University has positive copies of the 111 reels of the Cambridge-Michigan programme in the Seeley Historical Library.

The second set of documents belongs to the West German *Bundesarchiv* in Koblenz. In particular the "Senden Nachlass", a collection of personal letters received by Admiral Freiherr von Senden Bibran and a series of private memoranda and notes in his own hand, has been of great value. Occasional pieces of correspondence from other collections in the *Bundesarchiv* are also cited.

The third collection is that portion of the original German Naval Archives, which has been returned to the German authorities. The *Militärgeschichtliches Forschungsamt* in Freiburg has custody of these documents at present, and I was able to look at certain files, which were not filmed during the Cambridge-Michigan joint project.

The abbreviations listed below have been selected to correspond with the sub-divisions of the catalogue of the microfilms of the German Naval Archive and with the official designations of the documentary collections in the *Bundesarchiv* and the *Militärgeschichtliches Forschungsamt.* The letters or numbers which follow the main abbreviations are, in the case of official documents, those of the archivist of the original naval bureau or department. In some cases, the initial archivist added a title to the file, and where that is the case I have used that designation, e.g. "MK. I.f.1. *Flottengesetz*".

MK	Files of the *Marinekabinett* (Imperial Naval Cabinet)
ADMA	Files of the *Admiralstab der Marine, Abteilung A* (Admiralty Staff of the Navy, Section A)
ADMB	Files of the *Admiralstab der Marine, Abteilung B* (Admiralty Staff of the Navy, Section B)
RMA	Files of the *Reichsmarine-Amt* (Imperial Naval Office)
BA K	*Bundesarchiv-Militärarchiv, Kriegsmarine*
MGFA DZ	Documentary Section. *Militärgeschichtliches Forschungsamt*

The one significant published collection of documents which I have used is the selection of material from the German Foreign Ministry, officially made during the 1920's. It is abbreviated:

GP	*Die Grosse Politik der Europäischen Kabinette,* 1871-1914, *Sammlung der diplomatischen Akten des Auswärtigen Amtes,* edited by Johannes Lepsius, Albrecht Mendelssohn-Bartholdy, Friedrich Thimme, Berlin, 1923 and after.

Jonathan Steinberg
Cambridge, 1964

Contents

FOREWORD *page* 5
PREFACE 9
NOTES ON DOCUMENTARY SOURCES AND ABBREVIATIONS 11
INTRODUCTION: GERMANY AND THE NAVAL ARMS RACE 17
1. THE GERMAN NAVY, THE GERMAN NATION AND THE GERMAN STRUCTURE OF GOVERNMENT 31
   A. The Navy, The Nation and Nationalism 31
   B. The Navy, The Middle Class and Liberalism 36
   C. The Navy and the Constitution of the Empire 46
   D. The Navy and Social and Economic Change 56
   E. Conclusion 59
2. TIRPITZ'S FIRST CAMPAIGN FOR OFFICE 61
3. THE FALL OF HOLLMANN AND TIRPITZ'S APPOINTMENT 97
4. A NAVY AGAINST ENGLAND 125
5. THE NAVY LAW IN THE REICHSTAG 149
   A. The Final Preparations 149
   B. The First Reading of the Navy Law 163
   C. The Navy Law in the Committee Stage 174
   D. The Passage of the Navy Law 193
CONCLUSION 201
APPENDIX: The Tirpitz Memorandum of June 1897 208
BIBLIOGRAPHY 225
INDEX 229

List of Plates

	Rear-Admiral von Tirpitz in 1900	*frontispiece*
1.	Sketch for a cruiser III class	*facing page* 31
2.	S.M.S. *Kaiserin Augusta*	32
3.	S.M.S. *König Wilhelm*	32
4.	A session of the German Reichstag in 1890	33
5.	Kaiser Wilhelm II and his family, 1896	48
6.	Gustav von Schmoller	48
7.	S.M.S. *Hagen*	49
8.	S.M.S. *Kaiser Friedrich III*	49
9.	Albrecht von Stosch	64
10.	Alfred Tirpitz as a *Korvetten-Kapitän* in 1884	64
11.	Sketch for a battleship	65
12.	Table of ships built in Germany after 1893	80
13.	S.M.S. *Kurfürst Friedrich Wilhelm*	81
14.	S.M.S. *Brandenburg*	81
15.	Prince Heinrich of Prussia	96
16.	Prince Chlodwig von Hohenlohe-Schillingsfürst	96
17.	Landing manoeuvres at Wittdün in 1901	97
18.	S.M.S. *Baden*	97
19.	S.M.S. *Wörth*	112
20.	S.M.S. *Gefion*	112
21.	Tirpitz as a Grand Admiral in 1911	113
22.	Admiral Otto von Diederichs	113
23.	Autographed portrait of Tirpitz as a Grand Admiral	113
24.	South wing of the Schillingsfürst Palace	128
25.	Admiral von Tirpitz in his office	128
26.	Eugen Richter	129
27.	Cartoon of Eugen Richter German	129

28. The *Bundesrat* (Federal Council) of the German Empire in 1900 *facing page* 144
29. August Bebel and Paul Singer 144
30. Ships of the High Seas Battle Fleet at anchor, 1899 145
31. Fleet manoeuvres, 1907 145
32. Cartoon showing Tirpitz, Hohenlohe and Admiral von Senden Bibran 206

The publishers would like to thank the following who have supplied photographs used in the book: Ullstein Bilderdienst, for the frontispiece and 4, 5, 6, 15, 16, 17, 21, 22, 23, 26, 27, 28, 29, 30, 31; the Bundesarchiv, for 1, 7, 8, 11, 12, 13, 19, 32; the Imperial War Museum, for 2, 3, 14, 18, 20; and Belser Verlag, for 9, 10, 24, 25, taken from their book *Tirpitz* by Ulrich von Hassel.

INTRODUCTION

Germany and the Naval Arms Race

During the second half of the nineteenth century, those nations able to build a fleet of heavy, protected warships, driven by coal-burning engines, came into possession of a new, mobile and astoundingly effective instrument of power. For the first time in human history ships were no longer dependent on wind and weather. Nations in Europe could exert force in remote parts of the world with far greater accuracy and reliability than ever before. By the end of the century, the great steel ships with their huge guns had grown into floating fortresses. "Showing the flag" and paying courtesy calls became as much a part of a naval commander's duty as were his tactical manoeuvres and exercises. The gunboat and the battle fleet joined the more traditional devices of diplomacy, and the possession of a presentable fleet became the hall-mark of international respectability.

These developments took place during a period when the disparity between the developed and under-developed societies of the world was widening dangerously, and they accentuated the relative inequalities of power in the world by binding it more closely together. The latent disparity became stridently manifest when European guns boomed off the China coast or cruisers anchored in African river deltas. Among the developed nations, inequalities of power and differing rates of economic and industrial growth were also becoming obvious. "As a result of the combination of these two developments there existed during the first half of the twentieth century a greater inequality of effective power between all the world's different areas and states, a greater political disequilibrium on a wider scale, than men had perhaps ever to contend with."[1]

Within this context of world-wide disequilibrium, the Anglo-

[1] F. H. Hinsley, *Power and the Pursuit of Peace*, Cambridge, 1963, p. 218.

German naval arms race has a special place. Although it reflected the broad developments in the changing situation and distribution of power in the world, it had certain specific features of its own. It was part of what can only be described as the struggle for hegemony in Europe. By the 1890s Germany's colossal industrial and economic expansion had begun to burst the framework of the continental balance of power. By comparison with her neighbours, Germany was rapidly becoming a European super-power and by 1900 she "approached a degree of material primacy in Europe which no power had possessed since 1815—but did so at a time when her power beyond Europe was negligible and when the prospects of enlarging it there were rapidly diminishing."[2] Germany's growth would, perhaps, have provoked the traditional British reluctance to permit the continent to be dominated by a single power in any case, but the decision to build a first-class fleet made British rivalry and resistance a certainty. The first German Navy Law of 1898 was the point of no return in this process, although nobody in Britain and scarcely a handful of men in Germany realized it.

The decision to give Germany a first-class fleet was not the only reason for introducing the Navy Law of 1898. That decision by itself was neither unreasonable nor unjustified. In the context of the period, it was probably inevitable. All the other powers were building furiously, and British naval supremacy was equally threatened every time a keel was laid by any one of them. But in one significant respect, the character of the German Navy Law was different. It alone challenged British hegemony directly and it did so by calling for a powerful fleet of battleships to be stationed in the North Sea. The Navy Law, or *Flottengesetz*, of 1898 had a distinct anti-British bias. In his first audience with Kaiser Wilhelm II on June 15, 1897, Admiral Tirpitz, its creator, made that quite clear. The object of the German battle-fleet was to give Germany a measure of naval power against Great Britain.[3] When he submitted his memorandum, he was well aware that the Kaiser's most influential adviser, Admiral Gustav Freiherr von Senden Bibran, had long been convinced that Great Britain was the real enemy

[2] *Ibid.*, p. 301.

[3] See Appendix: *Allgemeine Gesichtspunkte bei der Feststellung unserer Flottenstärke nach Schiffsklassen und -typen*, June, 1897. This memo, marked "very secret", was found

Continued on page 19

against whom Germany must prepare, and that the Kaiser himself now accepted such a view.[4]

Satisfying the Kaiser and the Admirals was one thing, and getting a bill through the Reichstag was another. Tirpitz knew that he was taking on a demanding task. He would have to alter the entire direction of Germany's previous naval programme and substitute battleships for the cruisers demanded by his predecessor. But even the cruiser programme had not been popular. In March of 1896 Tirpitz, watching the struggle in the Reichstag, wrote angrily to Admiral Senden, the Kaiser's Naval Cabinet chief, "Our representation in the Reichstag and the whole situation could hardly be more unfortunate. The State Secretary of the Foreign Ministry represents the Navy, blows a fanfare for cruisers and shoots at sparrows with his biggest guns. What sort of powder will impress the Reichstag later when the really serious demands are made? The State Secretary of the Imperial Naval Office beats himself on the breast and says, 'As long as I stand here, no boundless plans (i.e., no battleships) will be proposed.' Then in April the wicked uncle comes. . . . That's the situation and you will be in the best position to know whether it would not be better to let the present State Secretary stay in office for a few more years."[5]

That Tirpitz was not happy about being "the wicked uncle" was understandable. His fears for the future were soon confirmed. In March of 1897, Admiral Hollmann, the State Secretary of the Imperial Naval Office, suffered a crushing defeat in the Reichstag and lost his job in disgrace. The conflict over naval

Continued from page 18
in the files of the Imperial Naval Cabinet, MK.I.f.1, "Flottengesetz". All comments had been erased on the cover and it may well have been intended for destruction. By mistake it appears to have been caught up among handwritten drafts of the White Paper, which was submitted with the Draft Bill of the Navy Law in November, 1897, possibly because of the similarity of the handwriting of the various documents. This memo was first mentioned by Bernhard Michalik ("Probleme des deutschen Flottenbaus", a published dissertation, Breslau, 1931). The Kaiser also discussed his ideas about a plan for an invasion of England (see Chapter Four, Note 16, p. 129, and my article, "A German Plan for the Invasion of Holland and Belgium, 1897", *The Historical Journal*, Cambridge, 1963, Volume Six, Number One). Tirpitz had no use for such nonsense. He meant business.

[4] For Senden's attitude toward England, see his interesting letter to Vice-Admiral Valois, Chapter Four, Note 10, p. 127.

[5] Tirpitz to Senden, Letter of March 20, 1896, BA K 08-7/1, "Senden Nachlass".

expansion became so bitter that well-informed insiders, including the Chancellor, Prince Hohenlohe, were afraid of a constitutional crisis, possibly even of a *coup d'état*. In April of 1897, Baron Holstein, the grey eminence of the Foreign Ministry, wrote to his friend Paul von Hatzfeldt, German Ambassador in London: "With the Kaiser, the Navy Question now takes precedence over everything. Senden is said to dominate him completely. After the negative attitude of the Reichstag—which after all granted 58 out of the 70 million that were demanded—His Majesty refuses to send ships anywhere . . . The internal situation is very depressing. The Kaiser wants a fleet like that of England—with 28 first-class battleships—and wants to direct his whole domestic policy to that end, i.e., to a fight."[6]

Despite the obstacles, the "wicked uncle" managed to get his law through the Reichstag during the following year without a *coup d'état* and without a serious fight. He concealed the real purpose of the Navy Law during the debates in order to avoid unnecessary opposition, and he continued to do so until his hand was forced in the struggle over the second Navy Law, the *Flottengesetz* of 1900. He succeeded when almost anyone would have predicted failure. Admiral Tirpitz was a consummate politician. His Bill had the clarity and economy which earlier naval plans lacked because he had a fully developed theory of power. It enabled him to construct a Bill which was small in its demands and yet absolutely resolute in its underlying purpose. This theory was the famous "risk theory". In essence it was a shrewd and subtle attempt, the first of its kind, to use the potentialities of a new instrument of force, the Navy, to achieve a diplomatic re-alignment. Tirpitz was the first modern strategist to see that an arms race can be used as a kind of lever to force other powers to move in a desired direction. "We require", he wrote in his first memorandum for the Kaiser, "a certain measure of naval power as a political factor against England."[7] The only way to get it was to build as many battleships as possible and to threaten England with a powerful German fleet

[6] Holstein to Paul von Hatzfeldt, April 14, 1897, *The Holstein Papers, The Memoirs, Diaries and Correspondence of Friedrich von Holstein*, ed. by Norman Rich and M. H. Fisher, Cambridge, 1955-63, Vol. IV, No. 610, p. 28.
[7] See Appendix, Paragraph 2, and Footnote 3, above (p. 18).

"between Heligoland and the Thames".[8] Such a fleet would, Tirpitz maintained, limit the risk to Germany of a sudden punitive attack by the English. The risk theory was both an offensive and a defensive strategy, a lever and a deterrent.

If the Navy were to serve as a political lever and military deterrent, it must be concentrated in Germany's home waters. A fleet in the North Sea threatened England directly and at the same time protected Germany's vulnerable naval bases. There was a paradox in the risk theory which Tirpitz was slow to see. By concentrating her fleet in home waters, Germany tempted Britain to destroy the fleet before it grew large enough to act as an effective political lever. German fears of a "Copenhagen" (that is, a repeat of Britain's punitive destruction of the Danish fleet in 1807) were self-confirming. By building a fleet to assert herself against the dominant naval power, Germany merely increased her own vulnerability to a sudden naval attack. The paradox in the risk theory produced a vicious circle in German defence policy. Every increase in the risk for England increased the risk to Germany.

After 1900 the lever against England began to work. The relentless pressures of the arms race forced England to shift her defences, but in exactly the opposite way to the one desired. Instead of propelling England in Germany's direction or attracting the Franco-Russian alliance into the German orbit, the expanding German Navy helped to push all the other powers together. The initial dilemma became more complex. When England gradually abandoned its traditional policy of isolation and eventually joined France in an effort to restrain German pressure, Tirpitz's strategy had done precisely what he believed it would not do. In place of the relatively minor risk of a "Copenhagen", Tirpitz's lever had introduced the fearful prospect of war on two fronts and against the major naval power at the same time.

The pressure on Britain mounted steadily, as Tirpitz had planned, but the ultimate objective retreated, always dancing just beyond his reach. The "danger zone", through which Germany's growing fleet would have to pass, lengthened with each additional battleship. The now familiar treadmill of the

[8] Appendix, Paragraph 4, and Alfred von Tirpitz, *Erinnerungen*, Leipzig, 1920, p. 80.

arms race turned faster and faster, and the gap between Britain and Germany narrowed slightly. German diplomacy gradually lost some of its freedom to manoeuvre as the fleet swelled in size, and something very like panic began to seize the civilian leadership of the Reich. There seemed to be no way out of the trap into which Tirpitz's building programme had spilled them. They began to blame the means which he had chosen. Diplomats, politicians and journalists ceased to praise and began to attack the inflexible Navy Laws which committed the Empire to a fixed expansion of its naval strength. They complained that the laws were imposing a dangerous rigidity on Germany's military growth. They blamed the means but refused to abandon the ends. Germany was the innocent victim of British envy and not of their determination to achieve equality on the seas with Great Britain. When British papers spoke of the "German menace", the Kaiser hotly denied such charges. "We challenge nobody!" he wrote in English on the margin of one such article in 1905. "It is British vainness (*sic!*) and overheated fancy that styles our building so."[9] The fact remained that it was impossible to accept the ultimate objectives of Tirpitz's building programme and to condemn the means by which he meant to accomplish them. When his former supporters, especially among the professors, began to turn against him, he remained unmoved. "There was no other way to world power except to build a fleet. The greatest achievements are never granted to a people for nothing."[10]

Some historians have failed to see this distinction between ends and means. They have argued that the choice of fixed navy legislation was by itself the cause of Germany's entanglement in the arms race, or, as Professor Hubatsch suggests, that technology had made itself independent and was running away with the men involved. "The Navy Laws like the Schlieffen Plan and the clockwork mechanism of mobilization became independent of the necessarily flexible diplomatic and political influences."[11] This hypothesis has a certain attraction, especially for German

[9] Kaiser's handwritten marginal comments in English on an article in *The Navy and Military Record*, November 23, 1905, from the files of the Admiralty Staff (ADMA II. E.30).
[10] Tirpitz, *op. cit.*, p. 199.
[11] Walther Hubatsch, *Die Ära Tirpitz*, Gottingen, 1955, p. 83.

historians for whom the problem of the moral responsibility of Germany for the First World War has been such a torment, but it will not stand close examination. Machines are run by men. The Schlieffen Plan was consciously adopted and tenaciously adhered to. There was nothing automatic or inevitable about it. Under the elder Moltke, no such plan was ever adopted, and Bismarck said in 1887 that Germany would never begin a war with the violation of a European treaty.[12] By 1897, when the Schlieffen Plan was first formulated and the Schröder Plan to invade Belgium and Holland was being considered by the naval authorities, this was no longer true. A mixture of aggressive optimism and fearful pessimism began to move men to think up defensive strategies, which depended on violent, sudden attacks, violations of neutrality or risky adventures. Not even Moltke's famous refusal to call off the Schlieffen Plan on the night of August 1, 1914, can be blamed entirely on technology.[13] In the case of the Navy Laws, Professor Hubatsch's suggestion is even more misleading. The amendments to the *Flottengesetz* of 1898 were always conscious political decisions. There was nothing automatic or mechanical about them. Obviously the use of fixed naval laws gave the arms race a certain rigidity and posed very real problems for the diplomacy of the Empire, but technology as such cannot explain either the treadmill quality of the arms race, nor the bitter determination to carry on with it.

The argument that technology was an independent causal factor in the arms race is based on a fundamental confusion between strategy and tactics. The Tirpitz building programme was, as he himself put it, "applied strategy". The use of fixed Navy Laws were merely his tactics for out-manoeuvring the Reichstag and for assuring continuity in construction. Failure to see this has led some historians to see Tirpitz purely as a

[12] Gerhard Ritter, *Staatskunst und Kriegshandwerk*, Munich, 1954 and 1960, Vol. II, p. 243.

[13] Barbara W. Tuchman, *The Guns of August*, New York, 1962, p. 80. "When Moltke's 'It cannot be done' was revealed after the war in his memoirs, General von Staab, Chief of the Railway Division, was so incensed by what he considered a reproach upon his bureau, that he wrote a book to prove it could have been done. In pages of charts and graphs he demonstrated how, given notice on August 1, he could have deployed four out of the seven armies to the Eastern Front by August 15."

technician, a man obsessed by his own creation.[14] It has also distracted historians from studying the actual effects on international relations of the changes in technology themselves. Naval technology never became independent of the leadership, as Professor Hubatsch argues. What it did was to shift the lines of force and the relative positions of the great powers and thus to change the framework of diplomacy. The treadmill aspect of the Anglo-German arms race was not caused by technology but by the politics of the participants.

An entirely different interpretation of Tirpitz and the arms race is to be found in Gerhard Ritter's study of militarism in German society. Professor Ritter sees Tirpitz as the perfect example of his category, the militarist nature. He emphasizes the human and social elements of the problem to the exclusion of the strategic and technical. When he argues that "the well-known answer of the Imperial Naval Office—'Keep building until they have to come to us'—was the answer of the typical militarist", he misunderstands the very essence of the risk theory.[15] Tirpitz believed, and it was not an unreasonable belief, that in view of England's resources and attitudes she would surely prefer alliance with Germany either to financial ruin or to unpalatable agreements with her traditional enemies, France or Russia. "Keep building" was not fanatical militarism but a conscious strategy, conceived in advance and executed to perfection. By ignoring the rationality of Tirpitz's programme, however false its assumptions, Professor Ritter obscures rather than clarifies the issues of the Anglo-German arms race. The naval expansion was never more than a means to a political end: German hegemony of Europe and equality with Britain throughout the world. Professor Ritter's argument also ignores the domestic character of German "navalism". While the Navy

[14] An example of the typical cliché about Tirpitz can be found in a recent work by a group of German historians: "With him (Tirpitz) there came to power for the first time one of those men who have been created and distorted by the modern division of labour: the specialist, the technical expert . . ." (Wilhelm Schüssler, "Deutsche Weltpolitik 1890 bis 1914", in *Weltmachtstreben und Flottenbau*, ed. by W. Schüssler, Witten/Ruhr, 1956, p. 22). Professor Schüssler goes on to deny that Tirpitz had any interest in other than technical matters: "An deutschen Geist und deutscher Kultur wird kein Gedanke verschwendet." (*Ibid.*, p. 23.) This is a gross distortion of the personality of Tirpitz, as anyone who has read Tirpitz's own writings is forced to admit.

[15] Gerhard Ritter, *Staatskunst und Kriegshandwerk*, II, p. 201.

expanded to the enthusiastic applause of the prosperous middle classes, the Army's leaders peered out from their reactionary bastions at social changes which they were simply unable to understand or accept. Even after the war, the generals could not grasp that the failure of the Army to get sufficient funds from the Reichstag lay with its own inept leadership, not in Tirpitz's ruthlessness or in the Navy's greed, "which ate up all the funds".[16] Militarism must be defined far more subtly than Professor Ritter does, if the difference between Army and Navy is to be understood.

Both Professor Ritter and Professor Hubatsch overshoot the mark. Neither can explain why German society so willingly accepted the objectives of the Tirpitz programme and refused to abandon them even when the central paradox of the risk theory began to produce the wrong results. Even if technology had a life of its own or Tirpitz had been a pure technocrat or nothing but a militarist, that society had the power to alter his plans. There was a Reichstag which could have protested. It was elected by universal suffrage and was by comparison with the other parliaments of its day unquestionably one of the most representative. It voted on major pieces of Tirpitz's programme no less than five times between 1898 and 1914, and each time gave him virtually everything he wanted. There was a vigorous Press and an influential academic community. There was a civilian administration and there were the numerous parliaments in each of the constituent states of the Empire. A concerted resistance to the naval building programme from any one of these groups would have forced Tirpitz very quickly to modify his demands. There was no such resistance until the threat of war lay across the land, and even then the resistance was merely directed at the government which had bungled its diplomatic task rather than at the naval administration which had made that task so hard.

If it is useless to seek impersonal trends or automatic forces in the causes of the Anglo-German arms race, it is equally useless to seek historical scapegoats. The individuals who made the decisions belonged to their age and nation and their acts can only be understood in that context. This truism is all too often

[16] General K. von Einem, "Fürst Bülow und das deutsche Heer", in F. Thimme, *Front wider Bülow*, Munich, 1931, p. 155.

forgotten where Kaiser Wilhelm II is concerned. The Kaiser was admittedly one of those strange figures in history whose personalities have had more effect on the course of affairs than their deeds. He evidently generated a peculiar excitement in those around him and his lightning changes of disposition were like the flickering brilliance of a powerful electric storm. Historians have disagreed violently on the role which the Kaiser actually played. Erich Brandenburg believed that "on the whole Wilhelm II never really had permanent control, but by his sudden interventions caused confusion."[17] Others, like Erich Eyck, have seen the "personal regime" of Wilhelm II as *the* great evil of the post-Bismarckian Reich.[18]

On one point his contemporaries were entirely in agreement. From the beginning, the Kaiser was an important factor in Germany's growth as a sea-power. Holstein wrote that the plan to create a Navy equal to Britain's and the inability to brook opposition were "the two principles to which the Kaiser remained true throughout his reign."[19] The Kaiser's naval preoccupation was neither irrational nor foolish. There is no evidence whatever that his contemporaries regarded him as a freak or as a man impossible to deal with. They complained about his idiosyncrasies, his impulsiveness and his lack of good sense, but they saw those traits in the perspective which historians have too often ignored.

When the Kaiser pleaded for a large Navy, he was merely following an international fashion, however bombastically he chose to phrase his pleas. Marine technology naturally occupied his thoughts because it was one of the most dramatic frontiers of progress in the applied sciences. While Europe's armies were in many respects less flexible and mobile than they had been before the introduction of heavy ordnance, the navies were improving the speed, fire-power, efficiency and tactical usefulness of their ships at an incredible rate. As Sidney Low remarked in 1898, "the pestilent activity of the modern military and naval inventor is simply a cosmopolitan nuisance . . . it seems a pity that an international convention cannot be

[17] Erich Brandenburg, *Vom Bismarck zum Weltkriege*, Berlin, 1924, p. 18.
[18] Erich Eyck, *Das persönliche Regiment Wilhelms II*, Erlangen/Zurich, 1948.
[19] *The Holstein Papers*, Vol. 1, p. 174. See also William L. Langer, *The Diplomacy of Imperialism*, New York, 1935, Vol. II, pp. 428 ff.

arranged, whereby any individual proposing a new machine or device for warlike purposes should be immediately taken out and hanged."[20] The Kaiser was not the cause of the nuisance, although he might well have been high on Low's list of candidates for the noose. The fact was that Germany had to keep up with the latest naval developments if she were to remain a great power. How she kept up was not quite so clear. After all, the modern navy was still an experiment. No one knew with certainty whether the new designs and the new theories of attack and defence would work in practice. That the Kaiser demanded a Navy was inevitable; that the Navy should be chiefly directed against Great Britain was not.[21]

The changes in technology, the ominous disequilibrium in effective power throughout the world, the explosive growth of German power in Europe and the personalities of the individuals who faced these problems were all very real and important factors in the arms race, but they do not explain it. There were many possible responses to the set of difficulties besetting Germany in the 1890s. Why did her leaders choose Tirpitz's battle fleet? Why was that battle fleet directed mainly against Great Britain? Because Germans had come to want what Britain had and to believe that they could have it. Britain only became the enemy when men like Admiral Tirpitz and Admiral Senden demanded that Germany achieve the same position of power in the world which she had already begun to approach in Europe. Britain became the enemy when a great many Germans began to see her as the main obstacle to German greatness. Finally, Britain became the enemy because Germany's leaders accepted the view that two great trading nations could not co-exist and that German growth must lead to a struggle for survival between them.

Although these views became prevalent only in the period after the fall of Bismarck, they had roots which went deep into Germany's social and intellectual history. I believe that they became dominant in the 1890s because of the very nature of the

[20] A. J. Marder, *The Anatomy of British Sea Power, British Naval Policy, 1880–1905*, London, 1940, p. 8.

[21] "It must be emphasised again and again," Vice-Admiral von Mantey wrote to the historian, Hans Hallmann, in 1932, "that the Kaiser constantly stirred the flames of naval enthusiasm among the people and within the Navy itself. What was forged and took shape in those flames was a matter for the experts, the admirals . . ." (MGFA-DZ: III M 503/1 (7741), March 24, 1932).

German nation-state and that they found expression in Tirpitz's Navy because of its special position in that state. The strategy which led to the arms race falls into place once the relationship between the Navy and the nation is revealed. The Navy, the risk theory and the arms race become part of the social and intellectual history of the Reich as well as of its political history. They were not merely accidental manifestations of certain external trends. When the individual characteristics of German society in the nineteenth century are placed together with the military and diplomatic activity of the Reich, when the Navy takes its place in the struggle for German unification and nationhood, when the risk theory rejoins the intellectual traditions from which it emerged, an account of the arms race springs to life, which seems to me to make sense of Germany's part in that historical tragedy. It becomes increasingly clear that the one truly national institution in the unstable and unfinished German Empire was the very same institution at the heart of the struggle with Britain. Germany's diplomatic isolation is seen to be a consequence not of the blunders of her leadership but of the substance of her aspirations.

An arms race is, after all, an immense social, political, legal and economic process. Its influences penetrate every corner of the societies involved, and its attendant manifestations are simply too complex to fit the standard categories of historical analysis. Even if the subject of study is only one of the participants in such a race, as is the case here, the number of elements in that nation's social, cultural, economic and religious traditions which significantly affect the course of the arms race is very large. Without, for example, an understanding of German *Kultur*, the very words of Tirpitz's risk theory will be meaningless. Words like *Deutschtum*, *Weltgeltung*, *Weltmacht* and *Volk* were as important in the growth of the German Navy as Tirpitz's strategy. To take another example, unless the Navy is placed in the perspective of the struggle for national unification, we cannot understand why it could grow so rapidly after 1898. Thirdly, unless we distinguish between the social classes in Germany, we cannot explain the Navy's popularity and the Army's unpopularity. The fact that the Navy was middle class, liberal, nationalist and commercial, helps us to see why its fundamental strategy was aggressive and anti-British.

The embodiment of these domestic characteristics and aspirations in the Navy led to an arms race with Great Britain. The arms race did not just happen, nor was it the result of the machinations of evil men. It began as a product of a particular society, a representative, external manifestation of the internal dynamics which made that society a disturbing factor in the broader context of international relations in the period before the First World War. To say this is not to condemn Germany as such nor to deny that Great Britain was also responsible for the relentless acceleration of the naval struggle.[22] All that it implies is that the decision to introduce the *Flottengesetz* of 1898 created new tensions in the international situation which had not been there before and that these tensions were consciously accepted by the German military and political leadership as part of the risks which lay across the path to German greatness. The idea that the Navy would be both a political lever with which Germany could force an improvement in her international situation and, at the same time, a deterrent was in itself not necessarily false or misguided. In the hands of the men of Wilhelmine Germany and in the context of that society as it faced the rest of the world, it led to a disaster from which the world has not yet recovered.

The Navy Law of 1898 was the first step in this process. With it, the course was set and the forces mobilized. Its passage in April of that year was without question the most important event in the domestic politics of Imperial Germany between the fall of Bismarck and the beginning of the twentieth century. In it, all the problems of that society came to the surface, and through it, they were projected onto the world scene. It marked a shift in the balance of international forces by which Europe had been kept in check since the Congress of Vienna. Its motto was the Kaiser's challenge: "Aus dem deutschen Reich ist ein Weltreich geworden" (The German Empire has become a world empire).

[22] In 1901, the German *Flottenverein* had 600,000 members and associates. The Navy League in Great Britain had 15,000 members and an annual expenditure of under £4,000. The colossal difference in scale of the two organizations underlines the contrast between the role of the Navy in the two societies. In Germany navalism was virtually a mass movement of its own. (Figures on the Navy League and *Flottenverein* from A. J. Marder, *op. cit.*, pp. 54 f.)

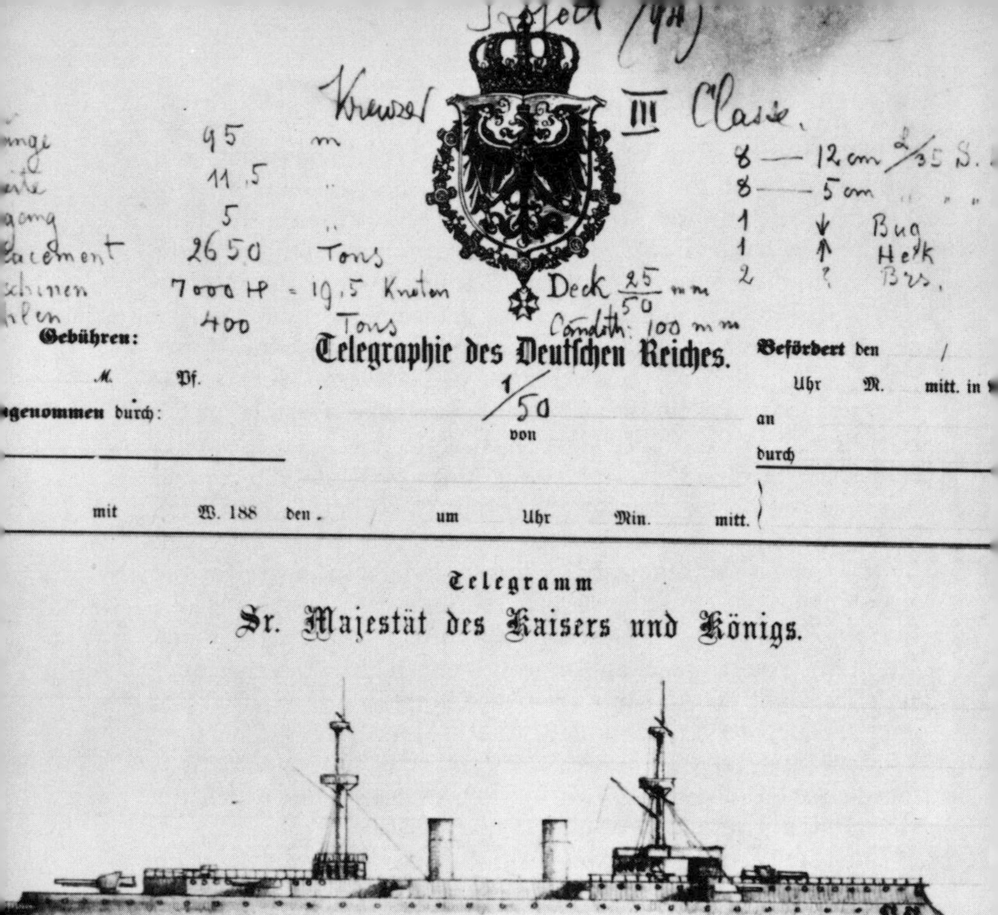

Kreuzer III Classe.

nge 95 m
ite 11.5 "
gang 5 "
acement 2650 Tons
chinen 7000 HP = 19.5 Knoten
hlen 400 Tons

8 — 12 cm L/35 S.
8 — 5 cm " "
1 ↓ Bug
1 ↑ Heck
2 ? Brs.

Deck 25/50 mm
Comdoth: 100 mm

Gebühren: M. Pf.

Telegraphie des Deutschen Reiches.

Befördert den / Uhr M. mitt. in

genommen durch:

1/50 von

an

durch

mit W. 188 den um Uhr Min. mitt.

Telegramm
Sr. Majestät des Kaisers und Königs.

Fjärland. 12/VII 94

V. 1

Sketch on a telegraph form for a cruiser III class, 2,650 tons, drawn and signed by Kaiser Wilhelm II in his own hand, July 12, 1894

1

The German Navy, The German Nation and The German Structure of Government

A. The Navy, The Nation and Nationalism

Without national unity, there could be no Navy in Germany. The simple facts of Germany's geography tied the fate of the Navy to that of the nation from the beginning of the unification movement. Before 1866, as indeed after 1945, the short northern coastal strip and the three main river basins were not controlled by one authority, and without such unified control German naval power had, and has, no real basis. Since geography had inescapably joined the German Navy and the German nation, the Navy naturally became entangled in the struggle for national identity. The rise and fall of the great *Schlachtflotte* is almost symbolic of the course of the German Empire itself. Now that Germany is once again divided, it is, perhaps, easier to see this relationship than in the days when a German nation-state was the obvious, self-evident and only form of government for the area. As early as 1919, Walther Rathenau speculated about the future of the united Germany: "If Germany explodes—and it is being consumed and strained in every way—the rage of our enemies will be stilled. A comfortable Confederation of the Rhine on a large scale stretching from Lake Constance to Hanover will be carefully constructed, and the nest of all evil, the Republic of Brandenburg, will be pushed out, outside of all German connections and the human community, a land of the Wends, which will be permitted either to return to savagery or to be ruled in the manner of Bela Kun."[1]

[1] Walther Rathenau, *Autonome Wirtschaft*, Jena, 1919, p. 4.

That this prophecy should be today's reality suggests that there was an inherent weakness in the German state from the beginning. The pomp and splendour of Bismarck's Reich concealed what has been rightly called an "inner fragility".[2] A nation had to be created late in the nineteenth century, where there had never been one before, out of elements with little in common, in a continent already delicately balanced and bursting with new forces. It is not surprising that the politics of the Empire of 1871 "had certain characteristics of an 'imperfect national state' and out of the awareness of this incompleteness many of its hasty decisions and inner tensions arose".[3] Bismarck, its creator, knew this only too well. His attitude is beautifully summed up in a letter to his wife written on October 20, 1870: "Tomorrow the South German Ministers are coming to debate the new 'Thousand Year Reich'."[4] His ironic contempt for his great work is, perhaps, its most perfect epitaph.

Within Bismarck's Empire, the Navy had a special position. Since it had not existed prior to 1871, it had to become an Imperial institution, and according to Article 53 of the Reich constitution, the Navy was explicitly stated to be an institution of the "Reich . . . under the supreme command of the Kaiser".[5] This made it unique in a country where even the postal, customs and railroad services were not national.[6] There was no German army, because the individual sovereigns retained certain powers over their own troops. According to the Versailles Treaty of Alliance of 1870, for example, "the Bavarian Army form(ed) an entirely separate component within the German federal army with an independent administration under the military sovereignty of His Majesty, the King of

[2] Theodor Schieder, *Das Deutsche Kaiserreich von 1871 als Nationalstaat*, Cologne and Opladen, 1961, p. 53.

[3] *Ibid.*, p. 39.

[4] Werner Richter, *Bismarck*, Frankfurt/Main, 1962, p. 236. English translation published by Macdonald, 1964.

[5] See p. 50 for the constitutional position of the Navy in detail.

[6] J. A. R. Marriott and C. G. Robertson, *The Evolution of Prussia*, Oxford, 1937, pp. 370 ff., contains a complete account of the so-called "Sonderrechte", or special rights, enjoyed by Bavaria, Saxony, Württemberg and Baden. The existence of individual sovereignties produced what a friend of Hohenlohe's called "Eisenbahn-Anarchie" on the railroads. Cf. Völderndorff to Hohenlohe, August 1899, in Prince Chlodwig zu Hohenlohe-Schillingsfürst, *Denkwürdigkeiten der Reichskanzlerzeit*, ed. by K. A. von Müller, Stuttgart/Berlin, 1931, p. 514.

S.M.S. "Kaiserin Augusta", cruiser II class, 1895, port broadside view, at anchor

S.M.S. "König Wilhelm", battleship II class (converted to cruiser), 1897, port broadside view, at anchor

A session of the German Reichstag in 1890: (1) Windthorst, leader of the Catholic Centre Party; (2) Richter, leader of the Radical Party; (3) Bennigsen, leader of the National Liberal Party; (4) Auer, prominent Social Democrat; (5) Bebel, leader of the Social Democratic Party; (6) von Vollmar, prominent Bavarian Social Democrat; (7) Singer, textile manufacturer turned Social Democrat; (8) Liebknecht, Social Democratic member of the Reichstag and editor of the Party's paper,

Bavaria."[7] As a result there was no national oath of allegiance for every German soldier,[8] no official national anthem and no universally observed national holiday. There was no "Government" in official terminology, only "The Associated Governments". The attempt in the 1890s to introduce a German cockade for the uniforms of all the military contingents nearly produced a constitutional crisis.[9] By comparison, the Navy's organization was simple and straightforward. It was undeniably national and centralized.

National life in the German Empire was plagued by uncertainty and incompleteness throughout its history. A unitary, modern state never existed in Wilhelmine Germany and often seemed no more than a pipe-dream impossible to fulfil. The Reich, which Bismarck founded, was always a hybrid and unsatisfactory compromise. For a truly conservative and monarchically-minded man like Freiherr von Hodenberg, leader of the Hanoverians in the Reichstag, there was no Germany. "I have been repeatedly struck by the fact", he said, "that here in this House members of the Bundesrath, yes, the Chancellor himself, in entirely official statements, have been using the expression 'Germany' instead of 'The German Empire'. Gentlemen, we are not Germany!"[10] For the Prussian conservative, the term "Kaiser" was sheer romantic nonsense. The Hohenzollerns were "Kings of Prussia" and words like "Reich", "Nation" and "Deutschland" were as distasteful as

[7] This independence extended to the maintenance of a separate General Staff and of a separate military justice. "The Reich sets the legal norms by which Bavaria is to exercise legal jurisdiction. What the Reich in our view cannot do is to exercise that jurisdiction itself" (Count Lerchenfeld, Plenipotentiary to the Bundesrath from the Kingdom of Bavaria in a written statement read to the Reichstag, December 16, 1897, *Stenographischer Bericht*, der Reichstag, 9. Legisl.-Periode, V. Session, 12. Sitzung, p. 311).

[8] The younger Moltke, after watching recruits being sworn in by a dozen different types of oaths, wrote in his diary that the lack of uniformity was symbolic of "our dismembered political set-up". (Generaloberst Helmuth von Moltke, *Erinnerungen, Briefe, Dokumente*, Stuttgart, 1922, p. 153.)

[9] Hutten-Czapski, writing to Hohenlohe, called the introduction of the German cockade "the most decisive measure initiated in the military area since 1870". (Letter to Hohenlohe, March 22, 1897, in Hohenlohe, *Denkwürdigkeiten*, p. 320.) Holstein said that the Prince Regent and the "gentle Grand Duke of Baden" were "outraged" by that action. (Holstein to Eulenburg, February 3, 1897, *The Holstein Papers*, IV, No. 599, p. 11.)

[10] *Stenographischer Bericht*, der Reichstag, 9. Legisl.-Periode, V. Session, 10. Sitzung, December 14, 1897, p. 230.

they were radical. The rabid nationalists were equally dissatisfied. "Here in Berlin, when the Pan-German League made an attempt to hold a large meeting, here in the Imperial capital, every possible trick was used to undermine it," cried a German Social Reform Party deputy. "I am personally convinced that the popular feeling in the German Empire long ago realised what was right . . . even if the popular movement is uncomfortable for the high diplomats and bureaucrats."[11] As late as 1907, Holstein feared "that in the right psychological circumstances the centrifugal forces will prove the stronger even in today's Germany . . . in a country like Germany which is not a block but a mosaic of tribes."[12]

The Navy was involved in this turmoil about national identity, not only because of its geographical and constitutional dependence on the success of the German nation-state, but also by its financial dependence on a Reichstag elected by universal suffrage. Each time it presented its budget, it confronted the whole spectrum of national disunion at once. The Reichstag elected in 1893 for five years happens to be the one which Tirpitz faced in November 1897, but its make-up is reasonably representative of the Reichstags elected between 1880 and 1900. It had to begin with two types of conservative (extreme agrarian and moderate), three types of liberal (National Liberal, Radical Union and Radical People's Party), a Catholic Centre party with 96 deputies of whom about one third were strong "states righters" from Bavaria, and it had 44 Social Democrats. It also had 52 deputies whose presence reflected the patchwork quality of Bismarck's Reich, that is, the 19 Poles, the 32 Hanoverians, Alsatians and Danes, and the 16 anti-Semites.[13] The composition of this Reichstag meant that there was neither a government nor a "national" majority. Only 153 deputies were left from the Bismarckian cartel of "Friends of the Reich", which he had put together in 1888 out of the two conservative parties and the National Liberals. Approximately 13 per cent of the deputies were entirely opposed to the Reich as it stood (Poles, Alsatians,

[11] *Ibid.*, p. 229.

[12] Holstein to Harden, January 6, 1907, in H. Rogge, *Holstein und Harden*, Munich, 1959, pp. 116 f.

[13] Figures from J. Alden Nichols, *Germany after Bismarck*, Cambridge, Mass., 1958, pp. 255 f.

etc.) for national reasons, another 10 per cent (the Social Democrats) for ideological reasons, another 24 per cent (the Centre) more or less opposed for religious reasons. In Bismarck's sense, more than half of the deputies in the Reichstag were "enemies of the Reich".[14]

Naval expansion depended on creating some sort of block out of the divided and chaotic parliamentary situation. One of the most bizarre manifestations of this problem was the courtship of the Polish members of the Reichstag by the Navy. "At the beginning of the 1890s, when liberals no longer acted on their love for the Navy and the Conservatives and Catholic Centre had not yet developed any positive feelings, the grotesque situation arose that the only party in the Reichstag which energetically demanded a fleet was the Polish group."[15] The irony of the position did not escape the other deputies, who soon dubbed the leader of the Polish party, Kosciol-Koscielski, "Unser Admiralski". It was ludicrous when Polish nationalists supported the national German Navy merely because it might be used against Russia, while the so-called "national" party, the Liberals, refused to support it at all.

The Polish episode is merely one of countless examples of the problem which national disunion presented to the naval leadership. Every argument in favour of naval growth was bound to generate opposition from some part of the chamber. To say that the Navy enhanced trade was to provoke conservative attacks on Caprivi's trade treaties or complaints about unfair advantages for commerce and industry against agriculture. Tirpitz's White Paper of 1897, *Die Seeinteressen des Deutschen Reichs*, crowed Dr. Barth, a Radical Union deputy, "destroyed the main argument for the extreme pretensions of the agrarian party", by showing that Germany was no longer an agricultural

[14] Given these figures it is difficult to argue that Bismarck's "cynical contempt for parliamentary liberalism and his insistence on authoritarian leadership kept the German middle class from active participation in government and precluded its growth to political maturity and responsible thinking" (Hans Kohn, *The Mind of Germany*, New York, 1960, p. 6). The middle class liberal parties were not strong enough to govern and were divided on almost every issue as early as the 1890s. Universal suffrage crushed them more effectively than Bismarck's authoritarianism. See p. 44 below.

[15] E. Kehr, "Schlachtflottenbau und Parteipolitik", *Historische Studien*, Vol. cxcvii, Berlin, 1930, p. 23.

country.[16] Radical Liberals resented the legal irresponsibility of the Navy. Catholics could use it as a bargaining position to obtain revision of the anti-Jesuit laws. Social Democrats saw the Navy as an imperialist instrument to oppress the working classes. The deputies representing national minorities could use it to demand redress of grievances. The politician who could successfully manipulate a Reichstag so composed had yet to arise.

B. The Navy, The Middle Class and Liberalism

The German Navy depended on the liberal movement and the allegiance of the middle class until the 1890s. This relationship shaped the service, infused it with certain characteristic middle class values and marked it off sharply from the Prussian Army. Long after the Navy was able to dispense with liberal political support, it remained closely associated with liberal ideas. These fundamental facts have often been overlooked. British and American historians have usually been too obsessed by the "Prussian menace" to notice that the Navy was neither Prussian nor conservative. German historians, usually men of the liberal middle classes themselves, have not wanted to see the relationship. It is far pleasanter to brand Tirpitz as a fanatic than to recognize him as a fellow pupil of one's own teachers. Those German historians who take seriously the relationship between the middle classes and the Navy come uncomfortably close to self-criticism. For the British or American historian it is hardly pleasant to recognize that reaction and aggression are not always quite as synonymous as liberals in the West like to imagine. If the belligerence of German naval expansion was a product of the liberal tradition in Germany, perhaps the "good" Germans so beloved of historical mythology are not so good after all, and the "bad Germans", the Junker militarists and reactionaries, not so bad.

That the German Navy was a child of German liberalism and the Revolution of 1848 is simply a fact. The Imperial Navy was born under the vaults of the Paulskirche, and its association with

[16] *Stenographischer Bericht,* der Reichstag, 9. Legisl.-Periode, V. Session, 4. Sitzung, December 6, 1897, p. 61.

the Revolution of 1848 remained part of its character until the end of the century. "The Left", wrote the *Vossische Zeitung* on March 10, 1897, "has no need to fear the accusation that it opposes the Navy. It can always point out that it was enthusiastic about a German Navy back in the days when such enthusiasm counted in government circles as a sure sign of revolutionary convictions." But the Revolution itself was a complicated phenomenon, simultaneously a liberal upheaval and a national act of devotion. "The struggle for the individual and the nation at the same time was the characteristic of the Revolution of 1848 . . . If the freedom of the individual was hampered by governments, they must be overthrown. If the freedom of the nation was hampered by external powers, they too would have to be destroyed."[17] These two aspects of German liberalism, its nationalism and its radicalism, influenced the growth of the Navy from the start.

The humiliation and resentment caused by the Danish war and the Prussian "sell-out" made the creation of the Imperial Navy seem particularly urgent. A committee set up under Prince Adalbert of Prussia during the winter of 1848/49 demanded the formation of a Navy of twenty ships of the line, twenty large and ten small cruisers, plus the requisite auxiliary vessels.[18] There was no hope of realizing such a programme with the means available at the time and the plans for the Imperial Navy suffered the same ignominious fate as the Reich of 1848 itself.[19]

The Revolution of 1848 was, thirdly, as much a lunge for power by the German middle classes as it was a call for freedom. On January 22, 1849, Dahlmann, the historian, addressing the Frankfurt Parliament, expressed their yearning for power in unequivocal terms. "The road to power is the only one, which will satisfy and fulfil the bubbling drive for freedom, for it is not mere freedom which the German seeks. It is for the most part the power which has been denied him for which he yearns."[20]

[17] E. Kehr, *op. cit.*, p. 3.
[18] Walther Hubatsch, *Die Ära Tirpitz*, p. 59.
[19] Prince Adalbert returned to Prussia where he agitated more or less unsuccessfully for a large expansion of the Prussian Navy. In 1860 Prussia attempted to negotiate an agreement with the Hanseatic cities for a joint defence of the Baltic coast, but the results were, if anything, less encouraging than those of 1848.
[20] Quoted in E. Kehr, *op. cit.*, p. 4.

It is not coincidental that these good, freedom-loving lawyers and academicians turned to the Navy as the means to attain that power, especially when circumstances conspired to keep them from power in real terms. As Professor Conze points out: ". . . only to such people could power, which as *one* of the foundations of politics is self-evident to any genuine politician and to any political leadership secure in its own traditions, appear as the *unique* political principle above all others."[21]

The experiences of 1848 left political liberalism in Germany three crucial concepts: ardent nationalism, political individualism and obsession with *Macht* (power). Although the national unity for which they yearned, the constitutional institutions which they admired and the political power after which they strove had all been denied them, German liberals continued to hope. They looked to England which was rich, powerful and free, and they wanted to have what English liberals had. They saw the great British fleet as a symbol of the power of a free, constitutional nation-state, while at home they remembered the bayonets of the Prussian infantry and Prussian cavalry storming revolutionary barricades.

All that German liberals had left was *Kultur*, but for them that meant a great deal. *Kultur* is an untranslatable term, meaning at once what we mean by "culture" and much more as well. It was not unlike the American expression, "way of life". It meant the German standard of living almost as much as it implied spiritual or philosophical values. Trade was civilizing and part of *Kultur*. Ships were expressions of the technical excellence of German workmen and were floating manifestations of German *Kultur*. Tirpitz, who belonged to the liberal tradition by birth and education, believed, for example, that ships were "*Kulturgeräte*" and that the sea was a great "*Kulturgebiet*".[22] In a sense, *Kultur* was an ideology of Germanism, an emotive commitment to some vaguely felt essence of the German spirit and an enthusiastic approval of that spirit's revelations, whether in a battleship or a Wagnerian myth.

Macht, *Kultur*, *Deutschtum* and *Nation* rapidly became for the

[21] Werner Conze, "Friedrich Naumann—Grundlagen und Ansatz seiner Politik in der national-sozialen Zeit", *Schicksalswege deutscher Vergangenheit*, Festschrift für S. Kaehler, Dusseldorf, 1950.

[22] Tirpitz, *op. cit.*, p. 16.

young naval officers after 1871 what aristocratic and monarchical sentiments had always been for the Prussian Army. It was natural for them to seek ideals for their new service from the liberal middle classes, not only because the traditions of German nationalism and historiography lent themselves so readily to the creation of a much subtler militarism than the crude arrogance of the Prussian Army, but also because these traditions were their own. The first two Chiefs of the Admiralty, Stosch and Caprivi, although both aristocrats and Prussian generals, were notoriously liberal by contemporary standards. Under them the new generation grew to maturity and among the younger naval officers there were fewer aristocratic associations. Alfred Tirpitz, for example, was born in 1849 into a solid, liberal, middle-class family. His father was a jurist and later state court judge, and his mother, Malwine Hartmann, was the daughter of a physician.[23] Admiral Müller, to take another example, was a Saxon, son of a chemistry professor and nephew of a young doctor who had fought heroically on the barricades in 1849.[24]

The Navy became a career for young men of middle-class backgrounds who were barred from advancement in the Prussian Army but who were ambitious and well trained. The very names of the famous admirals indicate solid bourgeois backgrounds. Hollmann, Hoffmann, Igenohl, Pohl, Scheer, Fischel, Schröder, Michaelis, etc. (the Kaiser eventually gave titles to most of them). Not only were these men without ancient lineage, but also without the caste prejudice, snobbery and aristocratic behaviour of the Army.[25]

The contrast between the two services did not escape the attention of Kaiser Wilhelm II. He was aware of the problem of

[23] There is no good biography of Tirpitz. See A. Schulze-Hinrichs, *Tirpitz*, Göttingen, 1958, which is a recital of all the old clichés, which neither world war has apparently been able to shake, or U. von Hassell, *Tirpitz*, Stuttgart, 1920, which is a book of reminiscences.

[24] Walter Görlitz, "Einleitung", *Kriegstagebücher, Aufzeichnungen und Briefe des Chefs des Marine-Kabinetts Admiral Georg Alexander von Müller, 1914–1918*, Göttingen, 1959, pp. 13 ff. English translation published by Macdonald, 1961.

[25] Naval personnel records reveal that between 1870 and 1894 there were only ten duels involving naval men (MK III, December 12, 1894). In a similar period of time in the Army, from the promulgation of the Courts of Honour Decree of May 2, 1874, to January 1, 1897, there were rarely fewer than four or five duels a year (K. Demeter, *Das deutsche Heer und seine Offiziere*, Berlin, 1930, pp. 147 ff.).

caste in the Prussian Army and occasionally pleaded with the regimental commanders to take a wider view of eligibility for officers' commissions. In a directive to the Prussian Minister of War in 1890, he wrote: "The aristocrat of birth can today no longer claim an exclusive right to supply the army with officers. The aristocrat of spirit . . . the sons of honourable bourgeois households . . . should and must be made available to the officer corps."[26] The Army rejected this appeal as it had so many others. Stubbornly, it defended its position and the commanding generals, especially the generals of the Guards, remained "the middle point of all the high aristocratic and reactionary movements in the Army".[27] In commenting on a conversation between the Kaiser and these generals in 1904, Zedlitz-Trützschler wrote in his diary: "The possibility of any sort of reform in our Army or in the officer corps never occurred to anyone . . . not a hint that the Army in its seclusion and narrow ideas had not kept up with developments in education . . ."[28] No change in this state of affairs took place until the eve of the war, but even then the Army and the Navy were marked by a striking difference in social composition.[29]

The new men of the Navy were tied to the middle class not only by birth and background but also by their activities. Command of the naval installations in Kiel and Wilhelmshaven, the administration of the Imperial Dockyards, where thousands

[26] Kaiser Wilhelm II, Directive to the Kriegsministerium, March 29, 1890, copy in Marinekabinett Files, MK III.

[27] Gerhard Ritter, *Staatskunst*, I, p. 220.

[28] Robert, Count Zedlitz-Trützschler, *Zwölf Jahre am deutschen Kaiserhof*, Berlin, 1924, p. 59.

[29] As late as 1914, 56 per cent of the Prussian army officers over the rank of colonel and slightly over 50 per cent of all the officers of the Great General Staff belonged to the nobility. (K. Demeter, *op. cit.*, pp. 34 f.) No chief of the General Staff nor any Minister of War before 1914 was of bourgeois origin. The contrast with the Navy is striking. Of the fifty-seven admirals and senior officers who served as heads of departments in the Admiralty Staff between 1899 and 1918, only seven belonged to the nobility and only three (Count Baudissin, Freiherr von Keyserlingk and Freiherr von Gagern) to the higher, titled nobility. (Kriegswissenshaftliche Abteilung der Marine, *Der Admiralstab der Kaiserlichen Marine*, Geheim, Berlin, 1936, p. 58.) At the Imperial Naval Office, the general pattern was much the same. Only six of the thirty-three naval officers on duty at the beginning of 1898, only two of the twelve department heads and none of the three admirals belonged to the nobility. ("Das Reichs-Marine-Amt", *Handbuch für das deutsche Reich auf das Jahr 1898*, Berlin, 1898, pp. 193 ff.)

of men found employment, the repair and engineering shops, the coastal batteries and harbour operations, weapons development and manufacture, were activities which naturally brought the naval officer and his civilian cousin together.[30] In Hamburg and Bremen, trade associations and clubs provided ideal agencies for the promotion of joint interests and the generation of political propaganda.

The Navy had natural social ties to yet another significant segment of the middle classes in Germany—the university professors. Wolfgang Marienfeld lists the names of 270 "Flotten-Professoren", who engaged in active production of propaganda for the Navy in the years between 1897 and 1906, either "by their own contributions or by prominence in the Navy League. The list does not include those who took part indirectly, especially those who were members of the German Colonial Society."[31] It reads like a *Who's Who* of German academic life. Lujo Brentano, Hans Delbrück, Otto Gierke, Paul Güssfeldt, Adolph Harnack, Paul Laband, Max Lenz, Reinhard von Lilienthal, Erich Marcks, Herman Oncken, Dietrich Schäfer, Theodor Schiemann, Gustav Schmoller, Werner Sombart, Max Weber, Ulrich von Wilamowitz-Moellendorff and Karl Woermann are just a few of the most famous of the 270 listed. They came from every faculty, including theologians both Catholic and Protestant, doctors of medicine, professors of chemistry and zoology as well as the lawyers, historians and economists. Tirpitz records gratefully his own debt to Treitschke, "that wonderful man . . . at whose side I sat

[30] Tirpitz was eager to widen and deepen this natural community of interests from the beginning of his career. In a letter to Senden, he argued against the separation of naval from commercial interests, opposed the "caste spirit which would be produced . . ." and recommended "that our sea officers in addition to the military side have the feeling that they must be Reich agents for our transatlantic, economic interests." (Tirpitz to Senden, Letter of 15 February, 1896, BA K 08-7/1, "Senden Nachlass".) In some cases, the contact between naval and commercial interests was secured through family ties. The brother of Henning von Holtzendorff, the admiral, was Arnd von Holtzendorff, a director of Albert Ballin's Hamburg-Amerika Line. Emil Georg von Stauss of the Deutsche Bank was the son-in-law of Admiral Müller. Clubs like the *Gesellschaft 1914* provided places where men like the Jewish bankers, Max Warburg and Carl Melchior, the Holtzendorff brothers, Admiral Müller, Hellferich, Zimmermann and others came together socially.

[31] Wolfgang Marienfeld, *Wissenschaft und Schlachtflottenbau in Deutschland, 1897–1906*, Beiheft 2 der *Marine Rundschau*, April, 1957, pp. 110 ff.

scratching notes on bits of paper", to Theodor Mommsen, "who wanted to give me ships but not a Navy Law", and to Dietrich Schäfer.[32]

These cultural affinities between the university professors and the Navy's leaders had deeper roots than simple membership of the same social class. The ties grew out of the very nature of German intellectual life, its ambivalence about the traditions and ideas of the West, its strong suspicion of absolute values and the authority of reason, and its philosophical admiration of the state and power, all of which are far too complicated to be dealt with in a study of this size.[33] Social Darwinism had transformed the German idealist tradition by the end of the nineteenth century into a particularly noxious doctrine of relentless struggle and mastery. The fact that so much of German philosophy was based on immanent rather than transcendental systems of thought further helped to undermine the authority of abstract principles of morality or law.[34] It is sufficient here to point out that all of these aspects of German intellectual life poured into the thinking of the naval leaders. Take this passage from Tirpitz's *Erinnerungen*, in which he tries to account for Germany's defeat in the First World War: "Equally responsible for our catastrophe is the receptivity of our intellectuals for Western culture. It is one-sided, since we long ago absorbed the old civilization of the West. Its contemporary, smooth, utilitarian and capitalist mass culture is less fruitful for the German nature than the square-headed idealism of the Russians and the Orient . . . To strengthen and spread German culture, it was necessary, above all, to establish our political independence of the Western powers . . ."[35]

[32] Tirpitz, *op. cit.*, p. 96.

[33] For a brilliant, if slightly chaotic, analysis of this complex problem, see Friedrich Heer, *Europäische Geistesgeschichte*, Stuttgart, 1953, pp. 563 ff.

[34] It is suggestive to see in this immanent tradition one of the sources of the rejection of abstract codes of morality, which was so common in the writings of military men in nineteenth century Germany. An example of this type was Bernhardi, who in *Deutschland und der nächste Krieg* wrote: "Law is no superhuman reality but an arbitrary invention of the human intellect. It has a different aspect to each people and treaties have validity only as long as they correspond to interests." (In Ritter, *Staatskunst*, II, p. 144.) Very similar arguments were used by Captain Schröder, the inventor of the naval plan for an invasion of England in 1897. See J. Steinberg, *op. cit.*

[35] Tirpitz, *op. cit.*, p. 150.

The final ingredient in this potent brew was supplied by the academic economists. Liberalism which to us is instinctively associated with free trade never had such connotations in German universities. German economists and economic historians believed that the secret of British success lay in Britain's sea power. As Reventlow, one of the most prominent of the naval propagandists, put it: "free-trading England did not prosper because of the 'free play of forces', but because it was the only 'force'."[36] German economists saw trade as a form of war or another expression of the darwinian struggle for survival.[37] Such a view of trade easily led to the famous "Handelsneid" theory, i.e., the view that commercial envy must inevitably lead Britain to attempt to destroy German commercial power. German academic economists could not envisage trade between highly developed nations in any other terms than hegemony and subjugation.

It does not require much imagination to see how easily these academic theories and the propaganda for naval expansion could be united. Nor was this a conscious and cynical application of convenient ideas. Germany's naval leaders adopted the view of history, theory of economics and philosophy of the state preached from university lecterns naturally, because these views were the prevalent attitudes of the social class to which they belonged by birth and education. Just as a natural community of interest arose between the commercial and industrial leaders and naval officers out of an identity of purpose and similarity of background and activity, so too a natural community of ideas developed for the same reasons between the admirals and professors.

By 1890 the new Navy had absorbed the entire standard of values of German bourgeois liberalism. It owed its survival through the lean years to liberal support, but that support was

[36] Ernst zu Reventlow, *Deutschlands Auswärtige Politik*, 3rd ed., Berlin, 1916, p. 93.
[37] The incapacity of German historians and economists to grasp the essence of free trade was reflected in the emergence of a kind of neo-mercantilism, "the so-called 'Historical Economists', led by Gustav Schmoller, Professor at Berlin after 1882. For Schmoller and his school, which had no counterpart in any other country, there were no economic laws valid for all time . . . Economic progress was equated with the efficiency of the nation's political institutions." (Professor C. H. Wilson, "Economic Conditions", *The New Cambridge Modern History*, Vol. XI, Cambridge, 1962, pp. 60 f. Cf. W. F. Bruck, *Social and Economic History of Germany, 1888–1938*, Cardiff, 1938, p. 37, and W. Marienfeld, *op. cit.*, pp. 22 ff.)

no longer enough. The inherent dilemmas of German liberalism had begun to destroy it. The nation-state constructed by Bismarck was hardly what liberals had envisaged. It did not square with liberal theories of representative government nor with their traditions of linguistic nationalism. It was a hybrid, patchwork structure, as we have already seen, and for orthodox liberals a thoroughly unsatisfactory one. They entered Bismarck's new nation-state with grave reservations, and they regarded it, once inside, with considerable suspicion. The curious constitution with its monarchical remnants but also with its universal suffrage proved too much for the movement to swallow.

The liberal political parties began to split as early as the 1870s. By the 1890s they had fallen apart. On the left were the orthodox liberals for whom representative government and political liberty remained the great goals; on the right the nationalistic liberals for whom the Empire, commerce, *Deutschtum* and *Kultur* were more important than political liberty. Both wings were being rapidly overtaken by the rise of Social Democracy. The left liberals had no attraction for the working classes, while the right liberals were employers, well-to-do professional men and academics who edged themselves closer to their former conservative enemies in the face of the red peril. Gradually the right-wing of the liberal movement and the landed nobility fused. The Prussian aristocracy offered a variety of attractions to the new industrialists. The glamorous world of titles and palaces, commissions in good regiments and influence at court, made the industrialists more national and less liberal. Their sons wanted to be gentlemen. "Only the man who wore the uniform with the silver pips on the shoulder was regarded as a 'real chap' . . . The imitation of aristocratic ways of behaviour and of the gruff tone of the mess took on positively ludicrous forms in bourgeois circles."[38]

It was also increasingly apparent that political liberalism would never be able to come to power. The position of Prussia within the federal union made that certain. Bismarck had built Prussian dominance into the Reich and in so doing had given the Prussian Landtag a disproportionate influence in German affairs. The antiquated and thoroughly unrepresentative

[38] Gerhard Ritter, *Staatskunst*, II, p. 129.

Prussian three-class voting system frustrated representative government, social reform, free trade and political liberalism, while giving the conservatives an influence out of all proportion to their voting strength.[39] After 1885, shrewd National Liberals saw the handwriting on the wall and increasingly voted with the conservatives.

Support for the Navy became less and less an automatic liberal response. Many of the left-wing liberals felt that the Navy had been snatched from them by the conservatives. Since the Reich was no longer theirs, the fleet could not be either. Yet they were unwilling to repudiate their initial allegiance to the Navy. As late as 1898 the old radical, Eugen Richter, who had become the bitterest critic of naval expansion, could not bring himself to deny his former attachment to the fleet. "The German Navy," he thundered, "emerged from the democratic, popular movement of the year 1848! (Quite true! Left.) In it the yearning for unity found for the first time a visible form."[40]

The problem took a different form for the right-wing National Liberals. They had consistently fought for the idea of the German nation, but as circumstances forced them further to the right, they fell into a dilemma. They saw the nation as "the united community of the free wills of men embodied in the state. This state was seized by the conservatives, who saw the truly national element of the state in its power structures."[41] The fear of socialism made National Liberals powerless to prevent the usurpation of the idea of the nation by the conservatives. As a result, they steadily lost support. "So far there has been no party in the Reichstag," the socialist, August Bebel, jeered, "which has so willingly supported every demand in the military and maritime fields as the National Liberal, and what has become of the National Liberal Party in the last 25 years? (Laughter. Lively applause on the Left.) Gentlemen, in the year 1874, Herr von Bennigsen, the leader of the party, could command more than 140 deputies, nearly half of the Reichstag. Today there are only fifty weak, little men . . . (Laughter) . . .

[39] For a particularly good account of the difficulty of governing in the Reich without the support of the Prussian Diet, see J. Alden Nichols, *op. cit.*, pp. 19 ff.

[40] *Stenographischer Bericht*, der Reichstag, 9 Legisl.-Periode, V. Session, 69. Sitzung, p. 1740, March 24, 1898.

[41] Theodor Schieder, *op. cit.*, p. 13.

a party in which there are hardly three men left who agree on a single question . . . (Prolonged laughter. Very good! on the Left)."[42]

This state of affairs constituted a very serious political obstacle to naval expansion. With the Radical People's Party in opposition and the National Liberal Party losing ground, the Navy could no longer count on enough votes in the Reichstag to get the annual estimates through. Bismarck's attempt to create a "cartel" of conservative and right-wing liberals collapsed when he fell, so that the period of naval growth in the 1890s coincided with the crumbling of the forces friendly to that expansion. An ironical situation developed. The Imperial Navy, the most thoroughly bourgeois, liberal institution of the Reich, came to depend on the anti-liberal Catholic Centre.

C. The Navy and the Constitution of the Empire

The German Empire was, as we have seen, a federal union. In that union the Navy occupied a peculiar position, constitutionally, politically and socially. Despite its favoured role as the only national institution, the Navy, like every other department of the Imperial Government, had to face certain problems which arose from the nature of the constitution itself. The great problem of any federal constitution is the division of sovereignty between the central government and the states. It cannot be avoided because in the end sovereignty is indivisible. Either the central government or the constituent states will eventually be forced to surrender sovereignty. Civil war or secession are the only alternatives, if neither gives in. These intrinsic problems of federalism were aggravated in the German case because it was a federal union of an unusual kind. It was not a league of equals, because Prussia substantially controlled it. On the other hand, Prussia's powers were limited. The Kings of Bavaria, Saxony and Württemberg retained a good many of the attributes of sovereignty. Operation within this federal structure was frustrating to all concerned. The Bavarians and other South Germans were in a position to obstruct the passage of legislation

[42] *Stenographischer Bericht*, der Reichstag, 9 Legisl.-Periode, V. Session, 5. Sitzung, p. 68, December 7, 1897.

and to prevent the execution of laws of the Reich within their territorial domains. The "states' rights" aspect of the federal system was aggravated, not only by the existence of the sovereign states, but by all the unsolved constitutional questions within each of them. There was considerable variation in the amount of voter participation and enfranchisement as well as in the political situations of the several German states. The south-west states were notoriously "democratic". There was "Red Saxony", with advanced social welfare programmes, and agrarian Prussia, where the three-class voting system assured an aristocratic, land-owning minority its permanent veto on social reform.

The periodic eruptions of crisis in the federal system were a constant source of disunion and dissension within the Empire. The Grand Duke of Baden, writing to Hohenlohe in 1897, could not conceal "the increasing anxieties of wide circles in the German Empire that the firm foundations of that Empire could be shattered . . . I must unfortunately confess that here in the South good national feeling is very much on the wane, and consequently political ideas are moving more and more to the left."[43] Instead of acting as a balance wheel, the federal system merely accelerated the centrifugal tendencies created by other issues. An important Imperial measure would often propel a national coalition party to spin off its constituent parts, as each group in turn reacted differently to the potentialities of the issue. The Centre Party, which was vital to the Navy, was always about to fly apart. During the 1890s, about a third of its more than one hundred Reichstag members were Bavarians who, in turn, were bitterly engaged in a struggle with the *Bauernbund* in the Bavarian Parliament. Since the *Bauernbund* was radical, democratic, aggressively agrarian and opposed to the growth of industry, "where the *Bauernbund* was dangerous to the Centre, the Centre's opposition to the fleet was stronger than elsewhere."[44] The foreign policy of the Reich was, according to Holstein, severely hampered by federalism. "If Bavaria should really succeed", he wrote, "in obstructing a measure, which both the Kaiser and the other German princes consider important, the German Reich will fall back into the days of the

[43] Hohenlohe, *op. cit.*, p. 369.
[44] E. Kehr, *op. cit.*, p. 135.

Confederation of the Rhine, and it would be understandable if our neighbours to the east and west built their plans in accordance with this state of affairs."[45]

The Bismarckian constitution was more of a hindrance than a help in the adjustment of sectional, political conflicts. The Kaiser's position was "constitutionally a peculiar one. He was not strictly a hereditary sovereign. He was not indeed a sovereign at all. Article XI states: 'The presidency of the union belongs to the King of Prussia who in this capacity shall be entitled German Emperor'. There was no German crown, no German civil list; the sovereignty was vested in the aggregate of the German governments as represented in the Bundesrath."[46] The official term for the government was "The Associated Governments of the German Empire". The Emperor's position and his powers, where not constitutionally defined, rested in reality on the power of Prussia and the wider privileges and rights which the King of Prussia enjoyed. "The legal position of the Kaiser in the Empire left considerable free play to constitutional interpretation, but in any event, it was not measurable by the normal standards of constitutionalism in the nineteenth century."[47] As King of Prussia, the Kaiser could act on a royal constitution in which the supremacy of the crown was indisputable. The union of his Royal Prussian and Imperial German prerogatives was imperfect and ill-defined. It is not really surprising that the Kaiser found his position as Emperor frustrating. In one of the many states' rights conflicts with the South German states, he burst out angrily, "The Kaiser has no rights . . . and in any case it is of no importance, I have eighteen Army Corps and I can handle South Germans."[48]

The position of the Reich Chancellor was, if anything, even more intolerable than that of the Kaiser. "The way things are going," wrote Hohenlohe in his diary in 1897, "cannot continue. If His Majesty wishes to rule by himself, I cannot act as his straw man . . . If H.M. alone and exclusively chooses the ministers, the government steadily loses consequence and authority . . . Without authority no government is possible. If

[45] Holstein's Memorandum, October 18, 1897, in Hohenlohe, *op. cit.*, p. 394.
[46] Marriott and Robertson, *op. cit.*, p. 372.
[47] Theodor Schieder, *op. cit.*, p. 82.
[48] Hohenlohe, *op. cit.*, p. 311.

Kaiser Wilhelm II and his family, 1896

Gustav von Schmoller, Professor of Economics at Berlin and founder of the "historical school" of economic theory, an influential advocate of Imperial expansion

S.M.S. "Hagen," coastal armoured ship (battleship IV class), 1894

S.M.S. "Kaiser Friedrich III", battleship I class, at the launching ceremony, July 1, 1896

I cannot get the Kaiser's agreement to measures which I regard as necessary then I have no authority . . . I cannot govern against public opinion and the Kaiser. To govern against both public opinion and the Kaiser is to be firmly planted in mid-air. Out of the question."[49] Hohenlohe's dilemma grew out of the peculiar nature of the office of Chancellor of the Reich, which Bismarck had designed to suit his own needs. The Chancellor was an appointee of the Emperor and as such entirely independent of the Reichstag. That was the theory. In practice without the consent of the Reichstag no legislation could be passed and the Chancellor could not govern. Even Bismarck himself could no longer operate his own constitution when the monarch chose to exercise more than nominal authority.[50] In Bismarck's view, the need to control royal authority would be more strongly felt by his successor, "because the same authority would not immediately be available to him, which my long tenure in the position of Minister-President and the confidence of the last two revered Emperors has amassed for me."[51] The prediction which Bismarck made was soon fulfilled. His successors, lacking his authority and personality, found themselves in the desperate position which Hohenlohe described.

Prussian traditions of military monarchy created awkward problems, not only for the Reich Chancellor who was usually a civilian, but also for the State Secretary of the Imperial Naval Office and the Minister of War, who were officers. The position of the Prussian Minister of War was an unusually delicate one. Prussian tradition rejected the insertion of a civilian between the Army and its supreme commander, the King of Prussia—Emperor of Germany. Since the Kaiser regarded the Army as his personal *Leibgarde*, the Minister of War ended up as the "whipping boy of the hybrid monarchical-constitutional system".[52] The members of the Reichstag mistrusted him because he was a general; generals mistrusted him because he was mixed up with parliamentarians; the Kaiser mistrusted him because his wishes often conflicted with those of the field commanders

[49] *Ibid.*, p. 342.
[50] Letter of resignation, Bismarck to Kaiser Wilhelm II, March 18, 1890, in Otto von Bismarck, *Mensch und Staat: Aus den Briefen, Reden und Schriften*, Munich, 1956, pp. 197 ff.
[51] *Ibid.*, p. 198.
[52] Gerhard Ritter, *Staatskunst*, I, p. 226.

and court entourage. His effectiveness was, as a result, sharply reduced and his authority limited.

The Navy's constitutional position differed in several respects from that of the Army. It was an institution of the Reich as such and its administrative head was an Imperial official, not a Prussian minister. According to Article 53 of the Constitution of 1871, "The Navy of the Reich is united under the supreme command of the Kaiser. The organization and structure of the same is within the jurisdiction of the Kaiser, who names the officers and civil servants of the Navy and receives a direct oath of allegiance, an oath also to be sworn by the other ranks."[53] Implicit in the Kaiser's power to nominate and to organize the Navy was the unresolved conflict between the rights of the monarch as supreme commander and the jurisdiction of the Reichstag as the source of funds, which made the situation of the Prussian Minister of War so very difficult. The Kaiser's *Kommandogewalt* (supreme authority) could be, and often was, used to play one force against the other and as such to act as a balance and arbiter between conflicting parties within the Navy. But inherent in the special position of the Kaiser was a dangerous temptation for the participants. "In this struggle," Tirpitz wrote, "they played the command prerogatives of the Supreme War Lord against me, which, they said, would be restricted, if the State Secretary, who was responsible to Parliament, received too much authority."[54] The effect of this manoeuvre was to elevate the Kaiser's power in the eyes of the public in order to pursue a different policy in the background. In the intra-departmental struggles in the period after Bismarck's fall, the Kaiser's powers of command became a grand fiction behind which each section of the Army or Navy followed its own, entirely individual course.

The relationship between a military minister and the Chancellor of the Reich was difficult to define. The Navy

[53] Cf. Walther Hubatsch, *Der Admiralstab und die obersten Marinebehörden in Deutschland, 1849–1945*, Frankfurt/Main, 1958, p. 34.

[54] Tirpitz, *op. cit.*, p. 122. Of course, when it suited him, Tirpitz was prepared to use the same device. (See pp. 69 f.) The irony of Tirpitz's later complaints on this point did not escape his contemporaries. As Admiral Seckendorff remarked in a letter to Senden, "How true were the words of old Stosch when he told Tirpitz, 'what you are attacking now, you will have to defend later!' " (Seckendorff to Senden, Letter of March 12, 1898, BA K 08-7/1, Vol. 7, "Senden Nachlass".)

ministers were officers who owed the Kaiser complete obedience, but they were also members of cabinets. In one of the many crises of leadership, the Kaiser ordered Admiral Hollmann to resign if the Budget Committee of the Reichstag refused to grant a requested sum of money. Poor Hollmann found himself in a terrible dilemma, because, as the Chancellor quickly pointed out of him, "he has no right to tender such a resignation on behalf of the cabinet . . . I told him . . . that he was not the responsible minister, but merely my State Secretary. The one responsible is I, and if anyone is going to raise a question of confidence, it has to be the Reich Chancellor."[55]

The two chief military ministers of the Army and Navy had little control over personnel in the two services. By an All-Highest Cabinet Order of April 28, 1885, Wilhelm I had determined that orders concerning personnel changes in the Army, new commands, leaves of absence and retirements, where no budgetary consent or legal authorization was required, were no longer to be countersigned by the Chancellor or the Minister of War.[56] The same rule applied to the Navy, and under Kaiser Wilhelm II it was vigorously enforced. The Kaiser's authority over military personnel further undermined the constitutional position of the Chancellor and the military ministers by creating an ill-defined area of jurisdiction and confusing the relationships of authority.[57]

The constitutional difficulties would have been hard to solve in any event, but they became impossible for men who had really neither enthusiasm for, nor allegiance to, constitutionalism. Certainly the devotion of the various Chancellors to the constitution was lukewarm and that of the Prussian Ministers of War non-existent. Hohenlohe's angry defence of the constitutional

[55] Hohenlohe, *op. cit.*, p. 312.

[56] A.K.O. Wilhelm I an den Reichskanzler, April 28, 1885, MK III.

[57] Rottenburg to Albedyll, Berlin, April 20, 1887, MK III. "His Highness (Bismarck) would be grateful for Your Excellency's opinion as to whether the responsible Minister of War is to be regarded as such or whether he is an organ for the transmission of military commands. The latter, in His Highness's view, would not be in conformity with constitutional considerations, since the Ministry of War in its entirety must be regarded as an institution responsible to Parliament . . . and the Minister of War is no longer, as he was before the Constitution, solely a general serving His Majesty the King, but now occupies a position subject to the criticism of Parliament."

position of the Chancellor during the crisis over Admiral Hollmann's resignation was actually a form of anti-constitutionalism. As he pointed out to the Kaiser, "the resignation demanded by Your Majesty in association with a parliamentary vote would result in our sliding imperceptibly into a parliamentary form of government and thus in our taking a course perilous for the Dynasty and the Empire. Parliament would be given a precedent and a means by which at any time the position of the Chancellor of the Reich might be shaken by unjustified, inappropriate decisions."[58] For such a man, the constitution of the Reich was an unpleasant reality, which monarchists like himself had to suffer.[59]

The weakness of the responsible officials of the Empire led to a growth in the strength of all those who were irresponsible. The sheer number of individuals who enjoyed the right of direct audience made it absolutely certain that the responsible officials would lose control over the course of events. Kaiser Wilhelm II's tendency to authorize conflicting plans and to act on whatever his most recent confidant had proposed merely made a bad situation worse. According to the generally accepted version of monarchical privilege, the Kaiser was entirely free to consult responsible or irresponsible persons as he saw fit. He was entitled to grant the rights of direct audience to any individual, just as he was entitled to demand special treatment for ruling princes and members of the royal family who happened to be serving in the armed forces.[60]

After Kaiser Wilhelm II became Emperor in 1888, the Navy, which had been unified under one Chief of the Admiralty, was

[58] Hohenlohe, *op. cit.*, p. 312.

[59] Tirpitz's tendency to submit his resignation whenever he was opposed was intensely repugnant to many of the senior naval officers. Prince Heinrich wrote to Senden: "I find this repeated threatening to resign not entirely loyal. In any case, a Monarch who had the courage to let a Prince Bismarck go, will not hesitate to accept the resignation of a Tirpitz if that is his wish." (Prince Heinrich to Senden, July 25, 1898, BA K 08-7/1, "Senden Nachlass".)

[60] According to the All-Highest Cabinet Order of November 11, 1900, MK XXXII, Vol. 2, personal adjutants could not be detached from duty in the suites of members of the royal family for any purpose whatsoever. In reply to a query from Naval Command, Baltic Sea, of April 26, 1900, the Chief of the Imperial Naval Cabinet informed all naval commands that "Princes serving *à la suite* could be assigned to relevant posts in the event of mobilization only on their own request". MK XXXII, Vol. 2.

chopped up into various administrative units (cf. Chapter Two, pp. 62 ff.). Grotesque situations arose as a result. In planning the Kaiser's Mediterranean tour in 1904, Admiral Senden Bibran, Chief of the Imperial Naval Cabinet, neglected to inform the Admiralty Staff that the Kaiser had decided to take the new cruiser *Friedrich Karl* as escort. Nobody had bothered to send copies of a single piece of the voluminous correspondence about the *Friedrich Karl* to the agency responsible for the deployment of Germany's fleet. The Admiralty Staff first learned of the absence of the newest and most powerful German cruiser during the major part of the summer from a casual request to arrange coaling facilities for the ship in Gibraltar.[61] If mobilization had occurred, the Admiralty Staff would have been blithely unaware that its strategic deployment included a vital ship which was not where it should have been.

Unity of command and purpose was further undermined by the special position of the Kaiser's Military and Naval Cabinets.[62] The two cabinets were personal administrative agencies of the Kaiser, and the chiefs were permanent members of the Emperor's entourage. An ambitious and active chief had the Kaiser's ear more frequently and less formally than anyone in the Navy or the Army. Tirpitz complained that "the cabinet chief was present at all official audiences with the responsible minister and it was natural that after his departure the Kaiser would discuss the matter in private. The cabinet chief had only to select the right moment and to adjust himself to the fantasy and temperament of the ruler to gain acceptance of his ideas." Since the cabinet chiefs deftly adapted their approach to the personality of the monarch, the Kaiser remained convinced that

[61] Cf. MK XXXVI, Vol. 22, Büchsel to Senden, March 9, 1904, and Memo by Senden, January 5, 1904, as well as letters, Senden to High Seas Fleet and Imperial Naval Office, January 9, 1904, January 19, 1904, January 25, 1904, February 2, 1904, February 6, 1904, February 7, 1904, February 21, 1904, telegrams of February 23, 1904, and February 24, 1904, and appropriate replies. The telegram March 7, 1904, from Usedom, Commander of the *Hohenzollern*, informing Senden that Gibraltar authorities had not been informed that a heavy cruiser was to accompany the Kaiser, was the first indication that a serious mistake had been made.

[62] On the role of the Naval Cabinet, see Walther Hubatsch, *Der Admiralstab*, pp. 49 ff. The literature on the Military Cabinet is voluminous; see especially Gordon Craig, *The Politics of the Prussian Army*, Oxford, 1955, pp. 226–30, and pp. 245 ff.

the cabinet chiefs were mere assistants carrying out his will in the form of written orders.[63]

The cabinet chief had other important opportunities to influence the course of decisions. The Chief of the Naval Cabinet had the apparently innocent job of preparing the arrangements for the Kaiser's cruises. Technically, the Oberhofmarschallamt had the responsibility for selecting the entourage, but on cruise the Chief of the Naval Cabinet could always manage to include a few friends and favourites, thus assuring such men a unique opportunity to enjoy an intimate association with the Kaiser.[64] The Naval Cabinet was responsible for personnel, decorations for foreign naval visitors, assignment to duties in the event of mobilization, the preparation of the Kaiser's naval correspondence and dozens of miscellaneous errands of a personal nature. Its position was so important that the public occasionally regarded the Chief of the Naval Cabinet as in some way being the head of the Navy.[65]

Another source of confusion for the responsible government arose from the privileged position of the naval and military attachés, whose reports usually went directly to the Kaiser, in some cases without the knowledge of the responsible ambassador. When the Kaiser embarrassed the Italian government in 1904 by arriving at the same time as the French President, it was not, as so many historians have claimed, a subtle demonstration by Bülow to remind Italy of the realities of the power situation. In fact, Bülow had nothing to do with the itinerary

[63] Tirpitz, *op. cit.*, p. 135. He conveniently omits from his memoirs any reference to the voluminous correspondence which he carried on with Senden before his appointment. In fact, had Tirpitz not used the indirect route to the Kaiser, which he condemns, he would never have become State Secretary at all.

[64] As an example, cf. Telegram, Senden to Admiral Freiherr von Seckendorff, MK XXXVI. Vol. 24. "Reisen Seiner Majestät", dated Berlin, February 20, 1905: "The Kaiser asked me for the Admirals whom I would suggest as guests on the HAPAG steamer to Naples. Have you any objections if I name you? Answer requested by tomorrow morning early, Senden." Seckendorff's reply was: "What a glorious prospect, if I should be considered . . ." For an ambitious man, it was the chance of a lifetime.

[65] Cf. The Mayor of Toenning's Memorandum to the Naval Cabinet, November 23, 1905, MK XI.c., and Senden's marginal comment: "This matter concerns the Imperial Naval Office and the Admiralty Staff. Apparently the Mayor of Toenning addressed himself to the Naval Cabinet in the belief that it was competent to make both a scientific and military appraisal of this question . . ." The question was one of coastal defence.

which was planned by an attaché and favourite of the Kaiser.[66] This incident was only one of many disastrous interventions by irresponsible military or naval attachés in the conduct of foreign policy. The civilian authorities could not control them, because in Prussian tradition no civilian could stand between a Prussian officer and his Supreme War Lord.

The really remarkable feature of the constitution of the German Empire was that it worked at all. Although it operated less and less successfully after Bismarck's powerful personality ceased to be its driving force, the fact remains that the Kaiser was able to find ministers and chancellors who managed to get something done, however frustrating they may have found the process. Although Tirpitz had to threaten to resign no less than four times within his first eighteen months of office, he did not have to carry out the threat, and remained in office for nearly twenty years. During peace-time Tirpitz never suffered a really serious defeat in his programme. It was only when war broke out that the constitution slowly collapsed. All its latent flaws and sources of confusion came to the surface, and Tirpitz's fate fulfilled the prophency which he had made more than thirty years earlier. "In that moment when we are placed before the question of our destiny . . . the Imperial Naval Office with one blow becomes a cipher."[67]

The constitution never operated smoothly even in its palmy days. There was always terrific friction in its machinery. More

[66] Letter of Colonel von Chelius to Count August Eulenburg, Oberhofmarschall of the Kaiser's court, Confidential, Rome, February 5, 1904, copy in the files of the Naval Cabinet, MK XXXVI. Vol. 22—"Since His Majesty the Kaiser showed me the favour of discussing his proposed trip to the Mediterranean privately and at the same time saw fit to order me to prepare a general plan of this trip, I have the honour to enclose for Your Excellency's kind attention a draft of the itinerary . . ." In the five page typewritten memorandum which Chelius enclosed, there is no mention of his consultation with the German Ambassador in Rome, with the Foreign Ministry or even with the Italian Foreign Ministry. In a private letter to August Eulenburg, he showed himself aware of the considerable diplomatic importance of the trip: "The construction of a draft presented certain difficulties, because a political factor had to be reckoned with: the possible simultaneous presence of the President of the French Republic . . . I did not mention this in the enclosure on purpose but have chosen instead to bring it to Your Excellency's attention informally, so that the enclosed itinerary could be presented, if necessary, independently of such considerations to His Majesty . . . If the return trip of His Majesty should begin at Genoa on April 30th, a simultaneous presence of both heads of state on Italian soil would be unavoidable . . ."

[67] Tirpitz to Senden, December 30, 1892, BA K 08-7/1, "Senden Nachlass".

heat than light was generated, and the government, even under Bismarck, seemed incapable of lurching out of one crisis without stumbling into another. The fiction of the central authority of the Kaiser prevented any genuine administrative reform, while it encouraged the different branches of government to follow their own exclusive policies. A man with an idea could get a great deal accomplished, but never quite enough to assure that the other branches of government were co-operating with him, never quite enough to gain real control. It was not surprising that the other powers found Germany's erratic and unpredictable behaviour most alarming and began to look for intricate, machiavellian explanations for what were all too often merely the products of un-coordinated activities of several conflicting departments.

This was the constitution with which Germany was supposed to solve the problems raised by the political divisions within and the dangerous imbalance abroad. This ramshackle, monarchical, federal, autocratic and yet democratic machine was expected to deal efficiently with all the tensions produced by the uncertainty of national identity, shifting political trends, the national minorities, religious divisions, technological changes and the growth of a modern public opinion.

D. The Navy and Social and Economic Change

All the difficulties discussed in the first three sections of this chapter were aggravated by the staggering explosion of population and industrial growth which shook Germany between 1860 and 1900. An agrarian society was transformed into a predominantly urban one within a generation. The social changes caused by this churning were vast. Between 1871 and 1910 the population of the German Empire rose from 41,000,000 to 65,000,000, and the number of people living in urban areas more than doubled.[68] Between 1871 and 1897, an annual rate of growth of population of one per cent per annum was maintained and only the constant flow of emigration, which reached a high point of 221,000 by 1881 and averaged more than 80,000

[68] Figures quoted from Marriott and Robertson, *op. cit.*, pp. 381 f.

throughout the period, prevented the situation from becoming explosive.[69]

The growth of the Social Democratic Party reflected these figures. Total Social Democratic votes rose from 493,258 in 1877 to 1,427,298 by 1890.[70] "In the elections of 1898, the S.P.D. received 2,111,073 or 27.23 per cent of the total... Proportional representation would have given the S.P.D. 108 instead of 56 seats... of the 397 seats in the Reichstag."[71] The surging growth of the working classes and their political party burst against the barriers of the Prussian dominated political structure. The antiquated three-class voting system in Prussia prevented the Prussian socialists from exercising an influence even remotely equivalent to their numbers and the firm grip of reactionary agrarians and frightened industrialists on the most important German state effectively throttled all attempts to adjust the political system to the new social realities. Acute observers like Max Weber retreated into ". . . a brave pessimism . . . the awareness of the curse of being born after a great political era..."[72]

For men like Friedrich Naumann and Gustav Schmoller, overseas expansion was the only way to escape the degradation of the working classes which the population explosion would necessarily produce. In a newspaper article, written on May 20, 1899, Dr. Schmoller analysed this problem: "We are the fastest growing nation in the world . . . If the 52 million Germans continue to increase in the future as in the past at the rate of 1 per cent per annum, by 1950 we shall have over 104 million Germans. How are we to feed these people in the homeland?... Proletarian conditions and pressure on wage levels of the worst sort must result if we do not summon up the energy to expand... If we do not participate in the grand power struggles in the world, we have no future . . . Bold steps abroad, a policy of reconciliation at home, return to the great ideas of social reform

[69] Das Reichs-Marine-Amt, *Die Seeinteressen des deutschen Reiches*, Berlin, 1897, Part One: "Bevölkerung, Einwanderung und Auswanderung", pp. 2 and 4, as well as pp. 6 ff. for direction of emigration by country.

[70] A. J. Berlau, *The German Social Democratic Party*, Columbia University, 1949, p. 40.

[71] *Ibid.*, p. 44.

[72] Werner Conze, "Friedrich Naumann: Grundlagen und Ansatz seiner Politik in der nationalsozialen Zeit", in *Schicksalswege deutscher Vergangenheit*, Festschrift für S. Kaehler, Dusseldorf, 1950, p. 358.

instead of petty repression . . . that is the lesson which the events in Samoa have taught us."[73]

Friedrich Naumann's National Social Party was in essence an attempt to spread this doctrine to the masses. He wanted "to teach the workers that they were simply shutting the gate to their own accession to power by persistently opposing the monarchy and especially by opposing Germany's Army and Navy".[74] Naumann believed that the population explosion and industrial efficiency would make Germany superior to all other powers. "The German race brings it; it brings Army, Navy, money and power . . . Modern gigantic instruments of power are only possible when an entire people has the budding juices of spring in its members."[75]

The Navy was ideally suited to mobilize such radical forces. It was the one national institution which was not marred by Prussian associations. It was industrial, powerful and progressive. Tirpitz dealt openly and fairly with Social Democrats, often running the risk of attack from men like Freiherr von Stumm and Count Klinckowström, for whom Tirpitz was a dangerous radical. "There are many honourable Social Democrats and radicals", he wrote, "who are true to the Fatherland and understand its national necessities."[76] His public relations officer, von Heeringen, treated Social Democratic journalists as courteously as bourgeois journalists. Information was supplied to the S.P.D. as to all political parties. Tirpitz was, after all, an employer on a large scale and well acquainted with the realities of the Socialist menace. He saw that the temper of the Social Democratic Party was changing. Kautzky and Schoenlank had written: "The child must be inoculated with the belief that none deserves to be called free who knows not . . . how to die for freedom. Should there be a need to keep a presumptuous enemy away from the homeland . . . the closed ranks of those who fight for their good cause will be ready to strike, and victory

[73] Dr. Gustav Schmoller, "Die Lehren von Samoa", newspaper leader, May 20, 1899, in the files of the Imperial Naval Office, MK XXIV.e.

[74] Erich Eyck, *op. cit.*, p. 158.

[75] Quoted in Werner Conze, *op. cit.*, p. 363.

[76] Tirpitz, *op. cit.*, p. 230. See also *Norddeutsche Allgemeine Zeitung*, February 1, 1899, for an editorial attack on Tirpitz, because he accepted a Socialist complaint about attempts by the Imperial Dockyards to influence workers in a by-election.

will be tied to their standards."[77] In the following year Holstein wrote to Bülow: "In the ten and a half years of the Kaiser's reign . . . Social Democracy, left in peace, has become fat and lethargic. Although companies still pay high enough dividends, workers' wages have risen. The Social Democratic leaders, Liebknecht, Bebel, Vollmar, Auer, are today comfortably-off bourgeois. Neither these men nor their followers represent a threat to the life of the Kaiser. They say, just as they did ten years ago: 'We are not really imperialist, but, if we have to have a Kaiser, we have the best possible'."[78]

E. Conclusion

The unusual position of the German Navy in the society of Imperial Germany gave it great sources of strength. No other German or Prussian institution could call on the same emotional associations with the nationalist movement. In a new nation-state as yet uncertain about its style, structure and identity, the Navy was unequivocally national and imperial. It had no particularist or states' rights inheritance to obstruct its growth. It could claim an honourable, liberal past and appeal to the rising industrial and commercial classes as a thoroughly middle class organization. To many radicals, it offered the universal panacea of colonial expansion and settlement, which, they believed, would ease, if not solve, domestic social problems. To the economists and historians it seemed the perfect instrument for the fulfilment of their neo-mercantilist or social darwinian theories of international relations. It could carry German *Kultur* to every corner of the globe and wrest for Germany that place among nations to which the German academic community believed she had been historically destined. "We do not by any means feel the need to stick our finger in every pie," as Bülow put it, "but on the other hand . . . the days when the German happily surrendered the land to one of his neighbours, to another the sea, and reserved for himself the heavens, where pure doctine was enthroned . . . (Laughter—Bravo!) Those

[77] Quoted in Berlau, *op. cit.*, p. 47.
[78] *The Holstein Papers*, IV, No. 736, July 30, 1900, p. 190.

days are over . . . In a word, we don't want to put anyone in the shade, but we too demand our place in the sun."[79]

There were certain weaknesses as well. The liberal parties were not strong enough to support a large naval programme by themselves. The Navy's alliance with the liberal, democratic, anti-clerical traditions made it unpalatable to the Catholic Centre Party which held the balance of power in the Reichstag. Its identity as a national and not a regional institution placed it at the mercy of a national parliament elected by universal suffrage. Every question which tore the fabric of German nationhood weakened the support for a national Navy. The bizarre constitutional structure and the confusion at the top of its own administration created a variety of obstacles to the formulation of a coherent building programme. The uncertainties caused by the rapid changes in naval technology obstructed the formulation of an underlying strategy. Indecision within the Navy made for erratic and contradictory political demands. Many diplomats opposed the fleet programme for fear of its effect on Anglo-German relations, and many Junker conservatives resented its associations with the trading and commercial interests, its industrial character and its bourgeois social composition.

Placating the Navy's enemies without alienating its friends was the problem at home. Stirring up naval enthusiasm without arousing foreign hostility was the problem abroad. Neither was an easy undertaking.

[79] *Stenographischer Bericht*, der Reichstag, 9. Legisl.-Periode, V. Session, 4. Sitzung December 6, 1897, p. 60.

2

Tirpitz's First Campaign for Office

"I believe that Tirpitz is the right man to push the Navy onwards in these difficult days."—*Admiral Senden*, March 1896.

The accession of Kaiser Wilhelm II to the throne on June 15, 1888, began a new era in German naval history. His grandfather, Wilhelm I, had been a soldier without any strong interest in naval affairs, and his father, Friedrich III, had come to the throne in the last months of a fatal illness so that his rule had been shadowy and brief. The young Kaiser, not yet thirty years old, was very fond of the sea and ships. "When the present Emperor was a boy, one of his favourite recreations was to sail a beautiful model of a British frigate on the lake at Potsdam . . . He once confessed that from his earliest youth onwards—'from the day when I ran about as a boy in Portsmouth dockyards, I have been greatly interested in British ships'."[1] During the early years of his reign he was given the unusual rank of Admiral of the Fleet of Her Majesty's Navy, a rank which he took seriously and enjoyed exercising. "One of the best days of my life . . . which I shall never forget", the Kaiser remarked years later, "was the day I inspected the Mediterranean Fleet, when I was on board the *Dreadnought*, and my flag was hoisted for the first time."[2]

His interest in British naval matters was more than ceremonial. He followed the development of construction techniques, the results of manoeuvres and tactical exercises and the performance of guns and equipment with concentrated attention, and had no reservations about expressing his criticisms of British naval efficiency. On February 21, 1891, Lord George

[1] Archibald S. Hurd, "The Kaiser's Dream of Sea Power", *Nineteenth Century and After*, August 1906, London, pp. 215 and 217.
[2] *Ibid.*, p. 218.

Hamilton, First Lord of the Admiralty, wrote to Salisbury that he had received a lengthy letter from the Kaiser, "on the subject of our heavy naval ordnance, in which His Majesty suggests certain administrative changes in our system . . . The letter His Majesty has written is only a fresh proof of his solicitude for the British Navy, but I trust I have shown that the rumours which have reached His Majesty are in many respects exaggerated."[3] Salisbury himself was not spared. The Kaiser, writing in English "as a simple British admiral", addressed a ten page letter to him: "I am a close and interested observer of what is going on in H.M. Navy to which to belong is my greatest pride . . . England's naval supremacy is in danger . . . The enclosed drawings which I submit to your Lordship are copies of those I made for H.M. the Queen and will show you how the French and Russians have distributed their fleets and what their shipbuilding programmes look like."[4] The Kaiser enjoyed the company of British naval officers and had many close friends in yachting circles, some of whom, like Admiral V. R. Montagu, received regular letters in the Kaiser's own hand.[5] Sir Edward Reed, a former Director of British Naval Construction, once remarked that he doubted whether any admiral in the British Navy was as "well informed concerning the most trivial detail of a ship or its machinery as the head of the German Navy."[6]

Within a few months of his accession to the throne, the Kaiser began a major reorganization of the Navy. The first victim of the new regime was General von Caprivi, Chief of the Admiralty from 1883 to 1888. "The real reason for Caprivi's departure," wrote Tirpitz, "was that the Kaiser wanted to

[3] Original letter, Lord George Hamilton to Lord Salisbury, handwritten, London, February 21, 1891, ADMB 1.1–12, with dozens of marginal notes in the Kaiser's hand. His final comment was: "This letter fully corresponds to Lord George's parliamentary speeches in which he invariably declares that on the whole everything in the Navy is the 'best in the world', and that all contrary opinions are either wrong or grossly *exaggerated.* But he has utterly failed 'on the whole' to prove my assertions as to the defects in Great Britain's heavy armaments are wrong and that his guns are good! W. I. et R." (In English in the original.)
[4] Kaiser Wilhelm II to Lord Salisbury, private and confidential, New Palace, December 20, 1893, MK, "Deckel", 1893 (in English in original).
[5] "The Montagu Correspondence", Special File, MK XXII.v, December 1903–February 1913.
[6] Archibald S. Hurd, *op. cit.*, p. 233.

divide the powers of the Admiralty in order to be able to intervene personally. Prince Bismarck, who in several collisions with Stosch had found such power in the hands of one man most uncomfortable, contributed unfortunately to this splintering of naval authority, which was harmful enough in peacetime but during the war was virtually fatal."[7]

When the new Chief of the Admiralty, Count Monts, set up a committee on August 16, 1888, "to work out a draft for the new organization of the main naval bureaux as commanded by All-Highest authority",[8] General Albrecht von Stosch, former Chief of the Admiralty, wrote a lengthy memorandum for Admiral Hollmann, the chairman, in which he urged the committee to accept a three-way division of naval functions on the model of the Army.[9] Stosch's point of view was unexpected, since he had vigorously opposed the activities of both the Army General Staff and the Military Cabinet. In the case of the Navy, he argued for the introduction of a structure which was bound to reproduce the same evils as those of the Army's organization. Stosch apparently believed that by separating active command from the responsibilities of long-term planning, it would be possible to create a super-ministry, which would control not only naval construction and strategy but also the development of merchant shipping and colonial expansion.[10]

The Kaiser decided, very likely for different reasons, to adopt for the Navy the three-way division of responsibility in practice in the Army, and by the All-Highest Cabinet Order of March 30, 1889, the Admiralty was dissolved. The solitary Chief of the Admiralty was replaced by a Chief of the High Command of the Navy with the rank and privileges of a Commanding General in the Army, a Chief of the Imperial Naval Cabinet and a State Secretary of the Imperial Naval

[7] Tirpitz, *Erinnerungen*, p. 38. This was, of course, written thirty years after the events. Tirpitz seems to have been for the split at the time. (Cf. Seckendorff to Senden, March 13, 1898, BA K 08-7/1, "Senden Nachlass"—"I have never believed that the position of the Chief of the High Command, which Count Monts began and Tirpitz as Chief of Staff carried out, was the right one.")

[8] Walther Hubatsch, *Der Admiralstab*, p. 50.

[9] F. B. M. Hollyday, *Bismarck's Rival, A Political Biography of Albrecht von Stosch*, Durham, North Carolina, 1960, p. 256.

[10] *Ibid.*, p. 257.

Office serving under the Reich Chancellor.[11] Unfortunately, the Kaiser failed to accept Stosch's suggestion that the Chief of the High Command be forbidden to communicate directly with the other departments of state, and the crucial proposal that the Chief of the Imperial Naval Cabinet be both a junior officer and subordinate to the State Secretary.[12]

Whether Stosch's conception of a responsible, all-powerful Navy Minister and subordinated commanders was prudent or not, it never had a hope of realization in practice. The Kaiser's reorganization of his personal entourage into the so-called *Grosses Hauptquartier*, one of his first official acts, had effectively destroyed the chances of such a hypothetical central agency for naval development, however unintentionally. Paragraph No. 6 of the *Ausführungsbestimmungen* to the All-Highest Cabinet Order of July 7, 1888 settled the principle that "Commanding Generals and those holding equal rank, as well as General Adjutants, Generals *à la suite* and A.D.C.s are empowered to make requests for an audience of the Kaiser directly to the A.D.C. on duty."[13] Every military insider had, in effect, virtually unlimited access to the Emperor's person. As long as the fiction of the Kaiser's "supreme authority" was maintained, a responsible and centralized Navy Ministry could never be realized. Any dissatisfied General or Admiral could undermine the Minister by appealing to the Kaiser directly. The new Chief of the Naval Cabinet, Captain Gustav Freiherr von Senden Bibran, refused to remain under the State Secretary's thumb or to accept a lesser status than that of the Chief of the Military Cabinet.[14] A naval triumvirate was created which was to cause Tirpitz more difficulty than all the anomalies of German political life, although without it he would never have come to power.

Expansion of the Navy was next on the Kaiser's agenda, but that was less easily accomplished. There were precedents from

[11] For the full text of the A.K.O., March 30, 1889, cf. MGFA-DZ:F. 6517.
[12] F. B. M. Hollyday, *op. cit.*, p. 256.
[13] No. 6, "Ausführungsbestimmung zu der A.K.O.", July 7, 1888, Potsdam, MK III, Copy in Naval Cabinet files.
[14] According to the All-Highest Cabinet Order creating the Naval Cabinet, the Chief was, in fact, given equal status to that of the Chief of the Military Cabinet and granted a regular weekly audience on Tuesdays at 11 a.m., when the Kaiser was in residence at Berlin or Potsdam. See Hubatsch, *Der Admiralstab*, p. 50, and Appendix 13, p. 236, for the full text of the Order.

Albrecht von Stosch, General of the Infantry and Chief of the Imperial Admiralty, 1872 to 1883

Alfred Tirpitz as a Korvetten-Kapitän in 1884

Sketch for a 10,000 ton battleship, drawn and signed by Kaiser Wilhelm II, dated May 21, 1891

the previous reign and there was also the Reichstag to consider. Under Wilhelm I, a naval construction programme had been initiated. "During the debate on the Imperial Budget for the Navy for 1872 the Reichstag voted, with reference to the plan for the foundation of the Navy adopted in 1867, that the Chancellor be requested to submit a comprehensive memorandum in which details be presented as to how far the said plan had been carried out and what sums would be required to carry it to completion."[15] Following this vote, the new Chief of the Admiralty, General von Stosch, prepared a plan, which Bismarck laid before the Reichstag on May 6, 1872. A ten year building plan was envisaged at a cost of 218,437,500 Marks. It called for the construction of 8 armoured frigates, 6 armoured corvettes, 7 monitors, 2 floating batteries, 20 light corvettes and a variety of miscellaneous smaller ships, including 10 large and 18 small torpedo boats.[16] The plan was enormous by comparison with the existing number of warships on duty. In a speech on May 27, 1873, Lasker expressed the feelings of the left-wing of the Liberals, when he argued that "today . . . it is rather like rolling down the side of a mountain. Surely it is time to put on the brakes and not continue to push forward."[17] Despite this opposition, the plan was adopted and carried out.

By 1883, the German Navy consisted of 7 armoured frigates—led by the *König Wilhelm* (9,757 tons)—and 4 armoured corvettes of the "Sachsen-Klasse" (7,400 tons), the first tactically unified group of identical warships constructed in Germany.[18] Personnel had grown from 160 officers and 3,300 men to 423 officers and 5,062 men.[19] Admittedly this force was tiny by comparison with England, which could boast more than sixty fighting ships in all,[20] but the Admiralty under Stosch could find satisfaction in having completed its initial assignment.

At the same time, certain fundamental principles of German naval strategy had been clearly conceived. "Without the

[15] "Denkschrift betreffend die Ausführung des Flottengründungsplansvon 1873", Abgeschlossen zum 1 Juli 1883, Kaiserliche Admiralität, Berlin, MK I.f.1, p. 3.
[16] *Ibid.*, p. 8.
[17] Quoted in Eckart Kehr, *Schlachtflottenbau und Parteipolitik*, p. 12.
[18] "Denkschrift betreffend die weitere Entwicklung der Kaiserlichen Marine", Kaiserliche Admiralität, Berlin, 1883, MK I.f.1, p. 24.
[19] *Ibid.*, pp. 11–13.
[20] *Ibid.*, p. 26.

background of armoured battleships, without the security of finding in case of need the support of a collected, battle-ready high seas fleet, the effectiveness of the ships in political service cannot correspond to the world position of the German Empire nor long be guaranteed."[21] The small ships or merchant vessels flying the Imperial flag would be protected indirectly by the big battle fleet at home. The knowledge that behind each light cruiser the massed power of the huge battle fleet was ready would make potential opponents think twice before they molested them. The other principle, which Stosch believed was involved in the construction of a battle fleet, was the famous concept of *Bündnisfähigkeit.* Again anticipating Tirpitz, Stosch argued that "if in a major war against a power with superior naval strength the German flag cannot maintain itself on its own, Germany can have no value for maritime allies . . . The most effective defence of the coasts of the Fatherland is without question a victory in a battle on the high seas."[22]

Tirpitz learned his lesson well under Stosch. In his twelve years at the Admiralty, Stosch inspired Tirpitz with the necessity of seeking a decisive battle in any successful naval strategy and of striving to give Germany a powerful home fleet upon which naval planning could be built. All his life Tirpitz remained an admirer of Stosch and in February of 1901 he ordered the two memoranda which Stosch had composed in 1883 to be circulated to all officers in the Imperial Naval Office. "Stosch", he wrote in his memoirs, "was way ahead of his time in the energy with which he drove our sea power forward after centuries of neglect . . . As early as the 1870s Stosch was convinced that we had to have colonies and that we could not exist for long without expansion."[23] Stosch's successor, General von Caprivi, was much less incisive in Tirpitz's view: "Despite his tactical and strategic understanding, he failed to develop a definite building programme, although he saw that the Navy could not continue to live from hand to mouth."[24] This criticism was again in the spirit of Stosch, who in one of the memoranda of 1883 had pleaded for the

[21] *Ibid.*, p. 4.
[22] *Ibid.*, p. 6.
[23] Tirpitz, *op. cit.*, p. 23.
[24] *Ibid.*, p. 25.

recognition that "a creation such as that of a German Navy cannot live from hand to mouth"[25]. The obstacle for both Stosch and Caprivi had been Bismarck. Stosch's disagreement with Bismarck cost him his office in 1883 and "his successor Caprivi never worked out a proper relationship to Bismarck".[26]

When Wilhelm II became Kaiser, he found that in the five years of Caprivi's tenure of office virtually nothing had been done to build on the foundation which Stosch had laid. After Caprivi was dismissed on July 5, 1888, his successor, Count Monts, managed to get the four first class battleships of the "Brandenburg Class" approved by the Reichstag during the winter of 1888-89.[27] Monts had only a short term of office because by the spring of 1889 the Admiralty no longer existed. In its place there were two agencies, the High Command and the Imperial Naval Office. Since the latter had the responsibility of dealing with the Reichstag and of preparing the budget, the building programme fell within its jurisdiction, but the development of strategy remained the function of the High Command. The unity of ship construction and military planning, which Stosch had strongly urged, was destroyed, and under Admiral Hollman, the Imperial Naval Office tended to build ships without consultation with the High Command. This state of affairs, and not the intervention of the Kaiser, was the cause of the appearance of anxieties about "limitless fleet plans", as Eugen Richter put it. Until strategy had been reunited with construction, the fleet would never have firm limits based on Germany's defence needs.

Before such needs could be recognized, something more than a reorganization of the naval hierarchy was required. Two primary questions had to be answered: who were the potential enemies and which of the available types of ships would be most appropriate against such enemies? In addition to the strategic objectives of the future Navy in war-time, there were considerations of peace-time service, the necessity felt in those years by all the powers "to show the flag" overseas and the

[25] "Denkschrift betreffend die weitere Entwicklung der Kaiserlichen Marine", Kaiserliche Admiralität, Berlin, 1883, MK I.f.1., p. 4.

[26] Günter Howe, "Gedanken zur deutschen Wehrpolitik zwischen 1871 und 1914" *Weltmachtstreben und Flottenbau*, p. 68.

[27] Walther Hubatsch, *Die Ära Tirpitz*, p. 62.

problem of protecting trade routes in both war and peace. None of these questions was simple and in reality they were never satisfactorily answered. The peculiar geographical position of Germany and its late arrival on the international scene made the construction of commerce raiders, as advocated by the French *jeune école*, unsuitable for the German Empire. Alternative strategies were not easy to find, because, aside from the contributions of the *jeune école*, the period was not a great one for advances in naval strategy in any of the world's navies. Engineering and marine technology were advancing so rapidly that strategic thinking, unable to absorb the entire significance of the changes, fell into partial paralysis. "In general the fleet's training remained more appropriate to the era of masts and yards than steam . . . and the ending of the long era of dependence on the wind for propulsion had been used, not to win the tactical freedom which it made possible, but to impose a higher degree of rigidity than ever before."[28]

When the Kaiser paid his annual visit to Kiel in 1891, the ideas of the naval leadership were far from ripe. On April 6, 1891, the leaders of the Navy entertained the Kaiser and the aged Field Marshal Moltke at an informal dinner. A lively discussion about the future of the Navy took place, which was characterized more by angry, bombastic gestures than by sober appreciation of the Navy's problems. Tirpitz was disgusted by the wild suggestions and by the table-pounding tone of the talk. "Diese Schweinerei muss aufhören" was the best the Navy's leaders could offer.[29] Except for the sense of frustration and the eagerness for change, the Navy's ideas had not advanced much beyond the mobilization plans worked out in the Admiralty under Caprivi. The enemy was assumed to be France or Russia or both, and the objective of German naval activity was to attain a partial victory over the French Atlantic Fleet within the first ten days of hostilities, by which time, it was assumed, the French Mediterranean Fleet would not yet have reached the North Atlantic.[30]

[28] Captain S. W. Roskill, *The Strategy of Sea Power*, London, 1962, p. 96.

[29] Rudolf Stadelmann, "Die Epoche der deutsch-englischen Flottenrivalität", in *Deutschland und Westeuropa*, pp. 89 f.

[30] For a discussion of strategy under Caprivi, cf. Walther Hubatsch, *Der Admiralstab*, pp. 44 ff.

At the beginning of 1892, Alfred Tirpitz, by then a captain, was appointed Chief of Staff to the Chief of the High Command of the Navy, with special responsibility for "the development of tactics for the High Seas Fleet".[31] Almost at once he began to transform the High Command. With his immensely powerful personality and his great charm, he converted his superiors and subordinates alike to his views. He drew his old comrades from the "Torpedo gang" together and with enthusiasm they began to work on a full-scale revision of the antiquated regulations for fleet exercises. "Tirpitz is a very energetic character," Admiral Senden wrote in a note to himself some years later. "He has too big a head of steam not to be a leader. He is ambitious, not choosy about his means, of a sanguine disposition. High as the heavens in his joys but never relaxing in his creative activity, no matter how crushed he may appear. He would never stand for treatment like that given to Admiral H. (Hollmann), for he is much too self-conscious and convinced of his own excellence . . . He has been very spoiled in his naval career and with the exception of the Chief of the Admiralty (Stosch) never had a superior who could match him."[32]

The new book of tactical exercises was nearly completed by December 28, 1892, when Tirpitz was unexpectedly called to an audience with the Kaiser. There he learned that Admiral Hollmann, State Secretary of the Imperial Naval Office, had demanded and achieved the right to edit and amend the tactical exercises. Tirpitz was furious. "For reasons of loyalty," he wrote to Senden, "I did not bring these views into the open at the recent audience of His Majesty, which I had already developed in conversation with you . . ."[33] He was determined "that such a case never occur again, where the State Secretary by means of a Cabinet Order designed by himself can throw out our entire, carefully constructed programme". He considered himself fully justified in attempting to pull strings behind the scenes "because the present State Secretary has adopted an

[31] A. Schulze-Hinrichs, *Tirpitz*, p. 20.
[32] "Aufzeichnung über Hollmann und Tirpitz", Note 3, BA K 08-7/1, "Senden Nachlass".
[33] Tirpitz to Senden, December 30, 1892, BA K 08-7/1, "Senden Nachlass", Confidential.

unworthy and factually unjustified attitude to the High Command", and he appealed to Senden "because conditions prevented me on account of the immediate consequences from speaking my mind ruthlessly in the presence of His Majesty . . . Since you personally have the inner responsibility for this matter and I personally must stand before the breach, in other words, since our interests run parallel, I thought that it was necessary and proper to put my views to you privately."[34]

Tirpitz attacked the rights of the State Secretary with every weapon at his command, using arguments later to be used against him by his opponents. Military matters which were "the direct expression of the supreme authority of the Kaiser" could not be administered by "a State Secretary, who, the way things are going, will undoubtedly become increasingly dependent on the Chancellor and on a Reichstag elected by universal suffrage."[35] He attacked the competence of the Imperial Naval Office to deal with matters affecting the tactics of the active fleet and, more interesting, he charged it with neglecting its proper functions. "Why does the I.N.O. not do anything about the burning question of reorganization of our dockyards? Why has it neglected our construction engineers and the German maritime industry in general? Why are the forces not gathered together to give the Navy a factually unassailable representation in the Reichstag? Obviously there are other factors to consider, but I must say honestly when I think of the way our case is presented that if I were a deputy and not a sea captain, but in all other respects a sensible chap, I would not grant one penny to this naval administration, because it is simply incapable of presenting really thought-out demands."[36]

The question of the competence of the Imperial Naval Office to exercise editorial control over purely military regulations remained one, but only one of the points at issue between the High Command and the Imperial Naval Office.[37] Strategy

[34] *Ibid.*, p. 5.
[35] *Ibid.*, p. 1.
[36] *Ibid.*, p. 3.
[37] It had still not been settled by the beginning of 1897. In a 36 page rebuttal of attacks from the High Command, Admiral Hollmann cited this issue as one of the dozen or more outstanding points of dispute between the two highest naval agencies. He argued: "It is not true that . . . regulations and instructions receive All-

Continued on page 71

and tactics was another source of disagreement. In this controversy too, Tirpitz tried to use his personal liaison with Senden. "Once again, I must ask you to look after the interests of the High Command and the hopes of our Navy to make some progress in the intellectual field," he wrote in 1893.[38] Although the first skirmishes between Tirpitz and Hollmann ended inconclusively, the lines were drawn for the bitter battles of 1896 and for the ultimate appointment of Tirpitz to Hollmann's position. Throughout the years 1893, 1894 and 1895, a steady guerrilla campaign was waged by the High Command to improve the position of the Chief of the High Command at the expense of the State Secretary.[39] In early 1895, Tirpitz and Senden gained another ally when Admiral Eduard von Knorr, a tough, irascible, red-headed old sea dog, was appointed Chief of the High Command of the Navy. That the combination Tirpitz-Knorr-Senden would ultimately prove too much for Admiral Hollmann was almost inevitable.[40]

Continued from page 70
Highest approval purely as an expression of the supreme military authority of the Kaiser. On the contrary, such approval is often given in association with the governmental power, often however to be seen as a manifestation of the latter only . . . and in the case of all regulations and instructions, organization, administration and technical questions will be touched." (Admiral Hollmann, *Immediatvortrag*, Berlin, January 21, 1897, p. 20. BA K 08-7/1, "Senden Nachlass".)

[38] Tirpitz to Senden, Berlin, January 11, 1893, BA K 08-7/1, "Senden Nachlass". Tirpitz's experiences as Chief of Staff reinforced the lessons he had learned from Stosch. He became firmly convinced of the pressing need for a strategy based on the development of a powerful fleet of battleships. After the manoeuvres of 1893 he began work on a memorandum, *Dienstschrift IX* of June 16, 1894, in which he expressed for the first time this fundamental component of his strategy. See Hans Hallmann, *Der Weg zum deutschen Schlachtflottenbau*, Stuttgart, 1933, p. 123, and W. Hubatsch, *Der Admiralstab*, p. 65.

[39] A bitterly fought point was the right of the High Command to deal directly with the Press. Senden managed to get the Kaiser's approval for an order empowering the High Command to provide the press with "reports or parts thereof, which have been made by the commanders of ships overseas on the general political situation, as well as the reproduction of such letters received by commanders from, say, a German living abroad, expressing the usefulness to trade and commerce of the presence of our warships or conversely the harm done to our countrymen there arising from the absence of such protection." (Senden to Chief of the High Command, January 23, 1894, MK III.)

[40] Bülow recalled (*Memoirs*, 1897–1903, English Ed., London, 1931, p. 65) Senden's singleminded devotion to the Navy. "Outside the Navy there existed nothing at all for this old fellow who had neither wife nor child, and had only a few friends . . . Admiral von Senden's love for the Navy went so far that in its interests he stuck to Admiral von Tirpitz whom he personally detested, because he thought he was the
Continued on page 72

Meanwhile the political situation was beginning to play into the hands of the naval cabal. Despite Caprivi's good intentions, the foreign relations of the Empire were deteriorating, while in domestic politics after 1892 the position of the Reich Chancellor was weakening as a result of repeated collisions between the Prussian Diet and the Reich government. By 1894, both foreign policy and Caprivi's position were crumbling. The assassination of President Sadi Carnot of France in 1894 frightened the Kaiser and the court entourage into hysterical demands for an anti-revolutionary law. Social reform was pushed aside, and the Kaiser and broad sections of the population succumbed to a "burst of political excitement . . . as Imperialism began to affect mass psychology".[41] On October 26, 1894, Caprivi resigned the Chancellorship, and the first phase of the post-Bismarckian era was over. His successor was the elderly Prince Chlodwig zu Hohenlohe-Schillingsfürst, a man chosen in order not to annoy the Kaiser.

The Kaiser's agitation for a massive increase in the fleet began to grow in intensity and volume. On January 8, 1895, the Kaiser made a speech to members of the Reichstag, in which he demanded a huge expansion of the fleet, but since he had heard both Hollmann's views on the necessity of building four new cruisers and the High Command's views on the necessity of building battleships, his speech was "like a gramophone record with two melodies playing at once".[42] On the 27th of the same month, the German Consul in Pretoria made an impassioned speech in which he swore that Germany was "the friend of the Boers".[43] On February 1, 1895, Baron Marschall, State Secretary at the Foreign Ministry, informed the British Ambassador that British complaints about German activity in the Transvaal were unfounded and that Germany regarded the Boer Republic as an "independent state".[44] Behind the scenes the High Command began to mount another full-scale

Continued from page 71
only man whose organizing ability and enthusiasm would ensure the swift and necessary expansion of the fleet."

[41] Werner Conze, *op. cit.*, p. 386.

[42] E. Kehr, *op. cit.*, p. 49.

[43] Herman Donner, *Die Vorgeschichte des Weltkrieges, Eine Sammlung aller wichtigsten Daten, 1870–1914*, Berlin, 1927.

[44] *Die Grosse Politik der Europäischen Kabinette, 1871–1914*, ed. by Thimme, Lepsius and Mendelssohn-Bartholdy, Berlin, 1921 ff., Vol. XI, No. 2577, pp. 3 ff.

attack on Admiral Hollmann. Holstein wrote apprehensively to Bülow on February 15, 1895: "A second attack is being directed against both Hollmann and Marschall. The Chief of the High Command, egged on by a few young place-seekers, has sent a memorandum with all sorts of cutting remarks about the Reich Navy and the Foreign Ministry to the Kaiser . . . Hollmann has threatened to resign, and Hohenlohe wrote to the Kaiser yesterday that he shares the views of Hollmann. This morning H.M. did not go to see either the Chancellor or Marschall, something he usually does after taking his walk; they say, too, that he is in a rotten mood. Naturally! All the people to whom he talks are anti-Government, and the latest method of the *Fronde*—that of praising the Kaiser at the expense of the government,—can hardly fail in its effect."[45]

Early in February, before the annual budget had been passed, the Kaiser used an unusual forum, the Royal Prussian Academy of War, to deliver a lengthy lecture on the need for a substantial expansion of the fleet. Accepting the premise that Germany would inevitably face enemies on two fronts in the next war, he demonstrated with elaborate charts and tables of statistics that both in respect of her merchant fleet and by comparison with the battle fleets of her probable enemies Germany was falling behind in her defences. "I believe," he told the officers, "that I have showed you with these figures that our Fatherland can demand that the necessary protection in maritime-military respect be provided for it and for its enormous interests abroad."[46] Turning to the dimensions of such a protection, he continued: "What must our demands be which we put to the Reichstag? . . . To begin with 9 cruisers 1st class, protected cruisers, above all replacement for the three flagships, in addition 15 cruisers 2nd class of the size of the *Kaiserin Augusta*, cruisers 4th class . . . 12."[47] If this big order were not filled, the Kaiser announced, "as the Chief of Staff of the High Command declared positively on his honour and conscience, the German battle fleet in 1899 will no longer be able to leave port."[48] Although Tirpitz was no doubt pleased

[45] *The Holstein Papers*, III, No. 443, p. 496, Holstein to Bülow, February 15, 1895.
[46] "Vortrag Seiner Majestät des Kaiser und König in der Königlichen Kriegs-Akademie zu Berlin", February 8, 1895, p. 7 (BA K 08-7/1, "Senden Nachlass").
[47] *Ibid.*, p. 19.
[48] *Ibid.*, p. 21.

to find himself so prominently quoted by his Imperial lord, he must have been taken aback to see his "honour and conscience" deployed in the cause of Hollmann's cruiser-building programme. The battle for the Imperial mind was evidently far from won.

Neither was the battle with the Reichstag. Hollmann's position, under fire internally from Senden and the High Command,[49] was absolutely dependent on an external success. Fortunately for him, Baron Marschall, who enjoyed the confidence of the majority of the deputies, pulled off a considerable coup and persuaded the Reichstag to pass an authorization on March 2nd enabling the State Secretary to begin building four cruisers. It was not the nine demanded by the Kaiser, but these four saved Hollmann's neck. Writing to Prince Radolin, German Ambassador in St. Petersburg, Holstein summarized the general situation of the Government: "During the past six weeks great efforts have been made here to get rid of Marschall. However, his position today is more secure than it was before. There are many factors that make him the most successful parliamentarian of the present cabinet . . . All the efforts on the part of M.'s opponents were frustrated by his success yesterday. The Kaiser is as happy as a lark about his four cruisers . . ."[50]

Meanwhile the Kaiser was intently following the course of the Sino-Japanese war. The small but efficient Japanese fleet rapidly established control of the seas. This was yet another demonstration of the importance of sea-power. The collapse of China might occur at any moment and trigger off a scramble for scraps of the dying Empire. "We dare not lose out in this business," the Kaiser wrote to the Chancellor as early as November 17, 1894, "nor allow ourselves to be surprised by events. We too need a firm base in China, where our trading turnover amounts to 400 million annually."[51] The actual dimensions of the Japanese victory and of the Japanese

[49] On February 25, the Kaiser was forced to issue another of the many All-Highest Cabinet Orders urging the two departments to co-operate with each other. (Quoted in RMA III. 1.5.2., Letter of the High Command, November 28, 1895.)

[50] *The Holstein Papers*, III, No. 452, p. 506, Holstein to Radolin, March 2, 1895.

[51] Kaiser Wilhelm II to Prince Hohenlohe, November 17, 1894, GP, Vol. IX, No. 2219, pp. 245 f.

demands at the peace conference in April, 1895, exceeded the Kaiser's expectations. The Japanese claim to Port Arthur and its hinterland, in State Secretary Marschall's words, "would bring China, or at least North China and Peking, into a protectorate relationship with Japan. Such high flown demands will certainly raise the question of the continued existence of China."[52]

When the Russian Foreign Minister, Lobanov, suggested that Germany join all the European powers in a combined protest to Japan, the German government jumped at the chance. Fear of the scramble for territory and of the possibility of an Anglo-Russian agreement over Germany's head, and a desire not to allow the newly established Franco-Russian alliance to consolidate itself, were the motives.[53] On April 17, 1895, the day of the signature of the Treaty, the Chief of the High Command of the Navy, Admiral von Knorr, wrote to Admiral Hollmann at the Imperial Naval Office informing him that a firm decision had been taken by the Kaiser and the Chancellor to join the other powers in a protest to Japan about the terms of the peace treaty, and on the following day Admiral von Knorr reported to the Kaiser that orders had been issued to the Cruiser Squadron in the Far East to take up positions in northern Chinese waters and to prepare to support Russia with force, if necessary.[54] The importance of this incident lay not so much in the substance of the German action as in its motivation. Policy was at last becoming 'world policy'. Germany demonstrated by her inclusion in the diplomatic protest that she too was a world power, no longer to be ignored. For the growth of the Navy, the incident had its uses. Naval power, and naval power alone, could guarantee the German position in the Far East.

When Great Britain refused to join the protest of the continental powers to Japan, the rift widened between Britain and Germany. The cordial relations of the Caprivi era deteriorated as the German drift towards Russia became obvious.

[52] Freiherr von Marschall, State Secretary of the Foreign Ministry, to Count von Hatzfeldt, German Ambassador in London, April 4, 1895, *ibid.*, No. 2233, p. 262.
[53] *Ibid.*, Nos. 2243–7, pp. 269 ff., and William L. Langer, *op. cit.*, Vol. I. pp. 182 ff.
[54] Letter, von Knorr to Hollmann, April 17, 1895, and von Knorr to the Kaiser, April 18, 1895, ADMB, I.1.11.

When the German Minister in Tokyo, Freiherr von Gutschmid, not only took part in the three power protest to the Japanese government but exceeded his French and Russian colleagues in belligerence, the British government was distinctly displeased. During the summer of 1895 Anglo-German relations went from bad to worse. The Kaiser's visit to Cowes was unsuccessful. The British Press was openly hostile to him and to his grandiose pretensions. Alfred von Kiderlen-Wächter wrote to Baron Holstein and described how much ill will the Kaiser had caused by insisting on bringing four German battleships with him: "H.M. gave the English a special treat by bringing along a fleet of four battleships and a dispatch-boat. They block the course of the racing vessels, every few moments they get an attack of *salutirium*, the sailors are flooding Cowes, the Queen has to invite the commanders, etc!"[55] The Kaiser and Lord Salisbury had a disagreement during the visit, which did not help to improve the atmosphere.

By October of 1895 Anglo-German relations were distinctly chilly and showed no signs of a thaw. On October 14th of that year, Sir Edward Malet, British Ambassador at Berlin, had an interview with State Secretary Marschall in which he protested about repeated German interventions in South Africa and gave expression to what the Kaiser furiously regarded as "threats".[56] While the South African problems continued to bubble, the Imperial Naval Office began to face its annual *via crucis* over the naval estimates. As Hollmann put the finishing touches on his demands for the 1896 fiscal year, the Associated Governments found themselves facing the eruption of an unpleasant crisis about reform of the antiquated and illiberal procedures for Army courts martial. Both naval expansion and reform of the Army's system of punishment were delicate and potentially explosive issues. Both questions stirred the Kaiser emotionally, and both raised constitutional uncertainties about the limits of the Emperor's powers as Commander-in-Chief. The reform of the Army's penal procedures affected the most reactionary and obscurantist group in German society, the officer corps, and produced angry

[55] *The Holstein Papers*, III, No. 482, p. 538, Kiderlen-Wächter to Holstein, August 7, 1895.
[56] GP, Vol. XI, No. 2578, pp. 5 ff.

sentiments on both sides. "A quarter of a century after the foundation of the German Empire there was no unified, let alone modern, penal procedure in the Army . . . The Prussian Military Code of Justice, issued in the pre-constitutional era (1845), was still in effect; it rested on the long discredited basis of secret and written inquisitorial procedures and was in operation everywhere in the Army except in Bavaria and Württemberg . . . The Military Cabinet as well as the majority of the generals resisted with the tenacity of a privileged caste any attempt to open the doors . . ."[57]

Prospects for a pleasant Reichstag session were not favourable when Hollmann informed the High Command of the Navy that the list of ships to be requested was ready[58]. Literally a day or two before the budget for the Navy was to be introduced, Admiral von Knorr let off his first salvo in what was to become a struggle for survival between the two most important naval officers. "I must express my regret", Knorr wrote, "that I have been given no opportunity to explain my views in All-Highest places, as is my duty, in this question so vital to the future of the Navy. Since Your Excellency has not even troubled to inform me of the reasons why the opinions of the High Command communicated to you initially with respect to the draft of the estimates for 1895/6, as well as the repeated and urgent arguments of the High Command of the Navy since that time, have not been respected, I am compelled to assume that Your Excellency refuses to recognize my right to cooperate on such matters . . ."[59] Admiral von Knorr had thrown down the gauntlet. It was now to be a fight to the finish and he informed Hollmann that he had submitted a memorandum to the Kaiser "expressing serious concern for the future of the Navy".

The memorandum of November 28, 1895, which von Knorr submitted, is a remarkable document. In it the first outlines of the future naval laws can be seen. It begins by noting that "for some time, and especially since the beginning of the 90s, not only our potential enemies, but all states which recognize

[57] Erich Eyck, *Wilhelm II*, p. 146.
[58] Hollmann to von Knorr, October 27, 1895, RMA III. 1.5.2.
[59] Letter, von Knorr to Hollmann, Berlin, November 28, 1895, *Very Secret*, RMA III.1.5.2.

the importance of a fleet for their world positions and economic interests, have been making great efforts to develop and expand their navies, in particular their battle fleets . . . For our remaining, antiquated armoured ships only one replacement has been authorized, so that the fleet finds itself in an extremely dangerous decline compared to the navies of other states."[60] Since "the French North Fleet and the Russian Baltic Fleet are our probable enemies",[61] the High Command argued, they had to compare the three powers: Russia, France and Germany. Based on the figures for 1896 and calculations of authorized new construction, the High Command arrived at distressing results: by 1901 France would have 9 or 10 new battleships and 10 old ones, Russia 10 new and 1 old, Germany 5 new and 1 old. "With each passing year these relationships become less favourable to us and by 1901 we shall not be equal in strength of our forces to either of the two opponents."[62] Under such circumstances, the High Command continued, the Kaiser Wilhelm Canal would be indefensible and thus strategically valueless and the Navy would be "equally unable . . . to fulfil its second objective, protection in war and peace of the overseas interests of Germany".[63]

Germany's fundamental naval strategy in the High Command's view had to be defensive with only occasional "offensive strikes". To carry out such limited defensive operations the fleet had to be at least thirty per cent stronger in material terms than either the French or Russian northern fleets.[64] Given both the premise and the soundness of the comparison, the High Command was now in a position to calculate how large a fleet Germany actually needed in precise terms. It was the end of the era of the "limitless fleet" and the beginning of a whole series of accurate, arithmetical assessments of Germany's objective naval strength measured by the strength of the enemy. This first figure, thirty per cent larger than either

[60] Das Oberkommando der Marine, "Stärkeverhältnis der deutschen Flotte gegenüber den Flotten unserer voraussichtlichen Gegner", Berlin, November 28, 1895, Copy, p. 1, RMA III. 1.5.2.
[61] *Ibid.*, p. 2.
[62] *Ibid.*, pp. 3 f.
[63] *Ibid.*, p. 9.
[64] *Ibid.*, p. 12.

opposing fleet, was not unreasonable, nor extravagantly large. Its significance lay less in its effect on the absolute size of the fleet than in its transformation of the framework within which the fleet could be objectively developed. Any changes in these arithmetical rules of thumb had to be changes in the fundamental strategic outlook of the Navy. The modest thirty per cent over the French or Russian fleets had given way by 1897 to a much more grandiose fifty per cent of the combined Franco-Russian fleets, which in time was replaced by the dynamic "building tempo" calculations of the Tirpitz era, two keels laid to three English and eventually three German keels to four English. Each new arithmetical comparison selected between 1895 and 1912 expanded the desirable size of the Navy, but once such a measurement had been fixed, the actual size of the fleet was, paradoxically, a function of the activity of Germany's opponent. Every expansion of the relevant foreign navies led in theory to an automatic German expansion as long as the principle of the fixed ratio of strength held. In this respect, the High Command was less aggressive than Tirpitz later became, because unlike the "risk theory" this principle left the initiative to Germany's opponents. If they built no ships, Germany built none. By contrast the "risk theory" involved German construction until the leverage of the German Home Fleet began to exert sufficient pressure on British policy. After that point had been reached, it would be enough to maintain a constant ratio.

For the moment, Germany would have to build to catch up with her probable enemies. Even to achieve the modest thirty per cent superiority meant an enormous increase in the sums needed from the Reichstag. "In view of the situation to which an unfriendly and unwilling popular assembly has brought us . . . only a building plan, limited in its aims and reduced to the necessary minimum, can prevent the gradual weakening of our military power at sea, but this building plan must be pursued with the greatest possible energy."[65] The choice of words displays the familiar Tirpitz style. (Tirpitz himself was no longer in Berlin. His tour of duty as Chief of Staff had ended.) Its emphases are typically the

[65] *Ibid.*, p. 21.

need for unity in strategy and construction and the importance of a vigorous campaign of popular education and propaganda. A diplomatic failure could be useful, if it could be shown that naval weakness had been the cause. "Only if the full truth is repeated again and again and the entire responsibility for our decline as a sea-power can be placed solely on the Reichstag, is a change in the present situation to be hoped for."[66]

The building plan which Admiral von Knorr proposed foresaw the expenditure of M32 millions per annum on construction over a thirteen year period, which was only a marginal increase on the average of M30 millions spent on ship-building during the previous five years.[67] This principle of demanding tiny increments, while concealing what Eugen Richter called "*das dicke Ende*", was a favourite ruse used by Tirpitz later. In this case, it could be shown legitimately that the annual costs were less than those of the French or Russian building schedules. The aim of the programme, a limited number of powerful ships, corresponded to the strategic principle that victory must be sought in a decisive battle in the home waters.[68] The number of different types was sharply reduced which made the plan cheaper and clearer in outline, while the primacy of the decisive struggle in home waters eliminated the need for a separate type of cruiser for overseas duty. Finally, the High Command attacked the Imperial Naval Office and urged the Kaiser to take steps to ensure co-operation between the two agencies, "since the lack of a definitely expressed organizational arrangement for the co-operation of the

[66] *Ibid.*, p. 23.

[67] *Ibid.*, *Anlage* 2, IV—The financial calculations were as follows:

Completion of *Ersatz Preussen*	18 million
„ „ *Ersatz Leipzig*	15 „
For 3 cruisers II Class (approved already) (10 million each)	30 „
For 12 battleships (20 million each)	240 „
For 3 armoured cruisers (7,000–7,500 tons) (12 million each)	36 „
For 12 protected cruisers IV Class (4 million each)	48 „
For 5 torpedo-boat divisions	30 „
For 5 gunboats	4 „
TOTAL:	M421 million

Average per annum appropriation required from April 1896 to April 1908: . . . . M32.4 million

[68] *Ibid.*, pp. 26 f.

Die Marine-Tabellen

Seiner Majestät des Kaisers Wilhelm.

Verkleinerte Facsimile-Nachbildung der Kaiserlichen Originale.

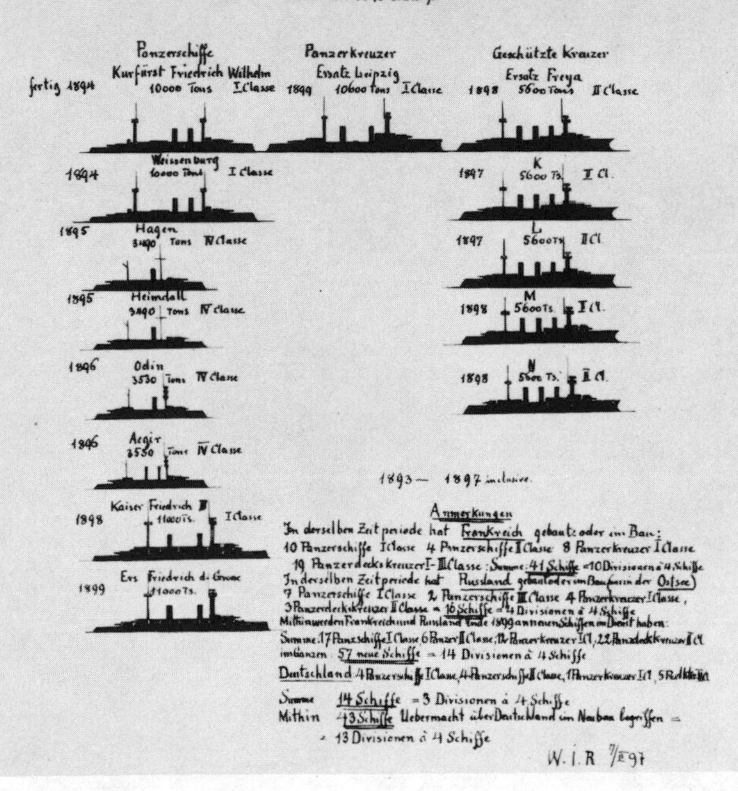

Anmerkungen

In derselben Zeitperiode hat Frankreich gebaut oder im Bau:
10 Panzerschiffe I Classe 4 Panzerschiffe II Classe 8 Panzerkreuzer I Classe
19 Panzerdeckskreuzer I–III Classe: Summe: 41 Schiffe = 10 Divisionen à 4 Schiffe
In derselben Zeitperiode hat Russland gebaut oder im Bau (nur in der Ostsee)
7 Panzerschiffe I Classe 2 Panzerschiffe III Classe 4 Panzerkreuzer I Classe,
3 Panzerdeckskreuzer II Classe = 16 Schiffe = 4 Divisionen à 4 Schiffe
Mithin werden Frankreich und Russland Ende 1899 an neuen Schiffen im Dienst haben:
Summe: 17 Panzschiffe I Classe, 6 Panzer II Classe, 12 Panzerkreuzer I Cl, 22 Panzdeckkreuzer I Cl
im Ganzen: 57 neue Schiffe = 14 Divisionen à 4 Schiffe
Deutschland 4 Panzerschiffe I Classe, 4 Panzerschiffe II Classe, 1 Panzerkreuzer I Cl, 5 [illegible]
Summe 14 Schiffe = 3 Divisionen à 4 Schiffe
Mithin 43 Schiffe Uebermacht über Deutschland im Neubau begriffen =
= 13 Divisionen à 4 Schiffe

W. I. R. 7/II 97

Table of ships built in Germany after 1893 prepared by Kaiser Wilhelm II, February 7, 1897

S.M.S. "Kurfürst Friedrich Wilhelm", battleship I class, at the Imperial Dockyard, Wilhelmshaven, 1894

S.M.S. "Brandenburg", battleship I class, 1895, starboard view from bow, at anchor

two highest naval offices has produced harmful results in this very important matter."[69]

The Kaiser was evidently impressed by the High Command's arguments and, when he came to Kiel on December 16, 1895, he called a meeting of all the naval chiefs at which he gave Admiral Hollman his new orders. The Imperial Naval Office was formally instructed: "(1) A plan is to be worked out for a ship-building programme to be carried out over a considerable number of years; (2) an increase in the number of battleships to twenty-five must be regarded as the minimum necessary in view of the new construction in the north fleets of our neighbouring enemies, as long as the "Siegfried Class" remains included in that number."[70] This was a triumph for the High Command. The argument that Germany's Navy must rest on a central fleet at home had carried the day. The figure of twenty-five battleships meant that two full squadrons plus a flag ship would be the core of that home fleet. Both principles were victories for Tirpitz's school of naval strategy.[71]

On the day following the big meeting in Kiel, Senden sent Tirpitz a confidential letter. He enclosed the order given to Hollmann and copies of the other relevant documents, and wrote that the Kaiser was aware of the problems involved in the passage of such a vast building programme. Senden invited Tirpitz to write a confidential report for the Kaiser about the way such a plan might be constructed "to build a basis for the future".[72] An audience with the Kaiser was to take place early in the new year. The future seemed clear at last, and Tirpitz was cheerful. On December 21st, he wrote hopefully to General von Stosch, his old mentor, of his vision of the transformation

[69] *Ibid.*, p. 29.

[70] "Allerhöchste Cabinets-Ordre an den Reichskanzler (RMA)", Kiel, December 16, 1895, RMA III 1.5.2.

[71] Although the High Command had scored a great success, the Kaiser had apparently still not got the point of the limited programme which had been placed before him, because he insisted on going ahead with a little idea of his own, a battleship of 9,000 tons with a speed of 18 knots. "An die Kaiserliche Werft zu Kiel, Aufgabe: Selbständige Ausarbeitung und Vorlage von Plänen betreffend ein Panzerschiff (seegehend)-9,000 tons Deplacement, 3 Maschinen, do. Schrauben, 1,000 tons Kohlen . . . 18 Knoten—4 24cm L/40 in Thürmen, 14 15cm L/40 S.K., 20 5cm S.K., 16 Maxim. S.K. . . . Wilhelm I.R. Konigl. Schloss, Kiel, 16.XII. 1895." (Written in Kaiser's hand), MK.I.10.c.

[72] Quoted in Hans Hallmann, *Der Weg zum deutschen Schlachtfottenbau*, pp. 169 f.

of Germany. No longer would the German lead "a parasitic existence", but soon "*civis Germanus sum*" would be heard all over the world.[73] The Kaiser was also filled with ideas of grandeur on the seas and on the 20th of the same month, he had the second of his two long interviews with Colonel Swaine, British military attaché in Berlin. As in the earlier interview in October, the Kaiser warned Swaine of the dangers of the British "policy of selfishness and bullying", and demanded that Britain join the Triple Alliance of Germany, Italy and Austria-Hungary. "For the sake of a few square miles full of negroes and palm trees, England had threatened her one real friend, the German Emperor, the grandson of Her Majesty the Queen of Great Britain and Ireland, with war."[74] Holstein was "utterly crushed by yesterday's conversation between H.M. and Swaine. H.M. said things which create a great threat of war for us . . . This can only lead to a crack-up."[75]

Ten days later the crack-up came. As the Kaiser had predicted, the blow fell in South Africa. The "few square miles full of negroes and palm trees" were about to provoke the first open break between Great Britain and the German Empire. On the last day of 1895 the Foreign Ministry received a cable from the German consul in Pretoria that a raid had been carried out on the Boer Republic by 800 armed men of the British Chartered Company, and that President Krüger was "counting on the intervention of Germany and France".[76] This invasion, the famous "Jameson Raid", ignited all the smouldering resentment of England which had been building up in Germany for more than a year. Even Holstein began to turn over the idea of a continental alliance against England.[77] The Kaiser was more impatient; he wanted dramatic action and not diplomatic realignment. The Minister of War, Bronsart

[73] Tirpitz, *op. cit.*, p. 52.

[74] Kaiser Wilhelm II to Reich Chancellor, Prince Hohenlohe, December 20, 1895, GP, X, No. 2572, p. 254, and Kaiser Wilhelm II to Freiherr von Marschall, October 25, 1895, GP, IX, No. 2579, pp. 8 ff.

[75] Holstein to Eulenburg, December 21, 1895, *The Holstein Papers*, Vol. III, No. 515, pp. 576 ff.

[76] German Consul in Pretoria, von Herff, to the Foreign Ministry, December 30, 1895, GP, XI, No. 2588, pp. 16 f.

[77] GP, XI, No. 2642, pp. 72 f., January 1, 1896, and the replies from the Ambassadors at Rome, Paris and St. Petersburg.

von Schellendorf, had an interview with him on January 2nd, during which the Kaiser lost his self-control and became so violent that Bronsart told the Chancellor: "If it had been anyone else, he (Bronsart) would have drawn his sword . . . The Minister of War thought that H.M.'s condition was not normal and he was very worried about the future."[78] The Kaiser's hysteria had not abated on the following day. At ten in the morning he appeared with his three admirals, Hollmann, Knorr and Senden, at the Reich Chancellor's palace to discuss the South African situation with Hohenlohe and Marschall. Wild and hysterical scenes took place. "The Kaiser wanted to mobilize the naval infantry, send troops from Germany to South Africa, or call an international conference, which would give him a protectorate over the Transvaal . . ."[79] After the conference had decided to send the famous telegram to President Krüger, Marschall said to Holstein, "You have no idea what proposals were made there, this is still the mildest."[80]

On the same day, January 3, 1896, Tirpitz completed his memorandum for the Kaiser. In it he declared his support in full for the programme submitted by the High Command. Two squadrons would represent "a considerable force even against a fleet of the first rank". He was convinced that "we shall be able to train ourselves in their tactical deployment quite easily as soon as they are actually available and unified".[81] He suggested certain alterations in the demands to be made of the Reichstag to simplify the structure of the fleet and to tip the scales even more heavily in favour of the home fleet. Two more battleships would be needed as reserve for the seventeen demanded by the High Command, three more heavy cruisers suitable for home and overseas duty and two fewer light cruisers of the third class. These alterations would involve an additional expenditure of M 64 million, but, Tirpitz believed, "such a measure would provide the best possible weapon against educated and ignorant Social Democrats".[82] Finally, Tirpitz outlined an early version of the "risk theory". "Even

[78] Hohenlohe, *op. cit.*, p. 151, Diary Entry, January 3, 1896.
[79] Erich Eyck, *op. cit.*, pp. 133 f.
[80] *The Holstein Papers*, IV, No. 608, p. 22.
[81] Quoted in Hans Hollmann, *Der Weg zum deutschen Schlachtflottenbau*, p. 173.
[82] *Ibid.*, p. 174.

the greatest sea state of Europe would be more conciliatory towards us if we were able to throw two or three highly trained squadrons into the political scales and correspondingly into the balance of conflict. We shall never achieve that using overseas cruisers."[83]

This was the programme which Tirpitz pursued without rest from that day until the outbreak of war in 1914. As he wrote to Stosch, "there is hope that the thread will be picked up where it was broken in 1883 . . . Our policy-makers fail to see that the alliance-worthiness of Germany even for European states is often to be found not in our Army but in the fleet . . . They simply do not understand the need for, and the importance of, sea power."[84]

Hollmann had in the meantime begun to carry out the orders received on December 16th and had formed a "Committee for the Further Development of the German Fleet", which began to meet at the end of December 1895.[85] In an earnest effort to restore good relations, Hollmann and von Knorr exchanged a series of letters covering the outstanding points of disagreement between them, and arrived fairly easily at compromises about the number of cruisers to be built under the plan and the sizes of the different cruiser classes.[86] With both sides showing good will, the work of the committee went ahead smoothly and, by the end of January, Hollmann was able to initial the first draft of the plan. Prospects for an end to the era of the "limitless fleet" had never been so rosy. A plan was going forward for a limited, but strategically useful, fleet, and the Imperial Naval Office began to consider the practical details and consequences. How much of the new fleet was to be kept on active duty at all times? How were orders to

[83] *Ibid.*, p. 175.

[84] Tirpitz to Stosch, February 12, 1896, Tirpitz, *op. cit.*, pp. 54 f.

[85] "Kommission zur Weiterentwicklung der deutschen Flotte" Order of December 18, 1895, signed by State Secretary Hollmann, RMA III. 1.5.2. Cf. RMA III. 1.5.2. "Kommission etc.", Direktion des Marine-Departements, for the Agenda, December 31, 1895, signed by Captain Büchsel, and also, "Denkschrift zum Immediatvortrag betreffend Vortrag an Aller-Höchsten Stelle über die Frist, die dem Schiffsbauprogramm zu Grunde gelegt werden soll", December 31, 1895, signed by Captain Fischel, Military Section, A, with replies by Hollmann, January 1, 1896, in margins. RMA III. 1.5.2.

[86] Letters of January 3 and 6, 1896, Hollmann to Knorr, as well as replies January 17 and 28, 1896, High Command to Imperial Naval Office, RMA III. 1.5.2.

be distributed among the shipyards? In view of the number of unsolved questions, the Committee concluded its first draft by pointing out that it was "necessary to assume that the first request for funds will not be made until the fiscal year 1897/8".[87]

At Court the atmosphere was quite different. The Kaiser had now decided that he had to have cruisers at once, in addition to the long-term building plan which he had approved in December. When Hohenlohe mildly suggested that this was impracticable, the Kaiser was extremely annoyed. "There is a distinction", he wrote to Hohenlohe on January 8, 1896, "between the fixed expansion plan for the Navy, as outlined in the Memorandum of the High Command of December 1st and my intentions as altered by Transvaal . . . My idea which has arisen as a consequence of Transvaal is a response to the desperate, immediate needs and is intended to fill a dangerous momentary gap . . . For the present problem a great plan is not required; we need an immediate measure, not new construction at home, but the purchase of armoured cruisers and cruisers wherever we can find them as soon as possible . . . At the same time, cruisers must be laid down in the homeland in numbers corresponding to the capacities of our dockyards."[88] Such ideas were, of course, politically quite fantastic and Hohenlohe knew it. Tirpitz was also very upset at the prospect of the High Command's victory of December 1895 going under in a welter of confused and absurd projects. On January 12th, Tirpitz called on Senden, who remarked drily in his diary: "Tirpitz was here. He was very dissatisfied that cruisers are now being demanded again and believes that, as a result, the whole programme will break up."[89] The next day Senden saw the Kaiser who was "furious with Hollmann that the demands of the Navy had not yet been put to the Reichstag; they had better be brought in before the 18th".[90]

Despite his objections, the ever-pliable Hohenlohe put out

[87] "Denkschrift, Abteilung A", January 28, 1896, approved by Hollmann. All other copies in possession of members of the Committee were to be destroyed on Hollmann's order and detailed work was to begin. RMA III. 1.5.2.
[88] Kaiser to Hohenlohe, January 8, 1896, Hohenlohe, *op. cit.*, pp. 153 f.
[89] Diary Entry of Admiral Senden, January 12, 1896, Eckart Kehr, *op. cit.*, Anhang IV, p. 464.
[90] *Ibid.*, Entry of January 13, 1896, p. 464.

feelers to the leaders of the Reichstag. A meeting was held on January 13th which indicated that "even at this moment there is not a trace of enthusiasm for enlarging the Navy. Such a bill would cause the Associated Governments a major defeat, which in the states of Europe, and especially in England, would be greeted with delight as a personal defeat for Your Majesty."[91] The Kaiser and Senden were beside themselves with rage. Senden informed the Kaiser that "Bennigsen of the National Liberals said he might have a few votes; Fritzen of the Centre said not one vote is for it, everyone was worried about loans, the people were already loaded with taxes; Levetzow of the Conservatives had no votes either; the Agrarians barely had their daily bread. As far as the Bundesrath is concerned, it is doubtful whether there is a majority there. The Chancellor requests that the idea be dropped. These are the facts: the King and Emperor has no majority in the Government, nor in the Bundesrath, nor in the Reichstag. This is an absolutely unbelievable state of affairs. How are we to be ruled and what will happen? I advise a change of personnel. We have to rebuild the Government from the ground up and put it on the basis of another programme. We must rule with one party only. Hollmann too must be more energetic . . . An energetic man with a broad view as State Secretary must bring about a change, perhaps Tirpitz."[92]

The Imperial temper was frayed to the point of hysteria by all these frustrations. On January 16th, Holstein sent a private telegram to Hatzfeldt, German Ambassador in London: "Great pressure is now being brought to bear on the Kaiser regarding an alleged English plan for a landing in Delagoa Bay. A large demand for additional funds for the Navy, which Prince Hohenlohe will not introduce because it has no prospect of passing, is today being used as a lever to overthrow the Prince, just as the Anti-Revolutionary Law was used in Caprivi's time. I am also afraid that if the Kaiser is not pacified about Delagoa by the day after tomorrow, he will deliver an extemporaneous speech to the members of the Reichstag that could have serious consequences."[93]

[91] Hohenlohe, *op. cit.*, pp. 156 f.
[92] Diary Entry, July 14, 1896, in E. Kehr, *op. cit.*, Anhang IV, p. 464.
[93] *The Holstein Papers*, Private Telegram, III, No. 522, p. 586.

The Kaiser's excitement was not entirely groundless. Reports from Great Britain were hardly calculated to calm his jittery nerves. German sailors had been assaulted on the Thames docks and German shops had been attacked by patriotic Englishmen. The British Press roared its disapproval of German intervention, and on January 7th, the Admiralty took steps to create a "Flying Squadron" to consist of two first-class battleships, two first-class and two second-class cruisers, and six destroyers. The squadron was ready to serve anywhere in the world at a moment's notice, and rumours were not scarce which pointed to Delagoa Bay as its first test of fire. On January 21st, the First Lord of the Admiralty, Mr. Goschen, put an end to the more expansive speculations by announcing that the flying squadron was actually going to Berehaven to await developments.[94] The Kaiser had already acted by the time this reassurance was made public. On January 16th, he dictated a cable to Admiral Senden which contained orders to remove the two third-class cruisers, *Kondor* and *Seeadler*, from their stations in Delagoa Bay. At the same time he ordered the High Command to recall the *Kaiser*, Germany's largest cruiser in the China Sea, as well as the *Arcona*, a second-class cruiser which had been temporarily attached to the Far Eastern Station.

Wilhelm II was certain that war with England might come at any moment, and he found the inertia of his government incredible. If his ministers could not see the gravity of the situation, he had no choice but to act himself. The orders to the High Command made this point entirely clear: "Today I informed Freiherr von Marschall that since the Reichstag is evidently unable to feel the burden of our national honour in the face of England and nobody interests himself in the Navy or shows any enthusiasm, and in view of the uncertain prospects for the spring, I can no longer weaken my fleet in home waters . . ."[95] Hohenlohe was dismayed. In a note to the Kaiser, he argued that recall of the two cruisers from Delagoa Bay at this time would be regarded by the world as flight from

[94] A. J. Marder, *op. cit.*, pp. 256 f.
[95] Official Telegram, Imperial Naval Cabinet to the Chief of the High Command, Berlin, January 16, 1896, ADMB I. 1–12.

the English,[96] although exactly what Hohenlohe expected two third-class cruisers of 1,640 tons armed with eight 4·1 inch quick-firing guns and two torpedo tubes to do against Britain's "Flying Squadron" is not clear. Von Knorr was torn between the military realities and the Chancellor's political assessment. For once, the Chief of the High Command of the Navy decided that it was wise to act constitutionally. Before carrying out the Kaiser's order he wrote to the Chancellor to ask: "Whether after Your Highness's audience of His Majesty another decision has been reached, so that in the event I can issue the corresponding orders?"[97] Holstein was also annoyed. "If the Kaiser makes it obvious that he thinks his fleet is too good for real world politics, the Reichstag will in that case certainly not approve anything for him."[98] But the Kaiser was adamant. "Today," he wrote to Hohenlohe on the 17th, "three strong English cruisers have arrived there (Delagoa). They are strong enough to paralyse the two ships even if they were to be used . . . I am therefore of the opinion that they should steam away as soon as possible."[99] After his consultation with the Chancellor, von Knorr had an audience with the Kaiser and managed to get the decisions modified. Only the *Kondor*, which had arrived on the 9th, would leave Delagoa Bay at the moment, while the *Seeadler* would remain.[100]

The recall of the ships from the Far East was settled by Hohenlohe, who pointed out that the *Kaiser* was the most powerful German ship in the Far East, and that Germany's position in that area depended on the "development of a strong maritime force. Only if we display our power continually before their eyes, and the possibility of using that power as well, can we arrive . . . at a realization of our wish to acquire a naval station in China."[101] It was an ironic twist that the peaceful old Chancellor had to remind the Chief of the High Command of the Navy's own desire for a coaling station. The argument convinced Knorr, because the order to recall the

[96] Hohenlohe, *op. cit.*, p. 160, Letter of January 17, 1896.
[97] Von Knorr to Hohenlohe, Berlin, January 16, 1896, ADMB I. 1–12.
[98] Holstein Memo, Hohenlohe, *op. cit.*, p. 160.
[99] Kaiser Wilhelm II to Hohenlohe, January 17, 1897, *ibid.*, p. 160.
[100] "Aktennotiz", no date, written in margin of letter of January 16, cf. Footnote 97.
[101] Hohenlohe to Knorr, "Delivered by hand", January 16, 1896, ADMB I. 1–12.

Arcona was rescinded and the return of the *Kaiser* was delayed.[102] Although Hohenlohe hoped that the crisis was now over, Marschall and Holstein were certain that it was not. "Every day," Hohenlohe wrote to his son on January 18th, "Marschall whips up Holstein to force me to have a row with the Kaiser . . . First the two gentlemen wanted me to demand that the Kaiser show me his after-dinner speech; now that the speech turns out to have been quite reasonable, they want to drive me into a conflict because of the Navy. Marschall, who is feeling big after his success in the Reichstag, seems to be cherishing hopes again about the Chancellorship."[103] Hohenlohe evidently believed that Marschall and Holstein had manufactured the crisis out of thin air, but he was wrong. The Kaiser was still determined to introduce the big Navy plan in the immediate future, despite the belief of the experts that it would not be feasible for at least a year and the Chancellor's belief that "it would be dangerous to talk further about enlarging the fleet and additional demands until the budget has been safely passed. Afterwards . . . we cannot do anything else except work out a plan and discuss it with H.M. . . ."[104] It was an open question whether the Kaiser would wait that long.

Holstein was extremely pessimistic. On January 25, 1896, he wrote to Eulenburg that the Kaiser was still in a state of pathological excitement. He was demanding vast appropriations for the fleet—his estimates ranged from 100 to 300 million—and he believed that by dissolving the Reichstag he could easily find people "who could arrange it".[105] On the evening of January 24th, Admiral Senden gave a beer party for a selected circle of the entourage. Admiral Hollmann, who was one of the guests, was collared by the Kaiser and treated to an ill-tempered display of petulance. Prince Hohenlohe, who received a full account from Hollmann, began to draw certain conclusions: "The Kaiser expressed himself in such a way that Hollmann was convinced the Kaiser hopes to find a Chancellor who will introduce big naval demands, then dissolve the Reichstag and eventually carry out a *coup d'état*. That's all

[102] "Aktennotiz" to Knorr's letter, January 16, 1896, cf. footnote 97.
[103] Hohenlohe, *op. cit.*, p. 161, January 18, 1896.
[104] *Ibid.*, Diary Entry, January 22, 1896.
[105] *The Holstein Papers,* III, No. 525, p. 589, Note 2.

right with me, . . . In any event I cannot see whom he will find to try out this experiment."[106]

While the political situation steadily worsened, Senden continued his efforts to dislodge Hollmann and to put Tirpitz in office. At the end of January he arranged an audience with the Kaiser for Tirpitz to discuss the memorandum of January 3rd. At this audience the Kaiser informed Tirpitz that he was to be Hollmann's successor and that the change of office would take place soon.[107] Tirpitz began to prepare for the new task. On February 8th, he wrote to Senden to suggest that the Ship Statistical Office and the Canal Department of the Reich Ministry of the Interior be absorbed into the Imperial Naval Office. With his characteristic enthusiasm, he began to develop "a series of measures against the prevailing ultra-bureaucracy, which would be ideal to create a favourable atmosphere for the I.N.O. We could thus work against the constant accusations of militarism through our acts, and the beginning could be made for the take-over of other sea interests. If the traffic in the canal rises, as I hope it will, the results will be entered in the profit ledger of the Navy."[108]

Senden was impressed by the energy and imagination which his bright young man was displaying and called in the Kaiser's Chief of the Civil Cabinet, Herman von Lucanus, to discuss the political feasibility of Tirpitz's proposals. Lucanus had reservations but Senden pointed out that "the peace-time tasks of the Navy were so different from those of the Army that it would be worth" the political risks involved in an expansion of the I.N.O. In seven points he outlined his vision of the programme for the I.N.O. Since the "Army was tied to the country by a thousand threads, tradition and appreciation of it were available." It would be necessary to find a "broader basis" for the Navy. The Hanseatic cities were useless because of "their particularist tendencies and parasitic standpoint about foreign trade." It would, thirdly, be necessary to "achieve contacts with sea interests and maritime circles, since recognition of the development of trade and commerce would provide a tool against the accusation of militarism". The

[106] Hohenlohe, *op. cit.*, p. 162, Diary Entry, January 25, 1896.
[107] Tirpitz, *op. cit.*, p. 60.
[108] Tirpitz to Senden, Kiel, February 8, 1896, BA K 08-7/1, "Senden Nachlass".

I.N.O. must have "a more positive State Secretary to face the Bundesrath and the Reichstag". The "branches of activity" of the new Imperial Naval Office would include "commercial fishing, professional magazines and journals, sea maps, control of accidents, the canal . . . These are all common interests today. The Navy wants to see them flourish, for its own advantage lies there too." This was "no mere bureaucratic benevolence, because the Navy's very existence depends on the prosperity of these interests". Finally, Senden concluded, there must be "*an absolute monarchy*. His Majesty to command how large the Navy to be; perhaps a special ministry for maritime affairs and colonies." The Army would take care of "revolutions within".[109]

Two days later in a long and revealing letter, Tirpitz replied to Senden's account of the conversation with Lucanus. On the whole he agreed with Senden's seven-point programme, but "on the political question, there are in fact objections. If we had an absolute monarchy, the Kaiser could by his own free choice, on the basis of suggestions from his advisers, simply say that the Navy should be this or that size. I might then consider it better to construct a special ministry for maritime affairs, and leave the battle fleet to itself. I shall pass over the question whether the caste spirit which would thereby be engendered in the service would be useful, especially for the Navy with its many relationships and situations overseas. Might it not, on the contrary, be worth recommending that our sea officers in addition to their military side also feel that they are Reich agents for our transatlantic, economic interests? I shall, as I say, leave this essentially psychological question on one side and instead stick to the fact that the Kaiser simply cannot operate according to his own wishes in the creation of a Navy, but must reckon with a series of other factors and with the will and wishes of the nation. We must set up our higher naval departments to fit this situation, whether we like it or not."[110] Nothing could have been more characteristic of the fundamental differences between Tirpitz, the middle class liberal, and the Silesian aristocrat and conservative, Baron

[109] "Aufzeichnung zum Gespräch mit S.E. von L.", February 13, 1896, BA K 08-7/1, "Senden Nachlass".

[110] Tirpitz to Senden, February 15, 1896, BA K 08-7/1, "Senden Nachlass".

Senden. Tirpitz wanted none of "that nervousness with which the Army is controlled" to affect the Navy.[111]

At the same time, the liberal admiral from the middle class was no less aggressive than the conservative Cabinet Chief in his attitude towards England. In a letter to Stosch on February 13th, he wrote: "England swallows rude behaviour from America . . . above all because America is an unpleasant enemy and Germany pays the bill, because at the moment it has no sea power worth mentioning."[112] Stosch too was full of bellicose sentiments. "If I were not such an old man," he wrote to a friend on the 14th, "I could be quite enthusiastic about a war."[113] And to Tirpitz, "Everything I have read of English action in recent days is based entirely on the assumption: we can destroy Germany with one blow. I have as a result begun to consider the question: how can we wage a successful war against England?"[114] During the last few weeks of his life, the old Chief of the Admiralty began to supply his star pupil with plans for such a war.[115]

While the foreign political crisis approached boiling point, the domestic situation was not encouraging. On February 7th, Dr. Ernst Lieber, leader of the Centre Party, mentioned "rumours about an extraordinary expansion of the fleet, which are connected with the telegram of His Majesty the Kaiser and the table talk in the White Room . . . Is there anything in the present condition of our foreign affairs, which might make such an adventurous fleet expansion necessary?"[116] Baron Marschall replying for the Associated Governments was forced to deny categorically that an additional naval Bill would be introduced in that session, which was precisely the opposite of the Kaiser's wishes. It was not surprising that Holstein was convinced that the Hohenlohe regime was nearing its final agony. In a letter to Eulenburg, two days after Lieber's question in the Reichstag, he wrote, "after Hohenlohe, if he is

[111] *Ibid.*
[112] Tirpitz to Stosch, February 13, 1896, Tirpitz, *op. cit.*, p. 55.
[113] F. B. M. Hollyday, *op. cit.*, p. 273.
[114] Stosch to Tirpitz, February 12, 1896, Tirpitz, *op. cit.*, p. 54.
[115] E. Schröder, "Albrecht von Stosch", *Historische Studien*, Vol. 353, Berlin, 1939, p. 105.
[116] *Stenographischer Bericht*, 12. Sitzung der II. Kommission (Budget), der Reichstag, IV. Session, February 7, 1896.

sacrificed between now and the next few months to a mood, or let us say a moment, we will get the Dissolution Chancellor, and if the elections, as is probable, go against the Government, he will be followed by the *coup d'état* Chancellor. Since the German Princes, as you know better than I, will not take part in an action against the Reich, the Kaiser will then be confronted with a choice between the Monts programme (war against Bavaria, etc.) and Jena, that is to say, beating a retreat. In one sense one can say that the advance on Jena has already begun, since, from what I hear, opinion in the Imperial entourage grows daily stronger in favour of a *coup d'état* against the Reich."[117]

Admiral Hollmann at the Imperial Naval Office was hanging by a thread. Senden had already manoeuvred Tirpitz into line as his successor with the Kaiser's blessing; the government of which Hollmann was a member was under terrific fire in the Reichstag, the Chancellor was rapidly losing control of the situation, and finally, on March 1st, Admiral von Knorr resumed his attacks on Hollmann by presenting a lengthy statement of his complaints at an audience with the Kaiser. He began by rejecting the numbers and types of the cruisers selected by Hollman for the building plan and argued for the simplicity of the High Command's original proposals. He urged the Kaiser to choose between 2nd class cruisers and 4th class, and complained bitterly about the failure of the Imperial Naval Office to consult the High Command about the designs for *Ersatz Leipzig*, *Freye*, "K" or "L" models. The Naval Office never answered his letters, he charged. "I first learned of these building plans from a letter of the Imperial Naval Office in which I was simply informed that the plans were now completed and had already been approved by Your Majesty."[118] A few days later Hollmann replied to the accusation. In the first place, he pointed out, the Kaiser had already made a final decision among the suggested types of cruisers in an audience on February 2, 1896. Secondly, it was only by the construction of several types of cruisers that the imperfections and advantages of the different types could be assessed. If the High Command's

[117] Holstein to Eulenburg, February 9, 1896, *The Holstein Papers*, III, No. 528, p. 593.
[118] "Immediatvorstellung", Oberkommando der Marine, Berlin, March 1, 1896. Copy in RMA III. 1.5.2.

suggestions were adopted, all the other types already in service would be left high and dry for the sake of one model, of which only the *Gefion* had actually been built. Finally, the German Navy would have to follow the trend already apparent in the construction of "improved" cruisers in the British Navy.[119]

While the top brass quarrelled before the Kaiser, the members of the joint naval subcommittees, which were drafting the Bill's provisions, began to quarrel as well. A meeting was held between Korvetten-Kapitän Rollmann of the Imperial Naval Office and Kapitän-Leutnant Lans of the High Command to try to solve certain disagreements on procedure, but Rollmann reported to the State Secretary that it had been unsuccessful.[120] The two groups soon became involved in fundamental questions about the types and numbers of ships to be included in the draft and about the percentage of ships to be kept on active duty. It was doubtful whether the joint subcommittees could continue to function, but on March 7th, Hollmann ordered them to go on despite the disagreement.[121]

From his privileged position, Senden also resumed his sniping against Hollmann. In a private note written in early March, very likely for use with the Kaiser, he wrote that Hollmann was "without initiative . . . shoves the blame onto the Chancellor who has not given him the proper orders, but he himself has done nothing at all to speed up the formulation of such orders . . . indecisive . . . the worthlessness of the man damages the Reich . . . His dismissal will take place most appropriately after the budget for 1896/7 has been approved, . . . His Majesty will have to be much more conciliatory in dealing with Tirpitz, to follow his suggestions, give him free room to operate, if their work together is to be profitable. I believe that Tirpitz is the right man to push the Navy onward in these difficult days."[122] Unfortunately these calculations were just a bit premature, because to Senden's consternation, Hollmann managed to convince the Reichstag that no large expansion for

[119] "Immediatbericht", Staatssekretär des Reich-Marine-Amts, March 5, 1896, RMA III. 1.5.2.

[120] Minute by Captain Rollmann of meeting, March 2, 1896, RMA III. 1.5.2.

[121] Order of State Secretary Hollmann, March 7, 1896, RMA III. 1.5.2.

[122] "Aufzeichnung über Hollmann", Handwritten and annotated: "Auf Befehl des Herrn Chefs als Geheim Sache aufzubewahren, Massmann, 3/4/96". Dated "März 1896", BA K 08-7/1, "Senden Nachlass".

the Navy was planned. The majority of the deputies, with whom Hollmann enjoyed fairly good relations, were prepared under the altered circumstances to accept Dr. Lieber's suggestion that "the best way to put an end to the limitless fleet plans is to support a sensible, carefully planned renewal and enlargement of our fleet."[123] Lieber's argument swung the Centre into line and one battleship, *Ersatz Friedrich der Grosse*, and three cruisers were approved by a solid majority.

Tirpitz, who saw his chances fade as Hollmann's position strengthened, was distressed by the unexpected turn of events. "Our representation in the Reichstag", he wrote angrily to Senden, "could hardly be more unfortunate. The State Secretary of the Foreign Ministry represents the Navy, blows a fanfare for cruisers and shoots at sparrows with his biggest guns. What sort of powder will impress the Reichstag later when the really serious demands are made? The State Secretary of the Imperial Naval Office beats himself on the breast and says, 'As long as I stand here, no boundless plans, *i.e.* no battleships, will be proposed'. Then in April the wicked uncle comes . . . According to people who know the situation in the Reichstag well, demands for battleships have been practically ruled out for years to come by this sort of tactic. Even Bennigsen (National-Liberal leader), who learned about naval matters from Stosch, seems to have come to the same opinion. That is the situation and you will be in the best position to know whether it would not be better to let the present State Secretary stay in office for a few more years."[124] Tirpitz's unwillingness to take on the unpleasant job of confronting the Reichstag with a big programme after Hollmann had sworn that no such programme would be introduced was understandable. Tirpitz never liked to go beyond the limits of the possible, and in the situation which confronted him at the end of March 1896, the only role that he could possibly play was that of imperial scapegoat. If the Kaiser dismissed Hollmann after a vote of confidence by the Reichstag, it could only be as a prelude to the widely rumoured *coup d'état*. As Holstein remarked in a letter to Radolin, "one cannot suddenly turn back world history 150 years".[125]

[123] E. Kehr, *op. cit.*, p. 60.
[124] Tirpitz to Senden, March 20, 1896, BA K 08-7/1, "Senden Nachlass".
[125] *The Holstein Papers*, III, No. 536, p. 601, Holstein to Radolin, March 22, 1896.

The Kaiser had, as usual, gone off on a cruise without settling any of the open questions about Tirpitz's and the Navy's future. Kiderlen-Wächter, who was on board as Foreign Ministry representative, reported that the Kaiser was in a good mood, busying himself with the sketches of his 9,000 ton battleship. "How the Reichstag will rejoice," he wrote, "and Hollmann, who already had so much trouble in talking H.M. out of his last idea, will be happier still. The last idea of the Kaiser's was very lovely, only it could not float."[126] The rage and fury of the first half of March had passed, and the Kaiser seemed less concerned to pick a fight himself than he had been a mere fortnight earlier. There was little left for Senden to do but to write to Tirpitz that their campaign had failed. "All the opinions of senior sea officers, to whom I spoke in Berlin," he wrote to Tirpitz from the royal yacht *Hohenzollern*, "were in agreement that only the present State Secretary offers any hope of getting the Navy Bill through peacefully. His Majesty shares the view expressed in your letter of March 20th, that a new State Secretary in the present parliamentary situation would arouse suspicion. It would be more difficult for him than for his predecessor to win confidence in parliamentary circles. His Majesty has therefore decided to refrain from a change at present, but wants you to be told that 'postponed' does not mean forever . . . The future will teach us whether the new Bill can be introduced successfully in the new fiscal year."[127] Shortly after this decision had been communicated, Tirpitz left Berlin to take over the command of the Cruiser Squadron in the China Sea.[128] The first phase of his campaign for office was over.

[126] *Ibid.*, No. 537, p. 603, Kiderlen-Wächter to Holstein, March 25, 1896. The details of this ship can be found in "Erläuterungen zu dem Entwurf eines seegehenden Panzerschiffs von 9,000 Tonnen", Kiel, March 14, 1896, MK I.10.c.

[127] Senden to Tirpitz, March 31, 1896, "Vertraulich", copy of original, BA K 08-7/1, "Senden Nachlass".

[128] In his *Erinnerungen*, Tirpitz passes quickly over this episode and distorts it in a very interesting way: "When Hollmann received a vote of confidence in the Reichstag, Prince Hohenlohe hesitated to change personnel" (p. 60). Prince Hohenlohe knew nothing of Tirpitz's appointment and neither did any of the responsible authorities of the Reich. Tirpitz evidently wished to conceal the slightly disreputable and certainly unconstitutional tactics which he and Senden pursued in trying to get him into power. In fact, he omits all mention of Senden's role in the matter and of the correspondence between them.

Prince Heinrich of Prussia, younger brother of Kaiser Wilhelm II, and a German Admiral—the first member of the Royal Family to become an active naval officer

Prince Chlodwig von Hohenlohe-Schillingsfürst, Chancellor of the Reich, 1894–1900, in 1895

Landing manoeuvres at Wittdün in 1901

S.M.S. "Baden", battleship I class of the 'Sachsen' class, 1901, starboard broadside view, at anchor

3

The Fall of Hollmann and Tirpitz's Appointment

The Krüger Telegram unleashed a tremendous outburst of anti-English sentiment and national emotion, but the position of the Navy and the government was little changed. As the smoke drifted away, both the Navy Bill and the legislative programme of Prince Hohenlohe were still firmly fixed at square one. The two most ominous issues, the big fleet programme and reform of the Army's code of justice, were still there, and the Kaiser made it quite clear that neither would be abandoned.[1] In the eyes of the closest companions of the Kaiser, the government had been feeble and would have to go. A government which had been unable to convince the Reichstag of the importance of a big fleet at the very moment when Germany was being humiliated for want of one had proved itself unworthy of the All-Highest confidence.

Rumours of intrigues by a "camarilla" of members of the court circle began to spread. "The Fatherland could be calm," Maximilian Harden wrote in *Die Zukunft* on May 9, 1896, "if it had only a fairy-tale camarilla of non-political courtiers to fear . . . as long as policy is firmly established by a united cabinet inspired with a firm will. The situation will become unstable if individual ministers feel the urge to play the 'caramilla game' themselves."[2] That some ministers should have felt such an urge was hardly surprising. Intrigue had always been the established weapon in the struggle between the Prussian monarchy and successive governments, and it was almost the only one suitable for use in matters affecting the Kaiser's

[1] Holstein to Karl von Lindenau, July 27, 1896, *The Holstein Papers*, III, No. 572, p. 635.
[2] Quoted in H. Rogge, *op. cit.*, pp. 55 f.

rights as Supreme War Lord, a title as grandiose as it was vague.

As the camarilla campaign grew in strength, Prince Hohenlohe's position as the Chancellor of the Reich became intolerable. He found himself forced into that "procrustean stretch", which Bismarck had defined as the inevitable posture of the Chancellor when Kaiser and Reichstag pulled in opposite directions. As the stretch widened, the Chancellor lost his freedom to manoeuvre. He could not choose between the two factors in the Government, because the constitution of the Reich and the spirit of its interpretation provided for no such choice. He could not govern without the Reichstag, but he was beholden to the Kaiser for his office. There was no way out of the dilemma without a concession by the Kaiser or a surrender by the Reichstag. Paralysis of the supreme executive officer of the Empire inevitably resulted. Hohenlohe's only weapon was the threat to resign, and its effect depended on the Kaiser's mood. Holstein busily urged Hohenlohe to use this ultimate weapon now. "If the Chancellor shows through the military courts martial question that in the end he will give way to constant pressure," Holstein observed in a letter to Lindenau, "he will be laying the basis for an insupportable future during the remainder of his tenure of office, because he will then be under constant pressure over the fleet question."[3]

The fact that both issues involved military policy weakened the Chancellor's position considerably. He had already been forced to give into the demands of the Chief of the High Command on the question of direct correspondence between naval attachés and the High Command.[4] If he could not resist pressure on such secondary aspects of civilian control of military policy, what hope had he of resisting on issues of principle? The realities of the military monarch outweighed the fiction of civilian control. A few years later, Eugen Richter summed up the problem: "Compare the number of audiences granted weekly to the Military Cabinet, the Naval Cabinet, the State Secretary of the Navy, the High Command, the Minister of War, with the few audiences granted by the

[3] Holstein to Lindenau, August 1, 1896, *The Holstein Papers*, III, No. 575, p. 640.
[4] Von Knorr to Reich Chancellor, Very Secret, May 22, 1896, ADMB I.1.A.1a.

Monarch to the entire civil administration . . . The position of the Reich Chancellor is such that when agreement has been reached by the State Secretary, the Naval Cabinet, the High Command and the Monarch, he finds himself facing accomplished facts . . ."[5] If Richter's analysis applied to issues on which the Chancellor could make some claim to a right of consultation, it applied even more to those issues on which Wilhelm II denied him such a right, and naval expansion was such an issue.

On May 28, 1896, the Kaiser issued an All-Highest Cabinet Order covering "those measures which must be taken to prepare for the introduction of a naval building programme."[6] The influence of Senden's ideas was obvious in the three principal objectives of the Order: "1. Education and instruction in broad segments of the population about the new tasks arising from the development of our sea interests" were to be stimulated; 2. Understanding was to be encouraged, "especially in educated circles, for the growth of our maritime fighting forces, which on the one hand offer the only healthy basis for the sea interests of the Reich and on the other advance the economic growth of Germany and improve the national welfare; 3. The tendencies in the people apparently already in favour of a further development of our sea interests and our maritime strength are to be comprehensively and emphatically promoted."[7] Needless to say, the Reich Chancellor was not consulted about the formulation of this Order, nor about His Majesty's decision "for tactical reasons" to put off the announcement and introduction of a Navy Bill in the Reichstag for the time being.[8]

More significant than the objectives which the Kaiser proposed were the means by which he believed they could be attained. In the form of explanatory comments to his Order of May 28th, he outlined an eight point programme for a full-scale propaganda campaign. Senden's influence is again

[5] *Stenographischer Bericht*, Der Reichstag, 9. Legisl.-Periode, V. Session, 7. Sitzung, March 28, 1898, p. 1831.
[6] "Ausführung zum Aller-Höchsten Kabinett-Ordre vom 28. Mai. 1896", Geheim Sache (1558/96 in I), MK I.f.1, "Persönlich", p. 1.
[7] *Ibid.*, p. 2.
[8] *Ibid.*, p. 3.

apparent both in the techniques suggested and in the tone of the argument. The eight points were conveyed to the Chief of the High Command and the State Secretary in the form of a "personal" memorandum, which was to serve as a guide to their activities. They were, firstly, to see that the active officer corps were promptly informed of the details of the building programme as soon as it had been approved by the Kaiser, and that senior officers accepted its principles as "the best for the attainment of the goal I have set for the fleet". Senior officers were to be encouraged to seek contact with trading firms and commercial groups, to gain influence in Chambers of Commerce and shipping companies, and to participate in commercial clubs and associations. "Tact and good education will assist in recognizing the necessary limits."[9] A special effort was to be made in the Hanseatic cities. The *Marine Rundschau* (The Navy Review) was to be broadened, popularized and published more often. It was to include translations, especially from English naval literature. Lectures were to be held and "material prepared by the Navy must be made available to suitable individuals for this purpose . . . The appearance of official agitation must be avoided. I should also like to recommend to you the strongest possible participation in favour of the fleet by that part of private industry which profits directly from it."[10] The Kaiser suggested that industrialists be encouraged "to work with their employees so that they in turn cast their votes for those candidates in elections who are prepared to promote the sea interests of the Reich."[11] Finally, the press activity inspired by the Navy was to be expanded. The Kaiser was prepared to provide the necessary personnel and "assistance from the All-Highest private funds".[12]

[9] *Ibid.*, p. 5. How far these techniques were conscious imitations of the propaganda and educational devices employed by the Navy League in Great Britain is not entirely clear. By January of 1896 the Navy League had, in Marder's words, "recovered from its attack of infantile paralysis, and had begun to play a conspicuous role in moulding public opinion on the needs of the Fleet". (A. J. Marder, *op. cit.*, p. 52.)

[10] *Ibid.*, p. 17.

[11] *Ibid.*, p. 20.

[12] *Ibid.*, p. 22. In his *Erinnerungen*, Tirpitz fails to mention the All-Highest Cabinet Order and the accompanying directives. Since he had left Berlin in early April, it

Continued on page 101

The one point on which the Kaiser had no clear ideas was the actual substance of the building plan which this propaganda campaign was to foster. With Tirpitz thousands of miles away, Hollmann's ideas began to reassert themselves. On June 29th, the Kaiser, the court entourage and Admiral Hollmann took part in a day's cruise to inspect the work on the North Sea–Baltic Canal. A heated discussion about the prospects of a long term building programme ensued. Hollmann argued that such a plan would never get through the Reichstag and General von Plessen supported this view. Hollmann was clearly convinced that naval expansion could only be carried out in small stages. He was certain that the Reichstag would reject grandiose, long term building plans, and he himself remained unconvinced of the need to concentrate exclusively on battleships. Technological change was too rapid to permit final decisions for one strategy or another. Senden objected strenuously, but he was over-ruled. As usual, the Kaiser followed the advice he had most recently heard. "The Kaiser said that he realized now that Hollmann was right. It was too late. They should have used the enthusiasm of the past year and the impression made by his speech on January 18th. The opportunity had been missed. Now they would have to give up the big plan, regard it merely as a study, lay it on one side and not speak of it any more. Senden was . . . utterly crushed . . . 'It is astonishing', he remarked, 'how quickly we capitulate as soon as a fight looks likely'."[13]

The Kaiser may have been willing to abandon the big battleship programme, but his Naval Cabinet Chief most decidedly was not. He continued to argue and plead for the building

Continued from page 100

is just possible that he never saw the documents, but he must have known of the Kaiser's and Senden's ideas along these lines. An argument for the assumption that he had a copy of the A.C.O., is that Hallmann (*Der Weg zum deutschen Schlachtflottenbau*, p. 255) mentions it, and Hallmann got his material from Tirpitz's personal papers.

[13] Hans Hallmann, *op. cit.*, p. 209. The following spring, Senden recorded a different version of the events in his notes. According to him, "when Hollmann had an audience on June 30 concerning the plan for an expansion of the Navy, he committed himself to the Kaiser to get the ships approved in the Reichstag but the plan must not be made public. The Kaiser gave in at that time . . ." ("Zu den Akten des Admiral Hollmanns", No. 10, Handwritten Memorandum by Admiral Senden, dated "März 1897", BA K 08-7/1, "Senden Nachlass".)

plan at every possible opportunity, even in England. "Senden was", Bülow recalled years later, "what the North Germans call '*stur*' (stubborn). He was also unfortunately extremely tactless . . . He loved to talk in London clubs, of how we would build a monster fleet, and when it was ready, then we would talk seriously to England."[14] The summer of 1896 was no exception. "This summer Senden said in England, as I am reliably informed," Holstein wrote to Kiderlen-Wächter, "that the great fleet programme must be pushed through and that the Kaiser intended to push it through. Hohenlohe, however, was too old for this sort of thing, and therefore the Kaiser was talking about bringing in new blood."[15] Senden's incessant agitation eventually began to worry "Phili" Eulenburg, the Kaiser's closest friend, who acted during these years as mediator between the court and the government. Under pressure from Holstein, "Phili" appealed to Wilhelm II directly. "For a long time now—and repeatedly," Eulenburg wrote, "Senden says in the officers' mess where he goes every day and always finds an eager public that in his view the Reichstag must appropriate 300 million to make the fleet into what we need—and the Reichstag, once we have dissolved it ten times or so, will approve everything we want."[16] Senden's aggressive attitude and tactless statements were obviously damaging to the government; Hohenlohe's chances to achieve a peaceful resolution of the Navy question in the Reichstag would soon disappear, if Senden continued to rant and rave. The newspapers were already reporting rumours about "limitless fleet plans" and also stories about Hollmann's successor. Tirpitz's name was so frequently mentioned in this connection that Prince Hohenlohe was compelled to issue a formal statement in the official *Reichsanzeiger* on September 12, 1896, "that a plan for the expansion of the fleet has not been presented by that flag officer either in All-Highest or in responsible circles . . . Rear Admiral Tirpitz has never been called upon to make such

[14] Bernhard von Bülow, *op. cit.*, p. 66.

[15] Holstein to Kiderlen-Wächter, August 13, 1896, *The Holstein Papers*, III, No. 582, p. 648.

[16] Philipp Eulenburg to Kaiser Wilhelm II, November 12, 1896, quoted in J. Haller, *Aus dem Leben des Fürsten Philipp zu Eulenburg-Hertefeldt*, Berlin, 1924, p. 250.

a plan and has never found himself in a position in which an order to work out such a plan could have been given to him. The inclusion of his name in newspaper polemics can hardly serve his own interests nor does it correspond to the customs of our military tradition to bring an officer in an irresponsible position into conflict with responsible authority."[17] That the Kaiser's own Cabinet Chief had been guilty of just such a breach of tradition added a certain irony to the statement, which in any case was not overly truthful.

The man of the hour was at that time carrying out his orders to "seek a place on the Chinese coast, where Germany could set up an economic and military base."[18] Although Tirpitz obviously enjoyed the chance to be back on active service after his four years in Berlin, his tour of duty as Flag Officer in Command of the Cruiser Squadron was not a great success. His schedule of manoeuvres and reconnaissance had been interrupted by the rebellion in the Philippines, which he regarded as a tempest in a teapot, and on July 23, 1896, S.M.S. *Iltis* sank while on a mission near Kiaochow. Unfavourable publicity was given to Tirpitz's sailing orders and, much more important, with the loss of the *Iltis*, he also lost Kapitän-Leutnant Otto Braun, an old friend from the "Torpedo Gang"

[17] Text quoted in H. Hallmann, *op. cit.*, p. 212.

[18] Tirpitz, *op. cit.*, p. 61. The history of the seizure of the port of Kiaochow by Germany is yet to be written. Tirpitz's account of it two decades later in his *Erinnerungen* is not complete. He writes that the Foreign Ministry, the Minister in Peking and his predecessor, Admiral Hoffmann, were all for Amoy because "they feared a Russian objection to our settling ourselves in the North", whereas "I came to the view that only the untouched pearl, Kiaochow, came in question". At the time he had some reservations: "In your letter, the statement that I had pleaded so warmly for Kiaochow surprises me. The Minister and Herr Detring seem to have given you this idea more than my report. All I said was that we should not cross Kiaochow off the list and merely wanted to get orders enabling me to carry out further investigation." (Tirpitz to Senden, Mirsbay, January 21, 1897, BA K 08-7/1, "Senden Nachlass".) Similarly in a report to the High Command, written on December 7, 1896, from Hong Kong, he suggested a settlement in the Yangtse valley or at Wusung. "If we want to accomplish something really great out here, we must get in there, as Your Excellency has already said . . . In the English colonial area, the incoming German immigrants simply disappear into the English national camp; thus a greater economic (and industrial) share of Greater Germany ("Alldeutschland") is denied us in this area. This process would at least be slowed down in the Yangste region if it does not become English politically. It almost seems as if England expects our intervention there . . ." (Tirpitz to von Knorr, December 7, 1896, ADMB III.1.13.)

days and "the one commander, whom I had available, apart from the flagship of course, to detach for independent reconnaissance".[19]

The year which Tirpitz had spent in the Far East had given him additional opportunity to think about Germany's position in the world and, in particular, about her relationship to Britain. In a letter to the Chief of the High Command in September, he warned that there was no easy solution to the problem of setting up and operating a base in China. "The question is entirely different for a state which does not possess the necessary measure of sea power and out here Germany will fall into that class for a long time to come."[20] In October, commenting on a report by one of his subordinates, he noted, "the Russian envoy in Peking, Count Cassini, believes that Kiaochow Bay is the only useful harbour and promising place for the future between Shanghai and Vladivostok. Because of its geographical position the place is wrong militarily for the Russians, in fact impossible. Since it would undoubtedly be useful for the Russians, if Germany were pushed into the English sphere, they will naturally always attempt to work to that end."[21] "As far as I can judge from my Asiatic perspective, our relationship to England is the main difficulty, which affects us in Europe as well. The difference over the Transvaal and, in my opinion, the absolutely useless newspaper war of last summer have considerably worsened the atmosphere for us in the Asiatic English community. I must confess, I have been unable to understand our newspapers like the *Kölner*, the *National-zeitung*, etc., not to mention how stupid their judgment of the power question is. If a collision between England and ourselves should take place, we are the ones now who will have to pay the bill . . . We shall run into fewer difficulties in solving our problems the heavier our military weight is out here. Unfortunately, the great development of the foreign fleets makes our strength look very small indeed."[22]

With respect to his own career, Tirpitz was not overly

[19] Tirpitz to Senden, January 21, 1897, BA K 08-7/1, "Senden Nachlass".
[20] Tirpitz to High Command, September 5, 1896, ADMB III.1.-8.
[21] Report by Oberlt. Michaelis to Chief of Squadron with marginal comments by Tirpitz, Nagasaki, October 7, 1896, ADMB III 1.-8.
[22] Tirpitz to Senden, January 21, 1897, cf. footnote 19.

distressed by the newspaper rumours about him as such, but he objected to the attempt "to shove the ominous threat of limitless fleet plans from the I.N.O. onto an active officer, such tactics are dangerous in principle, because one gives the officer in question at least a moral right to defend himself with the same weapon. Where will that lead?"[23] As late as January 1897 he seems to have believed that he would remain in the Far East for a long time and to have been quite content with that role. His moment had, he believed, come and gone for ever.

While Tirpitz was making his peace with his fate, events at home were conspiring to alter it. At the end of October 1896, the *Hamburger Nachrichten*, the house journal of Prince Bismarck's party of irreconcilables, shattered the government's confidence by publishing a thinly veiled account of Caprivi's failure to renew the Reinsurance Treaty with Russia. The political explosion which followed shook the entire nation. Bismarck, the great old man and founder of the Reich, had committed an act which, at the very least, was a colossal indiscretion and, in the eyes of some, came dangerously close to treason.[24] The effect of the publication was to rouse again the slumbering conflict between the Bismarckians and their opponents while rocking the already unstable position of Prince Hohenlohe's government. Sir Frank Lascelles, British Ambassador in Berlin, wrote to Lord Salisbury that the "revelations appeared to me to be more damaging to Prince Bismarck's reputation than to that of his successors, and . . . seemed to be indirectly aimed at the Emperor himself."[25] His Italian colleague, Count Lanza, agreed that "the attack was certainly directed against the Emperor but perhaps more especially against Baron Marschall, who has been instrumental in revising Prince Bismarck's tortuous policy."[26] In either case, the annoyance and discomfiture of the government was great. A revival of the stale controversy with the Bismarckians was the last thing which Hohenlohe and Marschall could have wished

[23] *Ibid.*
[24] Cf. Werner Richter, *op. cit.*, pp. 613 ff. (German edition), for an imaginative reconstruction of Bismarck's motives.
[25] Sir Frank Lascelles to the Marquess of Salisbury, October 30, 1896, *British Foreign Office Confidential Print* (copy in the Seeley Historical Library, Cambridge), Vol. 7218, No. 21.
[26] *Ibid.*, No. 22.

for on the very eve of the Reichstag debates on the Navy and reform of the military penal code. A conflict over Bismarck's action would certainly divide those who might normally expect to support the government on military questions.

In the meantime, Admiral Hollmann had been preparing his naval budget on the assumption that the idea of a Navy Law or a long-term building programme had been safely pigeon-holed. His ambitious budget followed the principle of experimentation with different ship types. While he requested an appropriation for one battleship, *Ersatz König Wilhelm*, it was a replacement of an existing ship rather than an addition to the total. Instead he concentrated on a great variety of lighter craft. His estimates included funds for two cruisers 2nd Class (Plans "O" and "P"), one cruiser 4th Class, one gunboat, one torpedo division and the full amount for the replacement of the *Iltis*. The extraordinary estimates (*i.e.*, the construction budget) amounted to M 70 million, the highest estimates ever submitted to the Reichstag.[27] Hollmann was demanding M 39,500,000 more than the previous year's estimates. Holstein was certain that "the Navy will simply have to accept the fact that cuts will be made in its demand for seventy million. The amount of these cuts will be in direct relationship with the bitterness which the constant insolent public pronouncements of Senden are arousing in all political and parliamentary circles . . . two days ago someone in the right wing of the National Liberal Party told Captain Borckenhagen, Chief of Staff of the High Command, that nobody could be astonished if the Reichstag looked upon the naval demands with suspicion when it heard the doctrine preached by authoritative people, especially by Admiral Senden, that our Navy had to be made ready for a war with England. I have no doubt that the cuts in the Navy's demands will once again make for a temporarily sultry atmosphere despite the winter weather. Nothing can be done about that however. No amount of persuasion would be able to remove the suspicion awakened in the Reichstag by statements emanating from Court, not to mention the speeches of Senden . . ."[28]

[27] Figures from H. Hallmann, *op. cit.*, pp. 213 f.

[28] Holstein to Eulenburg, November 30, 1896, *The Holstein Papers,* III, No. 587, pp. 656 f.

Hollmann must have felt that 'he had been there before', when the High Command once again chose his busiest moment to attack him from behind. On December 19, 1896, von Knorr had an audience in which he renewed the High Command's vendetta and rolled out the disputed question of the division of labour between the two highest naval bureaux.[29] Von Knorr's complaints covered virtually the whole range of activities carried out by the I.N.O. and the High Command, and touched on every sore point between them from the right to control the training of cadets to the right to communicate directly with the Reich ministries. This time, Hollmann was not prepared to be trifled with, and on December 28th, in a letter to von Knorr, he rejected all claims by the High Command to control press activity and announced his intention to apply for an All-Highest Cabinet Order forbidding any other naval agency from meddling in publicity matters.[30] Von Knorr replied in kind and demanded to be present at any audience at which Hollmann applied for such an order.[31] As usual, the High Command called on the Naval Cabinet to help in its campaign, and Senden was only too willing to oblige.[32] The month of January 1897 was filled with charges and counter-charges. Hollmann presented a 36-page report in reply to the High Command on the 21st, in which he accused the High Command of trying "to gain control of the entire development and supreme command over the entire Navy as well as the assumption of a series of rights which belong exclusively to Your Majesty . . . without having any share in the responsibilities which must be borne by the State Secretary . . . The contrast between the Kaiser's supreme military authority and administration has been artificially blown up. In the Navy, the governmental power emanates as directly from Your Majesty as the command power . . . the twenty-five sea officers of the Imperial Naval Office at whose head an admiral stands

[29] Immediatbericht des Oberkommandos—"Betreffend Abgrenzung des Geschäftsbereiches beider obersten Marinebehörden", BA K 08-7/1, "Senden Nachlass".

[30] Imperial Naval Office to High Command, December 28, 1896, MK III.

[31] High Command to Imperial Naval Office, January 7, 1897, MK III.

[32] Von Knorr to Senden, January 8, 1897, MK III. See also, Imperial Naval Office to High Command, January 16, 1897; Naval Cabinet to Imperial Naval Office, January 17, 1897, both in MK III.

come just as directly as the High Command from practical activities at sea and remain with certain exceptions just as long in their positions . . . For the Imperial Naval Office the same military identity must therefore be asserted as that which the High Command has so far claimed for itself alone."[33] Von Knorr, not to be outdone, appealed two days later to Senden "to be good enough to represent my position at an audience".[34]

Senden's dislike of Hollmann made life that much more difficult for the State Secretary. Senden and his civilian assistant, Geheimrath Massmann, sprinkled sarcastic and critical remarks in the margins of Hollmann's memoranda. On the memorandum of January 21st, Massmann wrote, "these (Hollmann's charges against the High Command) are grave accusations which should never have been expressed without a thorough examination of evidence, which could not in any case be produced."[35] Senden criticized Hollmann's memorandum of February 13, 1897, from every possible angle. The claim of the Imperial Naval Office to exclusive jurisdiction of publicity, Senden wrote angrily, "was a monopoly for the I.N.O. . . . would lame all freedom of speech in the Navy . . . All right, let him (Hollmann) prepare a programme and get busy doing what was laid down in the Order of May 28, 1896."[36] It was not surprising that by the second week in February, 1897, Korvetten-Kapitän Müller believed that Hollmann was on the way out. In a letter to Tirpitz, he wrote, "Admiral Hollmann is finished, and it is inconceivable that the course of the budget negotiations in the Reichstag will put him back in his easy chair at the I.N.O., Leipzigerplatz 13. Admiral Tirpitz as Hollmann's successor is settled, latest by the autumn of this year."[37]

Hohenlohe saw the danger to his State Secretary and turned

[33] *Immediatvortrag*, signed by Admiral Hollmann, Berlin, January 21, 1897, with comments by Geheimrath Massmann (Naval Cabinet), BA K 08-7/1, "Senden Nachlass", pp. 1, 4 f., 8 etc.

[34] Von Knorr to Senden, January 23, 1897, MK III. See also, Naval Cabinet to Imperial Naval Office, January 25, 1897, and Büchsel to von Knorr, January 31, 1897, both in MK III.

[35] Marginal comment on Hollmann's *Immediatvortrag*, January 21, 1897, p. 12, cf. footnote 33.

[36] "Immediatbericht des Reichs-Marine-Amts", February 13, 1897, pp. 3 ff.

[37] Müller to Tirpitz, February 9, 1897, quoted in H. Hallmann, *op. cit.*, p. 217.

to "Phili" Eulenburg for help. "Apparently the Kaiser is being influenced by experts and people outside of politics in Kiel. He seems to be toying with the idea of letting Hollmann go at the end of the year, because he is not the right man to carry the huge fleet plans through the Reichstag. I can tell you this here and now, that the monster fleet plan is a practical impossibility for the foreseeable future . . . If it were possible to make the atmosphere here even worse, the departure of the highly respected and popular Hollmann would do it. I consider the whole idea still-born, no matter which Navy Secretary or Reich Chancellor assumes the role of Godfather."[38] Holstein was also busy attempting to influence Eulenburg. "The Chancellor told me a little while ago," he wrote on February 3rd, " 'If the voters so much as suspect that the dreaded unlimited fleet programme is in prospect, this will have a quite fatal influence on the elections.' Either the Kaiser has not considered this or he has considered it and is steering towards a *coup d'état* in the interests of an anti-revolutionary law and a gigantic fleet. Which of the German Princes do you think will stand by the Kaiser in all this, now that the Kaiser has been accidentally or intentionally snubbing them since the previous autumn? . . . Just ask Monts what they are saying about the Kaiser in Munich."[39]

Eulenburg was distressed "by the great fleet plans, most of all by the prospect of losing the excellent Hollmann",[40] and in reply to Holstein hoped that, if Hollmann went, Senden might be his successor, because Senden was certain to make such a mess of things that the whole naval programme would be discredited for years to come.[41] Aside from expressions of regret, Eulenburg, who was at his ambassadorial post in Vienna for a change, was unable to accomplish very much. The Kaiser had "no doubt whatever", Holstein wrote to Bülow on February 17th, "and in this opinion he is probably supported by Senden and Co.—that it is only due to the ineptitude, ill-will and lack of interest on the part of the government that the money for the gigantic fleet hasn't yet been granted . . .

[38] Hohenlohe to Eulenburg, February 4, 1897, Hohenlohe, *op. cit.*, p. 297.
[39] Holstein to Eulenburg, February 3, 1897, *The Holstein Papers*, IV, No. 599, p. 11.
[40] Eulenburg to Hohenlohe, February 7, 1897, Hohenlohe, *op. cit.*, p. 298.
[41] Eulenburg to Holstein, February 7, 1897, *The Holstein Papers*, IV, No. 601, p. 14.

Hollmann, a splendid and courageous man, told the Kaiser straight out that as a result of this All-Highest table-talk, the chances of securing passage of this year's naval appropriations are as good as ruined. Moreover it was to be feared that the fact would be brought out that the charts sent directly from H.M. to the Reichstag which are intended to show the strength of the various European fleets are inaccurate. For H.M. omitted from the list all German ships he did not consider modern enough, even though they were still usable, whereas for the French and English fleets he included everything, even the most ancient barges."[42]

The political atmosphere was not improved by the Kaiser's speech to the Brandenburg Provincial Diet on February 26th. In the speech, which soon became notorious as the "*Handlanger Rede*", he claimed that Bismarck and Moltke had been mere "tools" in the hands of his immortal grandfather, Wilhelm I, "who in the Middle Ages would have been beatified". The effect of such tactless and tasteless comparisons was further to damage the imperial prestige and the prospects for favourable action on the naval estimates in the Reichstag. Once again, as in 1896, the Kaiser seemed determined to cause a really serious political crisis.

The prominent role which Wilhelm II played in the two clashes over naval expansion must be placed in perspective. It is important to remember that the crises were not only caused by the Kaiser's temperament or even by his "personal regime". The nature of the Reich constitution and the instability of the nation-state itself made every impetuous move by the Kaiser a governmental crisis. If the Chancellor, even a weak Chancellor like Prince Hohenlohe, had been able to depend on parliamentary support, if the responsible Ministers of War and the Navy had been really responsible, if the federal union had been either a league of equals or a more strongly unitary state, none of these difficulties with Kaiser Wilhelm II would have been so threatening. Secondly, the Kaiser's enthusiasm for expansion of the fleet was kept alive and encouraged by his immediate entourage. The byzantine atmosphere at court, "where the generals and courtiers dared not open their lips when the Kaiser asked for an opinion, where people froze in awe when

[42] Holstein to Bülow, February 17, 1897, *ibid.*, No. 605, pp. 18 f.

he entered . . .",[43] where adjutants kissed his hand when reporting for duty, where his favourites outdid each other in self-abasement, was hardly conducive to the formation of realistic political attitudes. Thirdly, the relentless determination of the High Command to have its own way was not of the Kaiser's making, and it was the constant sniping of Senden and von Knorr which ultimately destroyed Admiral Hollmann, not the Kaiser's personal whim.

By the beginning of March 1897 the feud between the High Command and the Imperial Naval Office had reached a point at which co-operation was no longer possible. The Kaiser had seen both the suggestions of the High Command and of the I.N.O. and, according to Senden, "neither had received his approval. The All-Highest decided instead to call an Imperial Committee into being, which would work out jurisdictional regulations according to certain directives and in the light of the submissions . . . During the formulation of the directives it came to light that in the year . . . (Blank in the original) Reich Chancellor Count Caprivi had claimed the right to countersign a similar order. I considered it proper to make certain whether the present Chancellor was of the same opinion and on March 2, 1897, was received by him. The Chancellor considered the formation of an Imperial Committee to be an internal affair of the Navy . . . and rejected the idea of a countersignature."[44] Under pressure from Marschall and Holstein, Prince Hohenlohe wrote a letter the following day reversing his position and rejecting such a Committee as unconstitutional.[45] "On March 4th a very serious disagreement between the Kaiser and Admiral Hollmann arose at lunch in the officers' mess at Wilhelmshaven, in which the latter energetically denied the Kaiser's right to create such a Committee since the Reich Chancellor had spoken against it. The Kaiser claimed the right. On the return trip from Bremen to Berlin on the 5th, the affair was discussed by Lucanus and me in the presence of the Kaiser, and it was agreed that according to established Prussian

[43] K. F. Nowak, *Das Dritte Deutsche Kaiserreich*, Berlin, 1929 and 1931, Vol. II, p. 138.
[44] "Zu den Akten des Admiral Hollmanns", Memorandum written in Senden's hand, dated "März 1897", BA K 08-7/1, "Senden Nachlass".
[45] Diary entry, Hohenlohe, *op. cit.*, p. 311.

tradition a Royal Prince be placed at the head of the Committee, an authority on constitutional matters be appointed to aid him and the Committee attempt to sort out the constitutional questions. Everything else belonged within the Emperor's supreme military authority ("Kommandogewalt"). On the 6th, I talked over the affair with General von Hahnke [Chief of the Kaiser's Military Cabinet] who confirmed without hesitation the Kaiser's right to call for such an Imperial Committee . . ."[46] On the 7th Hohenlohe had an audience of the Kaiser. "To my surprise", he recorded in his diary, "His Majesty received me cordially, heard my remarks with approval and began to expatiate in a lengthy monologue on the tasks of the Navy . . . If the Reichstag did not appropriate the money, he would build on and send the bill to the Reichstag later . . . I drew the Kaiser's attention to the difference between Prussia and the Reich and said that in Prussia he had old rights which still exist except where restricted by the Prussian constitution; in the Reich the Kaiser had only those rights granted him by the constitution of 1871. The Kaiser remarked in the middle, 'The Kaiser has no rights'."[47]

Admiral Hollmann's position was almost hopeless. The intriguers were busily undermining his position in the rear, while his seventy million budget faced withering criticism in the Budget Committee of the Reichstag. Quite unexpectedly, he resurrected Admiral Stosch's old memorandum of 1873 which demanded the creation of two squadrons of seven ships-of-the-line each. In the form of a White Paper, he submitted it to the Budget Committee with a comparison showing how far short of the initial Stosch plan the existing fleet had fallen. It is not easy to unravel Hollmann's motives in this action, and most historians have simply dismissed it as a clumsy and tactless move. The timing was certainly not well chosen. Hollmann distributed the White Paper and comparative tables on March 5, 1897, while Dr. Ernst Lieber was attempting to salvage one more cruiser for the Imperial Naval Office. Lieber felt betrayed and cried furiously, "I am a very embarrassed European."[48] Hollmann had completely miscalculated Lieber's

[46] Cf. footnote 44.
[47] Diary entry, March 7, 1897, Hohenlohe, *op. cit.*, pp. 311 f.
[48] H. Hallmann, *op. cit.*, pp. 219 f.

S.M.S. "Wörth", battleship I class, on its trials, maintaining an average speed of 16·8 knots per hour

S.M.S. "Gefion", cruiser IV class, 1895, starboard broadside view, at anchor

Tirpitz as a Grand Admiral in 1911

Autographed portrait of Tirpitz as a Grand Admiral

v. Tirpitz
Großadmiral

Admiral Otto von Diederichs, Tirpitz's successor as Commander of the German cruiser squadron in the Far East

devotion to the Navy and underestimated his vanity. Eugen Richter was, on the other hand, delighted by the new document. Triumphantly he crowed, "this memorandum just distributed realizes all the fears of limitless fleet plans."[49] The implication was that the Navy spokesmen were too fickle to be trusted. The paper had nothing to recommend it at first glance. Neither Chancellor nor Bundesrath had seen it, so that it had no constitutional basis. It took as its starting point an old plan which employed antiquated types of ships, a plan never formally adopted by the Reichstag. With so many defects, Hollmann can hardly have taken it seriously. It is not impossible that he meant it as an object lesson to the Kaiser and the court circle. By demonstrating how violent parliamentary reaction was to the merest suggestion of a long-term fleet plan, he may have hoped to silence his critics and save his skin. If that was his intention, it proved to be a boomerang. Irritating Dr. Lieber was the great mistake. The chances of saving the substance of his budget were small without Lieber, and there was little hope now of such help.

The next meeting of the Budget Committe of the Reichstag took place on Monday, March 8, 1897. The atmosphere was ominous and the unexpected presence of the Chancellor himself contributed to the sense of crisis in the air. Prince Hohenlohe tried to pacify the members of the Committee by suggesting that the memorandum had no legislative importance. It was merely intended to convey information and to provide a useful comparison of the present fleet with the older plan. Hollmann, who spoke next, displayed, as *The Times* correspondent remarked, "considerable excitement and repeatedly struck the table with his fist."[50] Vainly Hollmann tried to restore the Committee's confidence in his stability and prudence, but Dr. Lieber was not to be had. There was, Lieber replied, no longer any mention in naval memoranda of the primacy of the Army in Germany's defences nor any restraint in the nature of the Navy's demands.

Hollmann's ordeal continued that evening at a stormy audience with the Kaiser. By now the poor man simply could

[49] *Stenographischer Bericht,* Budget-Kommission des Reichstags, 9. Legisl.-Periode, IV. Session, 25. Sitzung, March 5, 1897.
[50] *The Times,* London, March 9, 1897.

not put a foot right. By obeying the Kaiser's order to submit his resignation he succeeded in annoying the Chancellor. Prince Hohenlohe wrote in his diary, "His Majesty commanded him to put the question of confidence in the government as soon as naval estimates had been thrown out. He will not do such a thing without my permission. I told Hollmann he has no right to tender such a resignation on behalf of the cabinet. He is not the responsible minister but only my State Secretary. I am the responsible official and if anyone is to submit his resignation it has to be the Reich Chancellor."[51] On March 9, 1897, Prince Hohenlohe wrote to the Kaiser and pointed this out.[52] On the 12th, the Budget Committee ended its hearings by cutting twelve millions from the naval estimates, and Hollmann obediently submitted his resignation. The Chancellor forwarded it to the Kaiser with the comment that he could not accept it for reasons outlined in his letter of the 9th. As always the Kaiser lost his nerve in the face of resolute opposition. He told Senden on the 15th that "the negative decisions of the Budget Committee did not justify the submission of resignations. Reich Chancellor, Naval Office, Foreign Ministry and Treasury should commit themselves to an energetic effort to get the naval estimates passed in full session. Everything else could wait for a while."[53] The Kaiser was unwilling, however, to withdraw his threats about Hollmann's future. "The fact that the letter of resignation has become known in parliamentary circles," he told the Chancellor, ". . . will have a sobering effect on the Centre, the cause of the trouble."[54]

The Kaiser's tactics misfired. The naval estimates were given a second reading on March 18th and 19th and passed as revised in committee on the 20th. The Kaiser had been thwarted at every turn. Through Hohenlohe's resistance, he had been prevented from reorganizing the Navy as he chose,[55] and now the naval estimates had been cut sharply. Hohenlohe told the King of Saxony that intimates of the Kaiser were

[51] Diary entry, March 8, 1897, Hohenlohe, *op. cit.*, p. 312.

[52] Hohenlohe to Kaiser Wilhelm II, March 9, 1897, *ibid.*, pp. 312 f.

[53] Cf. footnote 44.

[54] Kaiser Wilhelm II to Hohenlohe, March 16, 1897, Hohenlohe, *op. cit.*, p. 319.

[55] Diary entry, March 8, 1897, *ibid.*, p. 312; Senden to Prince Heinrich, April 12, 1897, MK XXXXVI.1.a. "For reasons which lie outside the Navy, His Majesty

Continued on page 115

beginning to suggest government without the Reichstag in the style of Bismarck in 1861,[56] and in a letter to Eulenburg on March 25th, he wrote, "The High Command and the Naval Cabinet want to get rid of Hollmann and put a more pliable man in his place. That is why they urged H.M. to order Hollmann to raise the question of confidence . . . I had as a result a lengthy discussion with H.M. in which he declared that he did not want a change of Chancellor, he did not want a dissolution, because the atmosphere in Germany was not ripe for it, and he had never considered a *coup d'état*. That was very encouraging for me and I hoped that we might at least get an extra cruiser plus the battleship approved in the full session. His Majesty had talked to the deputy von Stumm before he saw me . . . Stumm asserted that he had orders from His Majesty, went into the Reichstag, and told everyone, the Kaiser would make a terrific hubbub if the Navy estimates were not approved, chase all the ministers away and all sorts of things along that line . . . The consequence was an extraordinary uproar in the Reichstag. The Centre, whose speaker had been at pains to push through a few more appropriations, grew skittish. The Bavarian ultramontanes, who had arrived in large numbers, told their friends that they were so threatened by the members of the Peasants' Party at home that they dare not approve more than the Budget Committee recommended. They threatened to walk out, and the party's spokesman and his friends, who were afraid of splitting the party, gave in."[57] A few days later, Dr. Lieber told the Chancellor that feeling against the Kaiser was great in the Centre Party, "Virtually embittered".[58]

Hollmann had reached the end of the line. On the 30th he had an audience at which the Kaiser granted him an extended leave of absence. He told Hohenlohe that "the Kaiser

Continued from page 114
has temporarily postponed a revision of the regulations governing the areas of jurisdiction of the two highest naval departments. Probably this question will continue open for the next few months."

[56] Diary entry, March 24, 1897, Hohenlohe, *op. cit.*, p. 321, "The King shook his head and said, the allied Princes would be needed for such a course, and they would never agree because they lacked the necessary confidence in the stability of the Kaiser's undertakings."

[57] Hohenlohe to Eulenburg, March 25, 1897, *ibid.*, pp. 322 f.

[58] Diary entry, March 27, 1897, *ibid.*, p. 323.

wanted to call Admiral Tirpitz to act as his deputy. He also told me that the Kaiser gave him the impression that he wanted to clear up everything and do away with the Chancellor and the entire ministry . . . It is evident that the Kaiser is completely under the influence of people who are trying to convince him that he can set the stage for a great era of conflict, alter the constitution of the Reich, do away with universal suffrage and have untold cruisers built."[59] A few days later, Holstein wrote to Bülow, "Our doom embodied in Admiral Tirpitz is closing in upon us. The Bismarck-Henckel-Waldersee inspired *Berliner Neuesten Nachrichten* is now calling him the 'Roon of the Navy' . . . a favourite idea of the Kaisers . . . to make war against England on land together with Transvaal from South-west Africa without involving the two fleets."[60] Holstein discovered on April 5th that Tirpitz had requested the Kaiser for a delay of the recall orders and gleefully passed on the news: "A sign of the times: Tirpitz, the Roon of the Navy, hesitates: he has just cabled he needs three months to get back to Berlin and then before he takes over another three months to get orientated. Apparently he has no desire to make himself *kaput* for life." Bülow wrote on the margin: "Tirpitz is very able, competent, but has no real confidence in His Majesty and is afraid of Senden. He will be pulling along with the rest of the Cabinet soon enough."[61]

The Kaiser and Senden were in no mood to wait while Tirpitz hesitated. On April 7, 1897, Senden wrote identical letters to the Chief of the High Command and to Rear-Admiral Büchsel, acting State Secretary, informing them that "His Majesty the Kaiser intends to have a draft for a law prepared which will indicate how large the number of ships and torpedo boats must be in view of the present effective strengths of our probable enemies." For this purpose both officers were ordered to prepare memoranda on the tasks of the Navy in war and peace, to be ready by April 12th.[62] On the 9th the Kaiser had

[59] Diary entry, March 30, 1897, *ibid.*, pp. 326 f.
[60] Holstein to Bülow, April 3, 1897, BA "Bülow Nachlass", Mappe 90, F. 286–296.
[61] Holstein to Bülow, April 5, 1897, *ibid.*, F. 298. See also MGFA-DZ: 2024. PG 65990, ADMC I. 3–8, *Immediatvortrag*, April 5, 1897. Knorr minuted: "Admiral Tirpitz is to receive the answer that his orders stand but leave has been approved."
[62] Senden to von Knorr, MK I.f.1, and to Büchsel, RMA III.1.5.3., both dated April 7, 1897.

a long conversation with the Chancellor in which the "principle was settled that the German fleet must be half as strong as the combined Franco-Russian fleets, that is, it must be *unconditionally* superior to the entire Russian Baltic Fleet, and it must be able to fend off successfully the French North Sea Fleet or the Channel Fleet which may be used in action in the North Sea."[63] The principle was to be used as a guide in the calculations for a "Peacetime Effective Strength Law" for the Navy. This principle marked a return to the fixed naval programme of the High Command's memorandum of November 28, 1895, although it involved a somewhat larger fixed ratio than the High Command's thirty per cent stronger than either the French or Russian fleets.

The political prospects for the passage of such an ambitious fixed Navy Law were not good. Relations between the Kaiser and the Federal German Princes were still strained because of the struggle over reform of the penal code, which continued unabated. The mood of the Reichstag was distinctly hostile, and the enthusiasm of the Chancellor and Baron Marschall for such a measure was small. Holstein complained to Paul Hatzfeldt, German Ambassador in London, "With the Kaiser, the Navy Question now takes precedence over everything. Senden is said to dominate him completely. After the negative attitude of the Reichstag, which after all granted fifty-eight of the seventy million that were demanded, H.M. refuses to send ships anywhere . . . The greatest bitterness all around against the Centre which voted against the naval appropriations; against England which has the greatest naval strength . . . The internal situation is very depressing. The Kaiser wants a fleet like that of England—with twenty-eight first class battleships—and wants to direct his entire domestic policy to that end, *i.e.* to a fight."[64] The atmosphere at court had become nearly hysterical, and even Prince Heinrich had been infected by the general attack of nerves. "On the foreign political horizon," he wrote to Senden from Kiel, "it looks very dark indeed. Will we have time for regattas this year?"[65]

[63] Kaiser Wilhelm II to Senden, handwritten by Kaiser, April 9, 1897, MK.I.f.1., and Senden to Büchsel, April 9, 1897, RMA III. 1.5.3.

[64] Holstein to Hatzfeldt, April 14, 1897, *The Holstein Papers*, IV, No. 610, p. 28.

[65] Prince Heinrich to Senden, April 13, 1897, handwritten, MK XXXVI. 1.a.

Continued on page 118

The domestic political situation was equally threatening. Kiderlen-Wächter told Holstein on April 25th that the Kaiser was "very annoyed" with Marschall, "and would gladly make use of any excuse to get rid of him."[66] On the 28th the Kaiser caused a rumpus of his own. In a telegram to his brother, Admiral Prince Heinrich of Prussia, he called the members of the Reichstag "vaterlandslose Gesellen" (unpatriotic rascals). Heinrich, though unlike his older brother, could often be as tactless. Pleased by the telegram, he read it aloud to the officers of his flagship, the *König Wilhelm.* Naturally the news leaked out and equally naturally there was a political uproar of the first order. Hohenlohe called an emergency meeting of the State Ministry to discuss methods of preventing questions on it in the Reichstag, and arranged a special meeting with Lieber of the Centre. "This is not a question of a private expression of opinion," he wrote in a memorandum, "but of defamation of the Reichstag. The telegram lost its private character when it was officially announced by an admiral on active service to the crew of an imperial warship . . . if I were a member of the Reichstag, I would move a vote of censure of His Majesty."[67] Lieber called on the Chancellor on April 29th and informed him that the danger of such a vote had been postponed for the moment, but sentiment in the Reichstag was still inflamed.[68] By staking his entire prestige, Hohenlohe managed to get an official denial by the Kaiser. Holstein was certain that the end of the monarchy was in sight or at least "a powerful landslide to the Left, into democracy."[69]

The Hohenlohe adminstration continued to stumble from

Continued from page 117
This outburst of war nerves and Anglophobia is a curious phenomenon and not easily explained. During the months of April and May of 1897, the Kaiser and his entourage seem to have been certain that a war with England was imminent. On May 31 the Kaiser ordered the High Command to work out a plan for a war against England, which eventually became the Schröder plan for the invasion of Holland and Belgium. MGFA-DZ: 2024. PG 62990a, ADMC I. 3–8, *Immediatvortrag,* ganz geheim, "Krieg gegen England"—"Reinschrift in C, Mappe Operationspläne", Berlin, May 31, 1897. See also J. Steinberg, "A German Plan for the Invasion of Holland and Belgium, 1897", *Historical Journal,* Volume Six, Number One, Cambridge, 1963.

[66] Kiderlen-Wächter to Holstein, Karlsruhe, April 25, 1897, *The Holstein Papers,* IV, No. 615, p. 34.

[67] "Aufzeichnung", Hohenlohe, *op. cit.,* p. 335.

[68] Diary entry, April 29, 1897, *ibid.,* pp. 332 f.

[69] Holstein to Hatzfeldt, May 4, 1897, *The Holstein Papers,* IV, No. 616, p. 36.

crisis to crisis. On May 13th, Prince Hohenlohe introduced the long-awaited Law of Association Amendment Bill, which, as he himself had formally promised, at last abolished the antiquated prohibitions forbidding the union of political societies. The trouble was that the bill added such a list of reactionary restrictions and reservations that the concession to free speech was virtually swamped. New police powers were given to the state to cancel, interrupt, harass and close political meetings. As *The Times* correspondent in Berlin explained, "in order to realize the significance of the bill it is necessary to bear in mind that political meetings in Prussia are attended by a police officer in uniform, who usually has a seat on the platform beside the chairman. He is as often as not a former non-commissioned officer of the army. According to the bill a man of this class may decide at any moment that a political meeting which is being addressed by a Virchow or a Mommsen is 'dangerous to public safety or peace'."[70] The bill's other provisions were equally unpalatable, and a storm of protest swept through the party political Press. Not even in that bastion of reaction, the Prussian Landtag, could the government command a majority for the legislation. The 86 National Liberals joined the Centre to form a solid phalanx of opposition. In the Reichstag reaction to the Prussian situation was spontaneous and rapid. On May 18th a resolution passed the House by 207 to 53. The text was tantamount to a vote of censure: "Associations of every kind may enter into union with one another. Provisions to the contrary in the laws of the several German states are hereby repealed."

Sheer incompetence had led the government into the most serious federal-state crisis of Hohenlohe's chancellorship. To make matters worse, the Tausch trial opened in Berlin on May 20th. It promised to be a sordid affair involving the political police and certain to compromise many prominent government and court personalities. On the 22nd, Hohenlohe decided that he could no longer continue in office. "The way the government is going", he wrote in his diary, "cannot continue. If His Majesty wishes to rule by himself, I cannot act as his straw man . . . If H.M. alone and exclusively chooses the ministers,

[70] *The Times*, London, May 14, 1897.

the government steadily loses consequence and authority. Without authority no government is possible. If I cannot get the Kaiser's agreement to measures which I regard as necessary, then I have no authority . . . I cannot govern against public opinion and the Kaiser. To govern against both public opinion and the Kaiser is to be firmly planted in mid-air."[71] On May 31, 1897, the Prince submitted his resignation over "the Kaiser's order to dismiss Boetticher", Hohenlohe's State Secretary of the Interior and Deputy Reich Chancellor.[72]

The High Command had, in the meantime, completed the memorandum on the tasks of the Navy in war and peace, which the Kaiser had ordered on April 7th. On May 2nd Admiral von Knorr presented the memorandum at a special audience. In his view the Navy had eight specific peace-time tasks, including protection of overseas trade, improvement of marine engineering, navigation and cartography, assisting Germany's colonial expansion, and "moral and material support for friendly powers (Transvaal, China against Japan)".[73] Turning to the objectives of the Navy in war, he noted four main points: "1. Achievement of command of the sea, destruction and blockade of the enemy forces, blockade of enemy coast-line; 2. Protection of our own, destruction of enemy maritime commerce; 3. Protection of our own, damaging or conquest of enemy colonies; 4. Direct support for operations of the Army and provision of troop transports."[74] Since France and Russia were the most probable opponents in such a war, the High Command felt that cruiser attacks would be unsuitable tactics, "because of the necessary limitations of our forces". Blockade as an objective must also be abandoned, because the sheer length of the French and Russian coasts ruled out the possibility of successful blockade by Germany, while the relatively short German coast-line literally invited an enemy blockade. The only sensible strategy would be for the German Navy to concentrate in its home waters and "to try

[71] Diary entry, May 22, 1897, Hohenlohe, *op. cit.*, p. 342.
[72] Diary entry, May 31, 1897, *ibid.*, p. 346.
[73] Vortrag des Oberkommandos der Marine, "Aufgaben der Marine im Krieg und Frieden", RMA III. 1.5.3.
[74] *Ibid.*, Section B.

to defeat the enemy in an open sea battle."[75] Should a war with England occur, "which we should hardly expect to fight alone, our value as an ally would be greatly increased for other sea powers."[76] Historical observation demonstrated that loss of sea power meant loss of trade and loss of trade would mean the end of Germany's world position, "because trade seeks out other routes and lands and never returns."[77]

Eight days later Admiral von Knorr presented an outline for a fixed Navy Law by which the general ideas described above were to be realized. "The measure of the strength required by our Navy arises from its peace-time and war-time tasks, the strength of our enemies and the operations designed to defeat them . . . the war-time tasks of the Navy, as outlined in the memorandum of the 2nd of this month, must be confined to the strategic defensive . . . as our probable enemies, according to your Majesty's order, are assumed to be France and Russia. For the operational planning, the basic principle obtains that command of the sea can only be achieved and maintained by a decisive battle on the high seas . . . Germany, which has always been and still is dependent on a mighty land army because of its geographical position and historical development, has every reason to demand that in the construction of an appropriate sea force the greatest possible economy be used. From this point of view the basic demand is justified that no warship is built by us which is not equally suited to service in the home fleet and for use overseas."[78] To fill this need, the High Command believed that two full squadrons of eight modern high seas battleships in one tactical unit, plus a second unit composed of three divisions of four battleships each, or a total of twenty-eight battleships, were needed. For each division of battleships, one armoured and three protected cruisers would be needed as escorts, and thus, for twenty-eight battleships (seven divisions), seven armoured and twenty-one protected cruisers would be needed. The comparative strengths of the two enemies and Germany would then be:

[75] *Ibid.*, p. 9.
[76] *Ibid.*, p. 10.
[77] *Ibid.*, p. 10.
[78] Immediatvortrag des Oberkommandos der Marine, Berlin, May 10, 1897, RMA III. 1.5.3.

Russia and France:	20 New Battleships	11 Old Battleships
Germany:	28 New Battleships	(12) Old Battleships
Russia and France:	16 Armoured Cruisers	26 Protected Cruisers
Germany:	7 (& 1) Armrd. Crsrs.	21 (& 21) Prtctd. Crsrs.

The battleships in brackets represented the four ships of the "Baden" Class and eight ships of the "Siegfried" Class, and the cruisers in brackets those ships already on overseas duty.[79]

During the following week the Imperial Naval Office, working feverishly, began to prepare the calculations of the cost of the plan as well as to pare down its size. The I.N.O. substituted a total of twenty-eight for the High Command's twenty-eight new plus twelve old. Even so the cost of the programme, excluding the cost of torpedo-boats, amounted to the awe-inspiring sum of M 675,900,000.[80] On May 19th, the Kaiser held a top-secret conference with his admirals in Wiesbaden, at which acting State Secretary Büchsel presented a memorandum covering the Naval Office's work on the High Command plan. The effect of the discussion was to water down the High Command's advocacy of battleships and to restore three rather than two types of cruisers. The whole programme was scaled down, and the law which was to embody it was to contain the provision "that the number of ships laid down in paragraph 2 shall be attained by April 1, 1910, at the latest."[81] Five days later on the 24th of May, 1897, the first "Sketch for a Law with respect to the German Fleet" was completed by Captain Fischel in the Imperial Naval Office. It contained the provisions covering the active life and replacement periods for the ships in each class, as well as the tonnage of each type. In Section IV, "Provision of Funds", the formula was used: "Until completion of this law the sums to be spent each year will be included in the Reich budget

[79] Tirpitz regarded the draft of the plan as "unworkable" (Tirpitz, *op. cit.*, p. 80). There was still in his view too much of the old cruiser philosophy left.

[80] Konstruktionsabteilung, Reichs-Marine-Amt, May 18, 1897, RMA III, 1.5.3.

[81] Handwritten Memorandum, signed by Captain Büchsel, acting State Secretary, May 20, 1897, RMA III. 1.5.3., with counter-signatures by section chiefs of the Imperial Naval Office.

estimates of that year."[82] The average sum required during the duration of the law was estimated at M 54,100,000, and over the years between 1897 and 1910 a total of M 832,800,000 would be spent on construction.[83]

There can be no doubt that the work done by the High Command and the Imperial Naval Office during April and May of 1897 marked a great step forward in the development of thinking in the German Navy. The principle had been firmly established that only a decisive battle in home waters offered Germany any hope of victory at sea. The relationship between strategy and tactics had been re-established by the introduction of the unified squadron with a fixed ratio of heavy and light cruiser escorts into the planning of a long-term building programme. The principle, first developed by Stosch, of the "alliance value" of a German fleet had been re-emphasized and effectively argued. The first formal calculations of the cost and phases of construction to achieve such an alliance-worthy fleet had been made, and the choice of a fixed Navy Law had been determined to be the appropriate political device for the implementation of the fleet building plan. There was only one thing lacking: the firm foundation of political and strategic unity. The fusion of military technology and political objectives was to be the great contribution of Tirpitz.

Tirpitz himself continued to take his time returning home. He travelled slowly across North America and in Salt Lake City gave a brief Press conference to a group of American journalists. They were interested to hear his reactions to the unfavourable opinions which the German opposition Press had expressed about his appointment. The Admiral warily refrained from any direct comment, in effect allowing his opponents to continue to prophesy doom. Although he later regretted his excessive circumspection,[84] he was probably wise to keep quiet at this crucial point in his career. The Chancellor's political difficulties could only embarrass him and obstruct the development of the Navy. It was just as well to be thousands of miles from the source of the trouble and even better

[82] Section IV, "Skizze für ein Gesetz betreffend die deutsche Flotte", signed by Captain Fischel, Section Chief A, May 24, 1897, RMA III. 1.5.3.
[83] *Ibid.*
[84] Tirpitz, *op. cit.*, p. 79.

to miss the final collapse of Prince Hohenlohe's authority. Tirpitz was able to return to Germany with a clean slate. He had not contributed one way or another to the Chancellor's decision to strike the flag and withdraw his resignation. He avoided the dangerous cross-fire between Court and Chancellory which had destroyed his predecessor and need not rejoice with the Kaiser on his victory. By coming home slowly, Tirpitz missed the final capitulation of the government on the Law of Association Amendment Bill and thus escaped the parliamentary crisis too. His uncanny political instinct had directed him perfectly. In retrospect, it almost seems staged—the leisurely progress through America, the careful silence and the superbly timed appearance in Berlin. It is hard to suppress the feeling that some invisible hand had arranged affairs in the Navy and in the nation to make Tirpitz's debut peculiarly auspicious. Yet it was not a dramatic, triumphal entrance. Another Navy minister had taken up his post. Only in retrospect has it become clear that the arrival of the new minister changed the course of European history.

4

A Navy Against England

In early June, 1897, Admiral Tirpitz arrived in Berlin to take up his new position as State Secretary of the Imperial Naval Office. From the beginning, he faced two distinct sets of problems. He had, first of all, to alter the existing sketch for a Navy Law to meet what he regarded as the real threat to Germany's growth as a sea power. Secondly, he had to devise some means of restoring public confidence in the steadiness and sobriety of the naval authorities. Only if he succeeded in both endeavours could he hope to face the Reichstag with some chance of seeing a fixed Navy Law passed. He had grave doubts about his abilities as a politician,[1] and was not feeling particularly strong physically. Prince Heinrich wrote to Senden: "I saw Tirpitz. He looks well, is in good spirits, but will have to go to Ems on doctor's orders, because one lung has been giving him trouble again."[2]

His physical condition required, and the political situation justified, a certain initial caution. Although Hohenlohe's surrender to the Kaiser's demands cleared the air, the Chancellor's problems were far from solved.[3] For Tirpitz, the government's difficulties were heaven sent. He could get on with his main job, while the Kaiser, the Chancellor, the courtiers and the politicians haggled over the new appointments. Throughout the month of June, negotiation continued. Finally, on June 18, 1897, an official announcement declared that the condition of Baron Marschall's health had made necessary his resignation as State Secretary of the Foreign Ministry and that Bernhard von Bülow, German Ambassador in Rome, had been appointed his successor. State Secretary Boetticher resigned officially as of July 1st and was replaced at the Ministry of the Interior by the

[1] Tirpitz, *op. cit.*, p. 79.
[2] Prince Heinrich to Senden, Kiel, June 6, 1897, BA K 08-7/1, "Senden Nachlass".
[3] Diary entry, June 3, 1897, Hohenlohe, *op. cit.*, p. 350.

former Imperial State Secretary of the Treasury, Anton Count Posadowsky-Wehner. Boetticher's post as Vice-President of the Prussian State Ministry was taken by Prussian Finance Minister von Miquel, and the former German Ambassador in Washington, Freiherr von Thielmann, took over as Reich State Secretary of the Treasury. Lieutenant-General von Podbielski became Reich State Secretary of the Post Office.[4] Tirpitz was officially named State Secretary of the Imperial Naval Office and Plenipotentiary to the Bundesrath on June 17th.[5] A complete turnover of the top personnel of the Reich had taken place and even Holstein had submitted his resignation, which was not accepted.[6] The "Chancellor crisis" was over.

On June 15, 1897, Tirpitz was received by the Kaiser. During the audience he presented a memorandum entitled "General Considerations on the Constitution of our Fleet according to Ship Classes and Designs".[7] Behind the apparently technical character of this memorandum, a fully developed strategy for Germany's Navy was concealed, which can be said without exaggeration to have changed the course of modern history. Tirpitz assumed that German ships must be built to meet "the most difficult situation in war into which our fleet can come". Germany must choose her ship designs with the greatest threat to her sea power in mind. There was simply not enough money to meet every threat. He had no doubt which was the greatest: "For Germany the most dangerous enemy at the present time is England. It is also the enemy against which we most urgently require a certain measure of naval force as a political power factor."[8] Since commerce raiding was hopeless against an enemy so richly endowed with overseas bases as Great Britain, "our fleet must be so constructed that it can unfold its greatest military potential between Heligoland and the Thames."[9] Such a fleet would be adequate

[4] *Ibid.*, pp. 364 ff., for details.
[5] Order of June 17, 1897, MK XI.c.1.
[6] Holstein to Bulöw, June 24, 1897, *The Holstein Papers*, IV, No. 624, p. 43.
[7] "Allgemeine Gesichtspunkte bei der Feststellung unserer Flotte nach Schiffsklassen und Schiffstypen", Very Secret, June 1897, MK I.f.1. The complete text of this historic memorandum can be found in the original in its entirety in Appendix One, pp. 208-23, of this study.
[8] *Ibid.*, Paragraph 2, see p. 209.
[9] *Ibid.*, Paragraph 4, see p. 209.

to deal with France or Russia, so that "for the moment we need not pay particular attention to those enemies in the determination of our ship classes . . . The military situation against England demands battleships in as great a number as possible."[10] In view of the present capacity of wharves, dockyards, personnel and training, Tirpitz believed that Germany must limit her objectives. It would be realistic to assume that by 1905 the Home Fleet could consist of two fully equipped modern squadrons of eight ships each, a flagship and two reserve battleships—nineteen battleships in all. While the original plan submitted by the Naval Office had been based on a more gradual expansion to 1910, Tirpitz felt confident that his objectives could be accomplished within seven years.

Once these premises had been established, Tirpitz went on to argue with persuasive clarity that a practical strategy against Great Britain necessarily led to a concentration of naval forces at home. In turn, this concentration must lead to a limitation on the number and types of cruisers. The problem with cruisers lay in the unsettled state of naval tactics. As he readily admitted, "we possess much less experience and certainty about the value and means of using scouting groups in association with the main body of the fleet than we do about the forces in the fighting line."[11] As a result of this uncertainty, he believed that the proportion of cruisers to battleships should be kept as low as possible, because the expenditure on cruisers represented "a reduction from the forces needed for the ultimate outcome". A large and a small cruiser were the only types which ought to be built. "Although probably more than necessary (to be sure, less than a commander might wish) for a

[10] *Ibid.*, Paragraphs 5 and 6, pp. 209–11. Admiral Senden advanced the same argument in correspondence with his old friend, Vice-Admiral Viktor Valois: "If we opted for cruiser warfare, the whole English fleet would be available to use against us militarily. If we develop ourselves for battleship warfare, the line from the Elbe to the Thames is the appropriate theatre of war . . . in other words, with our massed power to strike the weaker part of the total British sea force . . . If we succeed in creating a battle fleet, against which the available battle fleet of England is not sufficient to rule out *any* chance of a defeat, in that moment we shall at last have significance as a seapower ('*Seegeltung*') . . ." "Aufzeichnungen betr. Ansicht Valois über die deutsche Flottenpolitik gegen England", handwritten by Senden, dated 1898, BA K 08-7, "Senden Nachlass".

[11] Cf. Appendix, Paragraph 10, see p. 211.

German fleet to be built against England, we have accepted the number estimated earlier of six reconnaissance groups composed of six large and eighteen small cruisers . . . That makes in total a Home Fleet of

1 Fleet Flagship
2 squadrons of 8 battleships—19 battleships
2 ships as reserve material
1 squadron of 8 coastal armoured ships
6 large cruisers
18 small cruisers."[12]

No questions of prestige should be allowed to divert the Navy's attention from the relentless execution of the plan. "The fact that occasionally an individual cruiser overseas may be weaker than its opponent must never be considered important. Only the main theatre of war will be decisive. In this sense the selection of a ship design in peace-time is applied naval strategy. It will never be possible, in any event, to prevent a German ship occasionally confronting a stronger adversary. It is a delusion to imagine that it is possible to meet such an eventuality by the appropriate choice of ship types."[13]

The overseas service had to be kept within close limits. Tirpitz estimated that the minimum requirements for the overseas service were three large cruisers, nine small cruisers and four gunboats plus a reserve force, so that by 1905 the entire German fleet at home and abroad would contain:

19 battleships (2 as reserve)
8 armoured coastal ships
12 large cruisers (3 overseas reserve)
30 small cruisers (3 overseas reserve)
12 torpedo boat divisions.

"This fleet can be largely completed by 1905. The expenditure for shipbuilding, including guns and torpedo armaments, will amount to M 408 million or 58 million per annum, plus final payments after 1905 of 72 million. The ordinary estimates will be increased by 4 million per annum as well, thus reaching 86 million by the fiscal year 1904/5."[14]

[12] *Ibid.*, Paragraphs 13 and 14, see p. 215.
[13] *Ibid.*, Paragraph 16, p. 215–17.
[14] *Ibid.*, Paragraph 20, p. 219.

South wing of the Schillingsfürst Palace, built in 1750, home of Prince Hohenlohe and birthplace of the French Foreign Legion, 1791

Tirpitz in his office as State Secretary of the Imperial Naval Office on the Leipzigerplatz, Berlin

Eugen Richter, German Liberal parliamentarian, member of the Reichstag from 1871 to 1905, and leader from 1884 on of the Radical Party and from 1893 of the Radical Union

"Der rauhe Eugen," hostile cartoon of Eugen Richter in 1903

In a comparative table,[15] Tirpitz showed the Kaiser how his plan altered the previous Naval Office programme of May 24, 1897. The total displacement of ships to be built equipped with armoured plating was increased in the Tirpitz plan by sixteen per cent. The total tonnage of partly protected or unprotected warships was sharply reduced. The total cost of construction was cut by M 140 million, nearly seventeen per cent, and the length of the plan shortened by five years. If the Kaiser approved Tirpitz's alterations, he would in effect be getting a smaller but far more powerfully armed fleet with fewer classes, costing less, more quickly.

The Tirpitz memorandum of June 1897 is certainly the most remarkable document in the history of the German Navy. Within a few days, Tirpitz had given direction, logic, consistency and economy to what had taken the Imperial Naval Office more than two months to work out and the German Navy nearly a decade to ponder on. By fixing his sights relentlessly on England, Tirpitz made the whole plan leap into life. Parts fell into place and the fleet became in an instant the diplomatic and military tool for which the Kaiser had been so anxiously pleading. An annual appropriation of fifty-eight millions, not a pfennig more than the Reichstag had in fact approved for Admiral Hollmann, would yield a return in terms of politico-military leverage out of all proportion to the capital invested.[16] At last Germany would achieve abroad that greatness at sea for which the Kaiser yearned, while at home Tirpitz's plan would silence for ever the carping critics and their cries of "limitless fleets". The Kaiser had found his man and he knew it.

At Leipzigerplatz 13, Tirpitz had scarcely settled in before he began to reveal those extraordinary qualities which made him,

[15] See p. 222, for a copy of the comparative table.

[16] These facts support the assertions made by Rudolf Stadelmann in "Die Epoche der deutsch-englischen Flottenrivalität" (p. 101) that the German Navy was built against England. Professor Hubatsch in his able study, *Die Ära Tirpitz,* denies Stadelmann's point by arguing that "consideration of the most difficult situation in war and the most dangerous opponent is self-evident for any military planning" (p. 15, Note 5). Of course such planning goes on in defence staffs, but Professor Hubatsch ignores the active, positive intention behind Tirpitz's planning: the intention to *alter* the existing balance of forces in the world in Germany's favour and to achieve parity with Great Britain as a world power.

perhaps, the ablest administrator in the history of the German Empire. He had a superb sense of priorities and understood how to encourage initiative and distribute responsibility. During the first three months of his tenure of office, he was quite happy to permit Rear-Admiral Büchsel to act as his deputy in the day-to-day affairs of the Imperial Naval Office. Much of the time Tirpitz spent in his summer house at St. Blasien in the Black Forest, where he could be free to think.[17] He encouraged frank and open discussion between subordinates and superiors, an approach which has still yet to penetrate the German business and administrative world. He organized a "brains trust" and never meddled in the activities of its members. He believed that a chief should always be "*primus inter pares*", as he once wrote to Senden,[18] and that a successful organization must be a team. "I used to 'roll the material about', an expression about which I was often teased," he recalled years later, "and gave each of my co-workers the maximum of independence."[19] The very expression, "roll the material about", is more reminiscent of Madison Avenue in the 1960s than Berlin in the 1890s. Every year he and his wife gave a party for all the officers and civil servants in the I.N.O. to welcome new members of the team, "at which the host devoted himself to personal conversation with the guests at their individual little tables."[20] Because he was no ordinary chief, he got no ordinary performances from his subordinates.

One of Tirpitz's first orders, No. 2335 of June 19, 1897,[21] set the new era in motion. Tirpitz gave his subordinates a hair-raising task: within six days they were to revise all the figures for the naval estimates for the fiscal year 1898/99 in the light of the new plan. They had to calculate the cost for first instalments of ships to be built, estimate the number and cost of the increased personnel, correct the ordinary estimates and add up the totals unbelievably quickly. Normally, a revised draft of the estimates would take a month at least. At the same time, he set up the first of his many committees, one composed of

[17] Tirpitz, *op. cit.*, pp. 82 ff.
[18] Tirpitz to Senden, February 15, 1896, BA K 08-7/1, "Senden Nachlass".
[19] Tirpitz, *op. cit.*, p. 84.
[20] A. Schulze-Hinrichs, *op. cit.*, pp. 45 f.
[21] Order No. 2335, Geheim Sache, Berlin, June 19, 1897, RMA III. 1.5.3.

Korvetten-Kapitän Capelle, Herr Perels, head of the Administrative Section, and Herr Klein, a *Vortragender Rat* in the same Section, which was to draft the text of the law under his direction. "The work is to be kept *top secret!*" the order concluded. Two days earlier he had set up a "Section for News and General Parliamentary Affairs (M II)" and appointed another of his bright young men, Korvetten-Kapitän August von Heeringen, as its section chief. The choice, as usual with Tirpitz, was a happy one. Heeringen was a gifted and charming man, "who knew how to work on a conversation partner persuasively and irresistibly by using his considerable talents as a speaker."[22] The task of the News Section was agitation. It was to make contact with the Press, arrange publication of suitable articles, create a favourable climate in German public opinion for a powerful fleet by reaching the most influential and articulate segments of the society, in particular, the universities and professional associations, and to work with and on important deputies of the Reichstag.

The burst of purposeful activity at the Imperial Naval Office had not come a moment too soon, if Germany were to achieve the goal of leverage at sea against Great Britain. As if to remind Tirpitz and his staff of the magnitude of their task, the Admiralty staged a naval review at Spithead on June 26, 1897, to mark Queen Victoria's Diamond Jubilee. It was, as Professor Marder remarks, "the greatest display of naval force the world had ever seen. It was more than a mere review or naval pageant; it was a demonstration to the world of Britain's sea power as 165 modern fighting ships of all classes, the flower of the Royal Navy, passed in review before the Queen and her distinguished foreign visitors. There were thirty miles of ships in five lines, each over five miles in length. Not a single post abroad had been weakened to make the strong show at Spithead. Only the modern units in home waters were used."[23] The very idea of competing with such a maritime colossus had already forced France to slacken her naval programme, and France had been a principal naval power for more than two centuries. How could Germany, starting almost from scratch,

[22] E. Kehr, *op. cit.*, p. 110.
[23] A. J. Marder, *op. cit.*, p. 281.

hope to face such a show of force? Tirpitz knew the answer, and during the summer of 1897 he began to unfold his plan.

In the following weeks, Tirpitz recalled in his memoirs, "I assembled the men whom I had chosen to work with me on the Navy Law either in Ems or St. Blasien. Herr von Capelle's parliamentary experience, his critical faculty and his logical prose style provided the right balance for my nature which was more instinctive . . . He had the capacity, together with Dähnhardt, to cultivate urbane relations with the deputies and to master financial questions . . . He was as indispensable for my parliamentary work as the fiery von Heeringen was in the stirring up of the nation. Heeringen carried out the intellectual mobilization of the masses in an extremely tactful manner."[24] Back in Berlin, the work was carried out by an equally able team, some of whom Tirpitz had fortunately inherited with the job; men like Captain Fischel and Rear-Admiral Büchsel, later Chief of the Admiralty Staff, Pohl, Ingenohl, Coerper and Scheer, all of whom were later to become famous in the First World War. By the end of the month of June the Leipzigerplatz was humming with activity, while the brains trust directed affairs by remote control. Again and again, Tirpitz pressed home to his subordinates the fact that the relationship to England must always be their guiding motif. In a marginal comment on an older memorandum, he criticized his predecessor's arguments in favour of short building periods and early replacement provisions. "The main point is missing," he wrote. "The private dockyards must learn to build *quickly* in order to be competitive *against England*."[25] Yet he was no fanatic. His marginal comments reveal a man with great self-control. He often had to hold in the reins on his enthusiastic subordinates with comments such as: "then we shall have to accept our limits . . . More than what the Law provides for 1905 is out of the question . . . Very sad! One must not want too much . . ."[26] Slowly he forced them to accept the limits of the possible and to see that self-restraint was the shrewdest way of solving the political difficulties still facing them.

[24] Tirpitz, *op. cit.*, pp. 81 f.

[25] Handwritten marginal comment on Hollmann's *Denkschrift*, "Der Schiffsbestand etc.", p. 7, dated June 1897, RMA III. 1.5.3.

[26] "Korrevisions-Bemerkungen", September 7, 1897, RMA III. 1.5.3., Vol. 2.

Nothing like Tirpitz's first months in office had ever happened to the Navy in its entire history, and soon rumours of the extraordinary goings-on at Leipzigerplatz began to appear in the Press. His appointment had already been greeted by a wave of comment in leading newspapers. The *Hannover Courant* showed itself to be well informed by reporting that "the memorandum of Herr Tirpitz, which has been talked about of late, was less concerned with fleet expansion as such than with the question which ship types and classes should be considered in new construction." The opposition, *Kölnische Volkszeitung*, noticed an important consequence of the new appointment. Since Rear-Admiral Tirpitz was only thirteenth on the seniority lists of the Navy, only the younger officers could become section chiefs under him. The Imperial Naval Office would have a new, youthful spirit. The *Freisinnige Zeitung*, Eugen Richter's paper, saw a certain irony in the new direction of the Navy. In a leader on June 15th, it reminded readers that the Reichstag had been called "unpatriotic scoundrels" for refusing to appropriate two cruisers which the Navy itself no longer wanted. "One State Secretary builds lots of cruisers, the other lots of battleships. If these changes in the Navy's leadership continue, eventually we shall have a fine fleet of both."[27]

The opposition Press's complaints about the unsteadiness of the Navy's attitudes were not surprising, nor particularly alarming. Gradually Tirpitz realized that the opposition was playing into his hands. After all, he too wanted an end to the era of uncertainty in naval strategy. On July 28, 1897, the radical *Vossische Zeitung* reported the creation of a News Section in the I.N.O., and took the occasion to criticize naval muddle: "We believe that we can safely assume that the Reichstag will continue to reserve its judgment about appropriations for new building no matter how lively the press agitation of the naval administration may be, until a fleet plan, which is fixed, calculated for years ahead and is binding, can be laid before it." Tirpitz was delighted. "A very useful article", he noted in the margin for the attention of von Heeringen. "If we could

[27] Newspaper files of the Imperial Naval Office, RMA III. 1.5.3., Vol. 4. Tirpitz wrote "very important" on the margin of the *Freisinnige Zeitung* article.

only manage to have a few more opposition papers press for a fixed naval programme! . . ."[28]

The preparations for the draft of the law were going ahead according to Tirpitz's rigorous timetable. On June 26th, the first estimates for fiscal year 1898/99 were completed. Tirpitz decided the same day to ask for funds to begin building two new battleships, one large and two small cruisers and one torpedo boat division.[29] On June 29th Büchsel, his deputy, initialled the final selection of ship designs, and by July 2nd, Captain Fischel submitted to the drafting committee the first rough draft of the law itself.[30]

On July 19th, the drafting committee completed its revision of the figures, signed and submitted the draft to Büchsel. The committee were so rushed that they were forced to submit unfinished work. "It has so far only been possible to prepare a temporary draft," they noted, "because there was not enough time for a thorough revision in which all the groups in the house would have had to co-operate."[31] Büchsel, who had received a telegram from Tirpitz at St. Blasien, ordered Capelle and von Heeringen to report there in person, taking the draft with them. Work continued at St. Blasien and on August 8th, Tirpitz ordered three copies of the revised draft to be sent to him by the 13th, which he intended to use "in an audience with the Reich Chancellor".[32] One important revision had been in his mind from the beginning, and in the August draft the cut-off point of the law was officially moved forward from the 1st of April 1910 to the 1st of April 1905. The Home Fleet's effective strength of nineteen battleships was to be achieved five years earlier than originally planned. This meant an acceleration of the rate at which new ships would have to be added to the eight still usable. In effect, eleven new battleships would have to be completed in seven years, an increase of five over the number originally fixed for completion by that date.[33] In

[28] Newspaper file, July 28, 1897, RMA III. 1.5.3., Vol. 4.
[29] "Tatsachenbericht", Berlin, June 26, 1897, RMA III. 1.5.3.
[30] Minute of July 29, 1897, and "A" to Büchsel, Berlin, July 2, 1897, with tables, RMA III. 1.5.3.
[31] Perels and Capelle to Büchsel, Berlin, 19 July, 1897, RMA III. 1.5.3.
[32] Tirpitz, Memorandum, St. Blasien, 8 August, 1897, RMA III. 1.5.3., Vol. 2.
[33] Cf. Anlage 2, Memo of 2 July, 1897; Anlage 1, Memo of 19 July, and "Berechnungen zur Begründung zum Gesetzentwurf", August 1897, RMA III. 1.5.3., Vol. 2.

financial terms, the acceleration involved an increase in the total cost of the plan over its seven year life span from M 409 million to M 477 million (including expansion of the torpedo boat flotillas), or an increase in the construction estimates per annum from M 58,443,000 to M 68,200,000.[34]

It is worth noting that this acceleration, the first of many in Tirpitz's long career, necessarily involved an acceleration in the building rhythm (or as Tirpitz put it, "Bautempo") by which keels were to be laid. In the pre-Tirpitz version of the plan, only seven new battleships were to be commissioned by 1905. Beginning in the fiscal year 1898/99 two keels would have been laid, one in the following year, two in the next and so on. The leisurely 2:1:2:1 pattern was to continue until the fiscal year 1902/3, after which one keel per annum was all that was needed to meet the goal, of two squadrons, a flagship and two reserve battleships by 1910.[35] By pushing ahead more quickly, a greater strain would be placed on the capacity of the Imperial and private dockyards. The revised pattern of keels to be laid would be less regular, 2:2:1:2:1:1:2.[36] There was an obvious temptation to make the pattern of building more regular. It was a kind of inherent escalator clause in Tirpitz's programme, because "regular" could only mean more. For example, two keels per annum would mean fourteen new ships, or by 1905 a fleet of twenty-two (eight old and fourteen new) battleships, but twenty-two would not be enough to make up three full squadrons of eight each, so more would be needed, etc. Tirpitz knew that economies in construction costs could be achieved by a rational, even distribution of building contracts.[37] There was, consequently, a second temptation to accelerate the building programme, and Tirpitz often turned to this second argument in the following years. The programme was intrinsically expansive and the emphasis on "Bautempo" extremely dangerous. It introduced an inflexible factor into

[34] *Ibid.*, Anlage 3.

[35] Memorandum of July 2, 1897, Anlage 2, RMA III. 1.5.3.

[36] Reichs-Marine-Amt, "Begründung zum Gesetzentwurf betreffend die deutsche Flotte", November 1897, Artikel II, p. 15.

[37] With his usual thoroughness, Tirpitz prepared in advance of the Reichstag opening a series of statistical tables to counter the argument that "the establishment

Continued on page 136

the international relations of the Reich. As an example, one can take the August draft of the Navy Law. Tirpitz had made a technical correction in a draft. It was an internal, administrative act. Yet its consequence was to accelerate the tempo of the Anglo-German arms race by a ratio of 5:6, before the race had even begun. The fixed Navy Law as a political device was an "infernal machine". Once it got moving, it was very hard to slow down.

By the end of August, the draft of the Navy Law had reached the stage at which Tirpitz could present it to the Kaiser. On August 24th, at an audience in Cassel, the Kaiser agreed to the details about types and cost which Tirpitz presented.[38] Tirpitz could now begin to devote more time to other pressing problems. To begin with, he faced one difficulty partly of his own making: the persistent hostility of the High Command of the Navy to the Imperial Naval Office. As Chief of Staff, he had led a relentless campaign against the I.N.O., and provoked one crisis after another, only now to find himself in the same position as Admiral Hollmann. The whole vexed question of the division of labour between the two departments had been left in the air by Hohenlohe's rejection in March of the Kaiser's suggestion of a Crown Committee. Nothing had been altered by Tirpitz's appointment to the Imperial Naval Office, and the rivalry between the two branches was certain to break out again. As Seckendorff wrote to Senden in 1898, "How true were the words of old Stosch when he told Tirpitz, 'what you are attacking now, you will have to defend later!' "[39] Tirpitz might well rue the day that he had undermined Hollmann's authority and stirred the High Command to attack the I.N.O., but had he not done so, he would never have gained favour with

Continued from page 135
of the German fleet in the brief period of seven years would push the activity of private shipbuilders onto an artificially high level, which they would be unable to maintain after the expiration of the programme . . . To disarm this argument, I should like to be able to deliver proof that the future warship contracts will only make up a small portion of the current construction activity of the private dockyards . . ." (Draft of Letter to High Command, Berlin, October 29, 1897, with marginal minutes of the Construction and the General Naval Sections, RMA III. 1.5.3., Vol. 3.)

[38] "Immediatvortrag", Cassel, August 24, 1897, RMA III. 1.5.3., Vol. 2.

[39] Seckendorff to Senden, March 12, 1898, BA K 08-7/1, "Senden Nachlass".

the Kaiser and Senden. Not even a Tirpitz could escape the consequences of Germany's peculiar constitition.

Trouble with the High Command began as early as June 1897. On the 21st Büchsel drafted a letter to the High Command for Tirpitz's signature, conveying the details of the new plan approved by the Kaiser on the 15th. The Imperial Naval Office asked the High Command for details of their specifications for the cruiser design.[40] This letter crossed one from the High Command which contained "a few tables, compiled... as a preliminary basis for further discussions..." The compilations included a table of organization of the fleet for 1910, a calculation of the disposition of ships on active service for the same year and an estimate for the establishment of officers and crews corresponding to the table of organization. "May I request your Excellency most respectfully," the Chief of the High Command continued, "to permit me the favour of a reply to these calculations and to be good enough to communicate with me in respect to the time allowed for the completion of the new ships . . ." Tirpitz had not the faintest intention of allowing von Knorr to have a say in this matter. Captain Fischel noted on the margin of the letter: "The acting State Secretary has ordered that this letter is not to be answered for the time being. The State Secretary himself will choose a suitable time for a reply." Büchsel wrote alongside von Knorr's request for consultation: "To be sent a final draft only, and then discussions in a committee."[41]

Tirpitz was much too realistic to imagine that simply excluding von Knorr and the High Command from the preparations of the Navy Law would solve a problem which had dragged on since 1891. Besides, he needed von Knorr's help and certain facilities which the High Command could provide.[42] A truce was the only way out for the time being. As soon as the draft of the law had been safely presented to the Kaiser, Tirpitz called on von Knorr to work out a *modus*

[40] Büchsel to High Command, Handwritten draft, "Ganz Geheim", July 21, 1897, RMA III. 1.5.3.

[41] High Command to Imperial Naval Office, "Ganz Geheim"—"Eingang: den 24 Juni 1897", RMA III. 1.5.3., Vol. 2, with minutes on margin by Fischel and Büchsel.

[42] Statistics on naval activity overseas, studies in the Admiralty Staff Section of the

Continued on page 138

vivendi on the most bitterly contested question between them—control of naval propaganda. By using all his charm, he managed to get von Knorr to agree "to let certain rights rest, which I should not give up in a fundamental discussion of the jurisdictional question and which will revive in efficacy, when the preconditions disappear, on which my refusal to exercise them now rests."[43] This truce gave Tirpitz the freedom of action he needed, but only on the one issue of propaganda and agitation. The High Command continued to raise niggling objections to various aspects of Tirpitz's work,[44] and to respond to his requests with bad grace.[45] By February of 1898, he was forced to resort to drastic measures. In an audience of February 7, he proposed, and the Kaiser approved, an All-Highest Cabinet Order requiring the High Command "to confine its correspondence with the Imperial Naval Office to those items absolutely essential to the maintenance of the service". Again in March, the Kaiser repeated this order and forced the High Command "to let all discussions about cruiser types rest".[46] Tirpitz had won the first round of the battle with the High Command.

Intervention by the Reich Treasury was another threat to speedy and satisfactory completion of the drafting process. On August 1, 1897, Tirpitz ordered six copies to be prepared and sent "as soon as possible" to the Treasury.[47] Büchsel pressed the section chiefs to the greatest possible effort with comments

Continued from page 137
High Command on foreign navies, strategic studies and the like could only be obtained at short notice from the High Command. (Cf. Tirpitz to von Knorr, October 30, 1897, RMA III. 1.5.3., Vol. 3, for an example.)

[43] Von Knorr to Tirpitz, Berlin, August 24, 1897, MK III.

[44] High Command to Imperial Naval Office, November 26, 1897, RMA III. 1.5.3., Vol. 3. They objected to Tirpitz's tactical assumptions.

[45] "I cannot fail to point out that the exhausting and time-consuming work could only be completed by an extraordinary effort on the part of my staff and by putting off pressing and vital work of my own department . . ." (von Knorr to Tirpitz, Berlin, December 3, 1897, RMA III., Vol. 2). Tirpitz underlined the passage quoted and scrawled angrily on the bottom of the page: "Now, when the question of life or death is supposed to be fought out!"

[46] "Allerhöchste Kabinetts-Ordre", February 7, 1898, and March 7, 1898, MGFA-DZ: 7145, PG 68751. ADMC I. 3–8. For the rest of the organization crisis, see Walther Hubatsch, *Der Admiralstab*, pp. 81 ff., "Senden Nachlass" BA K 08-7, and Kriegswissenschaftliche Abteilung der Marine, *Der Admiralstab der Kaiserlichen Marine*, pp. 15 ff.

[47] Draft of letter to State Secretary, Reich Treasury, Secret, Bad Ems, August 1, 1897, received at Imperial Naval Office, August 4, 1897, RMA III. 1.5.3.

such as "very urgent", "finish today" and "at once".[48] By August 8, 1897, work was completed on the financial calculations and the drafts forwarded to the Treasury. As expected, Freiherr von Thielmann had his doubts. "I am far from certain, in view of the experiences in the last Reichstag session, whether it will be possible to introduce the draft of a law for the German fleet in the session about to begin. For the appropriation of the items included in the estimates for fiscal 1898/99, the introduction of such a law will not be of decisive importance." To both objections, Tirpitz and Büchsel had answers. Tirpitz saw in Thielmann's remarks the fact that he was "in principle agreeable to the idea of a law". Büchsel wrote, "unless we introduce a law, the estimates will not be approved because they will be mere demands for new ships . . . It is not just a question of the money for 1898/99, but of the burden placed on the years to come arising from the approval of construction of two new battleships, one large, two small cruisers and two gunboats and of the fundamental recognition of the idea of strengthening the Navy . . . It is really a question of vital principle: certainty in the further development of the Navy."[49]

A direct confrontation between the Naval Office and the Treasury would accomplish nothing. Instead Tirpitz used the same manoeuvre on Thielmann that he had successfully worked on von Knorr. He paid a call on the State Secretary on August 21st, and agreed to the formation of a joint interdepartmental committee. As a favour he got Thielmann to agree to postpone the first session until mid-September, "because the appropriate section chief will be away on duty until that time".[50] The appropriate section chief was Capelle, who was at St. Blasien with Tirpitz, but Thielmann could not know that. He was still obviously under the impression that the State Secretary of the Navy was an ordinary administrative opponent, with whom one discussed matters of principle in bureaucratic committees.[51] Having put off the Treasury until

[48] *Ibid.*, Minutes of August 4 and 7, initialled by Büchsel.

[49] Freiherr von Thielmann to Tirpitz, Berlin, August 16, 1897, with marginal comments in pencil by Büchsel and Tirpitz, RMA III. 1.5.3.

[50] Tirpitz to Thielmann, Berlin, August 22, 1897, RMA III. 1.5.3.

[51] "In the meantime, may I assume that following our verbal agreement your Excellency will take steps to obtain a decision of the Herr Reich Chancellor and to be good enough to communicate that decision to me in writing, whether it is the

Continued on page 140

the middle of September, Tirpitz was able to see the Kaiser and the Chancellor first. Having done that he could lay his cards on the table and inform Thielmann that the questions of principle had been decided long ago. The month's delay had given Tirpitz the time to go over Thielmann's head, and now all he had to do was to take up a position behind the Kaiser's orders. "With all the good will in the world", he told Thielmann, "I regret that I am unable to request the Reich Chancellor for any further decisions on a question which has already been decided on All-Highest level with the knowledge of the Reich Chancellor."[52] The Treasury was checkmated, and on September 14th, Thielmann confessed that ". . . information had not been received at the Treasury of the All-Highest approval of the introduction of the Navy Law (brought about without consultation with the financial authorities)."[53]

Tirpitz's relations with other members of the government were much better than with the High Command and Treasury. He gained the respect of that influential intriguer, Prussian Finance Minister von Miquel, who wanted to use the Kaiser's confidence in the Admiral to get imperial approval of the government's approach to the penal reform question. On the 23rd of August, one of the Chancellor's aides, Hutten-Czapski, wrote to Hohenlohe that Tirpitz had been busy politically. "From a long letter which Tirpitz wrote Miquel from Cassel, I get the impression that the former as *homo novus* has great influence at the moment. The Kaiser approved his very modest draft law without any objection, insisted however that this one must be passed 'unconditionally'."[54] Tirpitz himself made every effort to be pleasant to everyone, and with the work on the draft law far advanced, he began a series of visits to luminaries of the Reich. On the 24th he paid a call on Bismarck at Friedrichsruh. His mission had a double purpose, not only

Continued from page 139
case that your intention to submit a draft to the coming Reichstag is still in force or whether such a step is to be postponed in the light of the tactical considerations raised in my letter of the 16th." Thielmann to Tirpitz, Berlin, August 25, 1897, RMA III. 1.5.3.

[52] Tirpitz to Thielmann, St. Blasien, September 4, 1897, RMA III. 1.5.3.

[53] Thielmann to Tirpitz, Berlin, September 14, 1897, RMA III. 1.5.3., Vol. 2.

[54] Hutten-Czapski to Hohenlohe, Bad Homburg, August 23, 1897, Hohenlohe, *op. cit.*, p. 378.

to try to convince the suspicious old giant of the need for his programme, but also to get Bismarck to withdraw his "gruff" refusal to attend the launching of a ship to be named after him.[55] Bismarck, who had no sympathy with *Weltpolitik*, was not interested. He was an old man, tired and embittered, who just wanted "to be left alone".[56] The Grand Duke of Baden was more amiable. Tirpitz so impressed the old gentleman that the Grand Duke wrote to Hohenlohe congratulating him that "such an excellent personality had undertaken the advocacy of these great tasks, a man whose character and experience are equally splendid."[57] The Prince-Regent of Bavaria was next on the list, and on September 26th, Tirpitz, Capelle and von Heeringen paid an official visit to the Senate of the Free City of Hamburg.[58]

The objective of all these visits and meetings with princes and officials was to make sure of the support of the Bundesrath, before he submitted his draft law in its entirety. Hamburg was important as a centre of commercial activity, and the contacts which he made there led to a resolution of the German Chambers of Commerce urging the creation of a fleet. The activity of Adolf Woermann, one of the most prominent Hamburg business leaders, was to prove invaluable in the propaganda campaign of the months of December and January. Tirpitz stretched feelers out to important editors of leading South German newspapers. In July, Geheimrath Koch, travelling ostensibly in a private capacity, had made contact with the *Badische Landeszeitung*, the *Schwäbische Merkur* in Stuttgart, the *Allgemeine Zeitung* in Munich and the *Fränkische Morgenzeitung* in Nuremberg.[59] The Imperial Naval Office had arranged to have a reporter on board the flagship of the squadron which accompanied the Kaiser on his Russian trip from August 4th to the 14th, 1897. The reporter's job was "to write suitable newspaper articles which will encourage interest in the Navy

[55] Wilmowski to Hohenlohe, Berlin, August 24, 1897, *ibid.*, p. 379.
[56] Tirpitz, *op. cit.*, p. 92; cf. E. Kehr, *op. cit.*, p. 89, for Bismarck's interview in Harden's *Die Zukunft* of September 4, 1897.
[57] Grand Duke of Baden to Hohenlohe, August 23, 1897, Hohenlohe, *op. cit.*, p. 377.
[58] On the visit to Munich, cf. Anton Graf Monts, *Erinnerungen und Gedanken*, Berlin, 1932, p. 196; on the visit to Hamburg, cf. E. Kehr, *op. cit.*, p. 115.
[59] MGFA-DZ: 2221, PG 93934, RMA I. 1.1.-1, July 14, 1897.

among the public at large".[60] In the same period, von Heeringen made an extensive tour of German universities and spoke to dozens of distinguished professors, urging them to contribute to the agitation in favour of the projected Navy Law.[61]

Tirpitz's personal diplomacy coincided with a campaign in the opposition Press against the Navy Law. Eugen Richter's *Freisinnige Zeitung* was both the best informed and most implacable of Tirpitz's journalistic foes. By now the paper's editors had begun to notice how Tirpitz was using their complaints about naval confusion. "The semi-official press would like to make it appear," the *Freisinnige Zeitung* commented on October 5th, "that the projected seven-year naval programme is some sort of invention of the radical Press and in particular of Herr Eugen Richter. Only a few days ago the very same governmental organs declared with emphatic references to enquiries in informed circles that the government intend to commit the Reichstag by law to spend annually until 1905 the sum of sixty million marks for construction of new ships . . . A seven year naval law is denied at the moment, but it can no longer be denied that Tirpitz's plans for ship construction will require the sum of 410 million over seven years. The semi-official Press seems to think that it owes Herr Tirpitz a debt of gratitude that this demand for 410 million proves that the era of "limitless fleet plans" is over. This 410 million is in reality merely the hazy outline of a naval bay, the shore-line of which disappears in the limitless distance."[62]

The protests of the opposition were slowly being drowned out by the crescendo of agitation coming from every quarter. In September of 1897 the propaganda campaign of the German Colonial Society began. A large sum of money was raised and given to a central directory for agitation, which in the seven months between its formulation and the passage of the Navy Law organized 173 lectures and printed 140,000 pamphlets, including 2,000 copies of Captain Mahan's *The Influence of*

[60] Büchsel to Naval Cabinet, July 29, 1897, MK XXXVI.13, "Reisen Seiner Majestät".

[61] W. Marienfeld, *op. cit.*, pp. 7 f. See also, MGFA-DZ: 2221, PG 93935, RMA I. 1.1-1, Vol. 2, September 18, 1897, for contacts between the News Section and German Chambers of Commerce.

[62] "Zur Marinevorlage", *Die Freisinnige Zeitung*, Berlin, October 5, 1897.

Sea Power on History.[63] The Pan-German League greeted the Tirpitz programme with enthusiasm and Dr. A. Lehr, one of the leaders of the League, appeared regularly at Leipzigerplatz 13 to get information and propaganda material.[64] At the suggestion of Professor Gustav Schmoller, Ernst von Halle, then a *Privatdozent* and later Professor of Economics at the University of Berlin, was employed by the News Section of the I.N.O. to provide scientific information and arguments for the White Papers which accompanied the Navy Law, and also for the "Nauticus" pamphlets in which the arguments of the opposition were countered point by point.[65] The appearance on September 11th in London of the famous article in *The Saturday Review*, which closed with the words "*Germaniam esse delendam*", was a welcome demonstration of the "danger" facing Germany. By the beginning of October, the propaganda campaign had reached colossal proportions. Complaints about official agitation mounted in volume, until the government could no longer ignore them. The official *Norddeutsche Allgemeine Zeitung* published a categorical denial that a press bureau had been instituted in the Imperial Naval Office for the purpose of disseminating articles on the Navy throughout the country, in order to create artificially an agitation in favour of an increase in the fleet. Nobody was fooled. As the Berlin correspondent of *The Times* remarked, "this may be literally true, but, whatever the source, it is patent to every observer that the government organs are one and all in the enjoyment of daily inspiration which finds vent in pregnant paragraphs or elaborate disquisitions on the future of the navy."[66]

On October 4, 1897, Tirpitz presented a final draft of the Navy Law to the Chancellor, and on the 5th, the Kaiser issued an All-Highest Cabinet Order empowering him to present the draft to the Bundesrath.[67] On October 7th, a meeting of the Ministry of State discussed the draft in Berlin and decided to omit one provision (Article One, Paragraph 3), which called

[63] W. Marienfeld, *op. cit.*, p. 87; A. T. Mahan, *The Influence of Sea Power on History*, New York, 1890.
[64] A. Kruck, *Geschichte des Alldeutschen Verbands*, Wiesbaden, 1954, p. 29.
[65] E. Kehr, *op. cit.*, p. 102, and W. Marienfeld, *op. cit.*, pp. 79 f.
[66] *The Times*, London, October 6, 1897.
[67] Tirpitz to Hohenlohe, Berlin, October 4, 1897; A.K.O., Danzig, October 5, 1897; both in RMA III. 1.5.3., Vol. 2.

for the augmentation of the torpedo boat flotilla.[68] On the 11th the Kaiser approved the alteration and the technical specifications for the large cruiser designs.[69] On the 15th Korvetten-Kapitän Pohl circulated the information to all section chiefs in the I.N.O. that the Bill was complete and no more alterations would be accepted, and on the 19th Capelle forwarded the draft to the Reich Printing Office with a request that absolute secrecy be maintained.[70] With the exception of a final and unsuccessful meeting of the joint Treasury-Naval Office Committee on the 18th, all that remained for Tirpitz to do was to submit the printed draft to the Reich Chancellor.

The document, which Prince Hohenlohe submitted to the members of the Bundesrath on October 29, 1897,[71] contained the text of a "Law Concerning the German Fleet" and the "*Begründung zum Gesetzentwurf*", in which the arguments in favour of the law as well as detailed explanations of its individual provisions could be found.[72] The text of the law itself was simply stated in Article One, "*Schiffsbestand*", that the Imperial Navy was to have a fixed number of ships of each type. Section One of Article One listed them: 19 battleships, 8 coastal armoured ships, 12 large and 30 small cruisers. Other paragraphs of Section One covered training ships, a vague statement about torpedo boat divisions, special ships and gunboats. Section Two listed the number of ships already in existence on April 1, 1898, which were to be included in the total in Section One. Section Three of Article One was an important provision which Tirpitz took over in its entirety from the first version of the law of May 24, 1897. It fixed the active life of the individual ship classes at twenty-five years for battleships, twenty for large cruisers and fifteen for small cruisers,[73] and committed

[68] Staatsministerium, Berlin, Wednesday, October 7, 1897, and Minute of Captain Fischel, October 11, 1897, RMA III. 1.5.3., Vols. 2 and 3.

[69] "Immediatvortrag", October 11, 1897, R.M.A. III. 1.5.3., Vol. 2.

[70] "Bekanntmachung", M I, signed by Pohl, Berlin, October 15, 1897, RMA III. 1.5.3., Vol. 3, and Capelle to Reichsdrückerei, Berlin, October 19, 1897, R.M.A. III. 1.5.3., Vol. 3.

[71] Fürst Hohenlohe to Bundesrath and Büchsel to Ministry of Interior, Berlin, October 29, 1897, RMA III. 1.5.3., Vol. 3.

[72] "Gesetz betreffend die Deutsche Flotte" and "Begründung zum Gesetzentwurf betreffend die Deutsche Flotte", printed copy with handwritten corrections, October 1897, RMA III. 1.5.3., Vol. 2.

[73] In his memoirs, Tirpitz writes: "The effective life, as a result of a parliamentary

Continued on page 145

The "Bundesrat" (Federal Council) of the German Empire in 1900. Seated from left to right: Selkmann, von Neidhardt, Graf Lerchenfeld, Posadowsky, Hohenthal, Jagemann. Standing from left to right: von Bonin, Warnbühler, Klügmann, von Oertgen, Crams-Burgdorff, Freiherr von Stengel, Tirpitz, Paulssen

Social Democratic members of the Reichstag, August Bebel and Paul Singer, in Berlin, 1903

Ships of the High Seas Battle Fleet, at anchor in Kiel Harbour, 1899

Fleet manoeuvres, 1907

the Reichstag to appropriate replacement funds automatically. Section Four stated that the money for the programme was to be appropriated in equal instalments in the annual budget of the Reich. Article Two and Article Three covered the disposition and table of organization of the active fleet and the personnel required to man it.

The "*Begründung*", the justification for these provisions, began with the "General Argument: The necessity of fixing by law 1. the strength of the battle fleet in terms of ships, active service and personnel; 2. the time period in which the desired effective strength is to be reached; 3. the regular replacement of the existing ships."[74] By fixing these three provisions, Tirpitz knew that any Reichstag which passed such a law would necessarily tie itself more tightly in moral terms than it ever could have done by any monetary obligations. It would commit itself to a certain building programme by law. If the ships grew larger and more expensive, the Reichstag might well object, but having given legal sanction to a battle fleet of a certain size, it could hardly place monetary obstacles in the way of a changing technology.[75] The law was what Tirpitz called a "*lex imperfecta*", that is, an open-ended commitment to build whatever type of ships to fill the establishment the Naval Office claimed was militarily necessary. This point was, of course, concealed in the "*Begründung*"; the civilian deputies were unlikely to realize how big a hostage they were in fact giving to the rapidly changing demands of technology. "There is no infringement of the rights of the Reichstag because of the establishment by law of the size of the Navy and of the annual portion of the battle fleet on active service," the "*Begründung*" explained, "because the constitutional co-operation of the Reichstag in the legal resolution of these questions is preserved in full . . ."[76] Tirpitz's assumption

Continued from page 144
misunderstanding, was set at twenty-five years and was thus higher than the foreign navies. This led to an over-extended active life of our ships." (Tirpitz, *op. cit.*, p. 173.) The effective age of twenty-five years had been first settled by the "Skizze zum Gesetz" of May 24, 1897, and had been included without alteration in all successive drafts of the law. There was no question of "parliamentary misunderstanding".

[74] "Begründung zum Gesetzentwurf etc.", p. 1.

[75] Tirpitz, *op. cit.*, pp. 108 f.

[76] "Begründung zum Gesetzentwurf etc.", p. 5.

that bland assurances of a general nature would satisfy the Reichstag was one of his few mistakes.

"The task of the battle fleet is the defence of the coasts of the nation. Number and size of ships have been exclusively determined according to this principle. Against larger sea powers this fleet has merely the significance of a 'sortie fleet'. Any other objective is ruled out by the limited naval strength, which the law provides."[77] In this Section of the "*Begründung*", as in the assertion in his memoirs that "the plan for the battle fleet was composed without any thought of a war against England",[78] Tirpitz was absolutely untruthful as opposed to the half-truths which he served up to the Reichstag on the significance of the "*lex imperfecta*". While it was partly true to say that the Reichstag retained its financial control over the naval programme despite the fixed Navy Law, it was wholly false to say that a fleet composed mainly of battleships had "merely the significance of a 'sortie fleet' ". It is a measure of the success of Tirpitz's agitation that by 1900 he could drop the mask and proclaim openly the full implications of the "risk theory" and its anti-English bias.

In Part Two of the "*Begründung*", the individual requirements of the Navy were outlined with great precision and clarity. With reference to Article One, the Naval Office pointed out that of the nineteen battleships stipulated by the law only twelve were actually on hand and of these the four ships of the "Sachsen" Class were so antiquated that their replacement would be required by 1902/03.[79] Replacement of the four "Sachsen" Class battleships, construction of a flagship, four new and two reserve battleships made up a total of eleven new battleships to be built during the seven years. The order of construction was also outlined. Between April 1, 1898, and April 1, 1902, all seven of the new ships would be begun, and in the remaining years of the programme the replacement of the "Sachsen" Class would follow.[80] The total cost of the programme, as Eugen Richter's *Freisinnige Zeitung* rightly estimated, amounted to M 410,000,000 for construction alone,

[77] *Ibid.*, p. 11.
[78] Tirpitz, *op. cit.*, pp. 58 f.
[79] "Begründung zum Gesetzentwurf", p. 13.
[80] *Ibid.*, p. 15, "Tabelle: Vertheilung der Schiffsbauten über die Jahre."

plus an average increase in the ordinary estimates, caused by an increase in personnel and other expenses, of M 4,200,000 for each year of the plan.[81] The sum M 410,000,000 produced an average annual figure for construction of M 58,600,000 which was only M 500,000 more than the actual appropriations for the previous year. It was, of course, achieved by omitting the cost of the torpedo boat divisions from the tables. The cost of torpedo boats amounted to the tidy sum of M 44,100,000.[82] Truthfulness was certainly not the outstanding characteristic of the "*Begründung*".

Only Tirpitz and his closest associates knew how much the "*Begründung*" concealed behind its impressive façade of facts and figures. To the members of the Bundesrath, it must have seemed both convincing and straightforward. The modesty of the programme was remarkable. At no time during the seven year existence of the law would the budget rise above the sum of M 150 million, an increase of less than thirty per cent on the total budget actually appropriated (new construction and total operation) in March of 1897 by the previous session of the Reichstag. Its clarity was equally commendable. The Navy knew where it was going and how it intended to get there. As Bülow put it in his memoirs, "an entirely different wind blew from this Bill than from all the earlier naval Bills. A clear spirit and a strong will spoke through it. The entire project and all its provisions were of the same stuff."[83] Its political aspect was pacific and defensive. It spoke a language of restraint and realism after nearly ten years of imperial bombast and administrative confusion. At every point the Naval Office had opted for uniformity, even if it meant building smaller battleships than had already become fashionable in foreign fleets.[84] A relationship between strategy, tactics,

[81] *Ibid.*, p. 23, "Tabelle: Voraussichtliche Steigerung des Marine-Etats bis zum Jahre 1904/05."

[82] The calculation of the cost of the missing torpedo-boats is taken from Anlage 2, "Feststellung und Vertheilung der Kosten für Schiffsbau" of July 2, 1897 (RMA III. 1.5.3.), at which time the torpedo boats were still included in the Naval Office's calculations.

[83] Bülow, *op. cit.*, p. 115.

[84] "Denkschrift der militärischen Abtheilung zum Immediatvortrag", October 26, 1897, signed by Fischel, RMA III. 1.5.3. "Since the two new battleships to be requested for fiscal 1898/99 are intended to be the third and fourth ships of a

Continued on page 148

weapons development and cost had not only been established but convincingly presented for all to see.

The fact that it had an inner purpose known only to a few insiders and concealed from the civilian leadership of the Reich made the Navy Law attractive at court. Support from the Kaiser and Senden gave Tirpitz a freedom to manoeuvre which his predecessors under Wilhelm II had not enjoyed. The Kaiser and Senden were getting their "*Flotte gegen England*", while Bundesrath and Reichstag received a Bill which put an end to the "limitless fleet plans". The Federal Princes had been visited and mollified, agitation unfolded in a style hitherto unknown in Germany and the Hohenlohe government was strengthened by the removal of the explosive Navy question from the list of its differences with the Kaiser. All this had been accomplished in four months. Tirpitz had completed the first stage of the most brilliant political operation of the Wilhelmine era. The second stage was about to begin.

Continued from page 147
division in which *Kaiser Friedrich III* and *Ersatz König Wilhelm* are the first and second, . . . it is suggested that they be built according to the plans for *Ersatz König Wilhelm* . . ." Since *Ersatz König Wilhelm* had a displacement of 11,038 tons, this meant that the German battleships would be smaller than the contemporary British "Majestic" Class, which had a 15,000 ton displacement.

5

The Navy Law in the Reichstag

A. The Final Preparations

In November 1897 His Excellency Rear-Admiral Alfred Tirpitz, State Secretary of the Imperial Naval Office, was a political unknown. At the age of 48 and only thirteenth in seniority among German admirals, he was by no means the commanding figure that he became after 1905, but he had begun to look physically like the later Tirpitz. His smooth, round head was already hairless, save for a fringe at the sides, and by this time he had begun to wear the extraordinary forked beard soon to be popular with cartoonists. The same large, expressive eyes looked out from beneath heavy, arched eye-brows which all the photographs of the later *Grossadmiral* emphasize. Although the physical presence of the man and the serene aura of self-confidence remind one of the older and more famous Tirpitz, he was certainly not yet that man. He had yet to face the ordeal of the German Reichstag, and he had to test his personality in the cross-fire of parliamentary attack.

Socially, Tirpitz was an accomplished man of the world. He had none of the tactless obstinacy of Senden, nor the gruff crudity of von Knorr. Despite his years of active service, there was nothing of the grizzled sea-dog about him. He looked less the sailor than the solid, imperturbable managing director, fond of a good cigar and a choice wine. His manners were polished, his conversation graceful and his dress elegant. He was thoroughly at home in the salons of Berlin and Vienna; if anything, in the words of a Russian princess, he was "*trop de grand homme*". The smooth exterior concealed two contradictory characteristics: ruthless determination and nervous instability. While the former may almost be taken for granted in a man so successful in public life, the latter is unexpected. Herr Ulrich von Hassell, whose son married Tirpitz's eldest daughter, remarked on this characteristic in his biography of the Admiral. One of Tirpitz's old comrades remembered vividly how the young naval officer had suffered from nervous ailments. Before his marriage in 1884, he had been a victim of acute hypochondria. Herr von Hassell quoted the comrade who recalled that Tirpitz "complained incessantly about his health, often came late to table and announced that he would be quite unable to eat anything . . . He took medicines far more than even remotely necessary and fought with sleeplessness, as he always said. Often it would turn out that he had in fact slept through a terrific thunder-shower."[1] Herr von Hassell attributed the decline in Tirpitz's hysterical ailments to the sobering influence of his happy marriage to Marie Lipke, although the neurosis never disappeared entirely. Even as a seventy-year-old, Tirpitz continued to fret about his health and to worry his family with complaints. He was an immensely emotional man, profoundly devoted to his wife and children and passionately attached to his home. A certain romantic flair or love of the "primitive" led him to buy a small villa in the spectacular remoteness of the Sardinian port of Alghero, where, as Tirpitz's daughter wrote to her father-in-law, "one is so far from the world and civilization, in such primitive 'bandit-like' conditions that it is easy to imagine that one is enchanted."[2] For comfort and relaxation, he chose the crisp, mountain atmosphere of St. Blasien in the Black Forest at the family's house set dramatically on the rim of a deep, pine-covered gorge.

Tirpitz's massive physical appearance gave many of his contemporaries the impression of solidity and calm, but those who knew him well were not misled. As Senden shrewdly observed, Tirpitz was prone to great extremes of emotional elation and total depression.[3] He disliked direct confrontation and, contrary to the common impression, shied away from open, pitched battles. His preference for compromise seemed

[1] Ulrich von Hassell, *Tirpitz*, p. 215.

[2] *Ibid.*, p. 218.

[3] "High as the heavens in his joys . . . but never relaxing in his creative activities, no matter how crushed he may seem . . ." ("Aufzeichnung über Hollmann und Tirpitz", Notes in Senden's hand, March 1896, BA K 08-7, "Senden Nachlass".)

to a stubborn old Prussian like Holstein virtually the same as cowardice.[4] The accusation was as crude as it was unjust. Tirpitz could fight. When vexed beyond a certain point, he was sometimes capable of colossal outbursts of fighting spirit, but he usually preferred the more reliable facets of his nature, his charm, his glittering intellect, his irresistible persuasiveness, to the gruff, rude aggressiveness of Prussian tradition. He was *par excellence* the politician and the manipulator of men. His was the new style, the business-like amiability of the emerging industrialists and managers of large enterprises, which would soon replace the taciturn, gloomy and humourless rectitude of the older Prussian generation.

Bernhard von Bülow, State Secretary of the Foreign Ministry, was also a new man. It was not a coincidence that his appointment was an item on the same Bundesrath agenda which included Tirpitz's naval bill. For of all the men in the administration of the Reich in the late autumn of 1897, Tirpitz and Bülow were most representative of the new style. If possible, Bülow was even more elegant, more felicitous in speech and graceful in manner than Tirpitz. Bülow's polish was so glossy that critics justly wondered whether there was any substance to the man at all. Rounder, smoother and handsomer than Tirpitz, Bülow was the white hope of the Kaiser and the court circle in foreign affairs as Tirpitz was in naval affairs. Their partnership was to prove fatal and unequal, because, unlike Tirpitz, Bülow had no inner strength. Where Tirpitz's glossy surface masked a will of iron, lamed though it might be by emotional instability, Bülow's glittering exterior concealed an utter lack of force and purpose. In foreign affairs it was the Admiral who had the ideas while the diplomat had only the manners. The contrast between the old Prussian and the new Reich leadership could not have been more marked than by the striking difference between Bülow and his father, who for many years occupied the same office which his son now assumed. The elder Bülow, silent, withdrawn, self-effacing and efficient, served Bismarck so well that his name

[4] "Tirpitz has no stomach for a fight. At the time of Kiaochow he was in favour of yielding. When Bülow arrived in December 1897, the first thing he heard was Tirpitz saying: 'We shall probably have to get out of Kiaochow' . . . He has shown similar lack of nerve on other occasions . . ." (*The Holstein Papers*, January 11, 1902, IV, No. 792, p. 245.)

has virtually disappeared from the record of history. His son's name was to be forever associated with a policy of flamboyance and postures. "Bülow is a disaster for us," Albert Ballin wrote to General Waldersee in November 1903. "He spoils the Kaiser completely by saying nothing but the most flattering rubbish and thus bringing His Majesty to a boundless overestimation of himself."[5]

In November 1897 Bülow's faults were not yet apparent, while his obvious abilities were desperately needed. The Reich Chancellor, Prince Hohenlohe, was a man of seventy-seven years of age. He had never been a good speaker, nor a strong leader. With each year he lapsed further into feebleness of will and weary cynicism. His family, an ancient European princely dynasty, was as old and aristocratic as the Hohenzollern for whom he had a lazy contempt, and his relationship to its youthful head was easy-going and familiar. As Chancellor, he had been unable and in part unwilling to resist Wilhelm II. The reorganization of the cabinet had been done over his protest, and the old man swallowed it. He allowed himself to be robbed of his choice of spokesman, Freiherr von Marschall, and was now forced to accept Tirpitz's Navy Bill on top of all his other political worries. As compensation for Marschall's loss, he was given Bülow. His position had become intolerable, but he lacked the strength to alter it. Eugen Richter openly mocked him in the Reichstag. "If I imagine that the Herr Chancellor were really to speak his mind to us," Richter began, "he might say something rather like this: 'The whole business is not pretty, I admit that. But I am a weak man, much weaker than you imagine. I have sometimes been able to prevent things which would have led to dangerous developments in home and foreign affairs, but I cannot get anything positive done, even if I give my word to do so . . . If I get the Navy Law passed, then I shall have done my bit and I can go. Anyway I feel a lot better on my estates than in the Wilhelmstrasse or the Reichstag . . . (Prolonged Laughter)."[6]

The prospects for such a peacable end to the old Chancellor's career were not good. There were too many lingering conflicts

[5] Quoted in E. Eyck, *op. cit.*, p. 190.

[6] *Stenographischer Bericht*, der Reichstag, 9. Legisl.-Periode, V Session, 9. Sitzung, December 13, 1897, p. 193. That Richter's remarks accurately, almost literally,

Continued on page 153

and governmental commitments which Hohenlohe was too feeble to meet. There was, in the first place, the festering dissension between the Reich and Bavaria over the reform of the military penal code. If the Chancellor had any hopes in that direction, Dr. Lieber, the leader of the Centre Party, was quick to dispel them at an interview late in October. "Lieber is still willing to work for the Navy," the Chancellor noted, ". . . but he says that without a penal code settlement the Reichstag will be unapproachable and will not approve anything."[7] Unless the 96 Centre deputies supported the government, there was no hope for the Navy Law, but support from the Centre was likely to cost a great deal. Since the Centre Party's strength rested on Catholic Bavaria, Dr. Lieber was in a delicate position. Co-operation with the government required concrete evidence of official goodwill, not only toward the Bavarian separatists but also to Catholics throughout the Reich. Their legal rights were still encumbered by much of the hostile legislation of Bismarck's anti-Catholic *Kulturkampf*. Lieber's freedom to manoeuvre was severely limited as long as there was no indication that full civil rights for Roman Catholic monastic and teaching orders would be restored. Lieber's dazzling image of the Centre as the government party and himself as quasi-prime minister collided with the cruel fact of the existence of such repressive legislation. Powerful, ultramontane priests and prelates were just waiting for Lieber to make a wrong move so they could overthrow his authority.

The reception of Tirpitz's Navy Bill in parliament was consequently uncertain. Surveying the scene, Bülow added up those who might support the Bill. "So far the Conservatives had no particular inclination for the creation of a big fleet. The Centreists would agree to it but would demand a big *douceur* for their consent. We could only be sure of the National Liberals and a section of the Radicals, the 'courtiers' under Rickert and Barth, but hardly of Eugen Richter with his narrow and somewhat philistine ideas. We could naturally reckon on

Continued from page 152
reflected Hohenlohe's thoughts can be seen in an entry in the Chancellor's diaries from October 17, in which the old man outlines three possible ways in which he might submit his resignation. (Hohenlohe, *op. cit.*, pp. 392 f.)

[7] Diary entry, October 28, 1897, *ibid.*, p. 397.

the violent opposition of the Social Democrats."[8] If Bülow's estimate was correct, the Navy Law could only command 162 votes of the 199 needed for a majority.

Hohenlohe's troubles were by no means confined to domestic affairs. The Kaiser, Senden and the Naval High Command were still clamouring for a coaling station and naval base on the Chinese coast. That this could not be acquired without introducing new strains into Germany's relations with either Russia or Great Britain or both was only too clear to the Chancellor. Meanwhile in the China Sea, Admiral Diederichs, Tirpitz's successor as commander of the cruiser squadron, had been alarmingly active. Unlike Tirpitz, Diederichs had no hesitations about a site for a German base. He wanted Kiaochow. On October 31st, the High Command received a cable from S.M.S. *Bussard* in Hankow that officers and men of the *Cormoran* had been insulted by a mob of Chinese. Von Holtzendorff, the Chief of Staff, suggested that "the incident might offer a suitable occasion for more serious negotiations with China and for a new approach to Russia."[9] The Kaiser approved the suggestion on the following day and immediately raised the issue with Bülow. As Holstein reported a little while later, the Kaiser spoke "very indignantly about the flaccid policy of the Foreign Ministry which had not understood how to exploit the favourable opportunities which had repeatedly presented themselves in recent years (as I said, the chief obstacle to any action was the fact that the Navy had not decided where it was to take place)."[10] Since Diederichs had convinced the Kaiser that Kiaochow Bay was the right spot, the Foreign Ministry found itself very much on the defensive. The problem about Kiaochow was its position in what was clearly the Russian sphere of influence in China. There were certain long-standing Russian claims to the bay and any action to acquire or to seize it would lead to an estrangement from Russia at the very moment when agitation for a big fleet might alienate England.

The news of the murder of German missionaries in Shantung,

[8] Bernhard von Bülow, *Memoirs*, p. 56.

[9] Von Holtzendorff to von Knorr, October 31, 1897, 7.30 p.m., MGFA-DZ: 2204. PG 65990a. ADMC I. 3-8, with minute by von Koester on results of an audience on November 1, 1897.

[10] Holstein to Hatzfeldt, November 13, 1897, *The Holstein Papers*, IV, No. 630, p. 49.

which arrived in Berlin on November 5th, was the last straw. The Kaiser demanded action at once and at any price.[11] Tirpitz was distressed by the prospect. His worst fears were confirmed when a strong Russian protest was received in Berlin on the 9th.[12] As soon as the news reached him, he sent a telegram to the Chancellor: "Regard the action against China as unfavourable for the Navy Bill and in the proposed form very dangerous. The consequences of this sort of action must lead to serious threat of hostilities. Request by return permission for audience with Your Highness."[13] His protest came too late. Admiral Diederichs had already set sail for Kiaochow Bay, where he anchored on November 12th and issued a proclamation announcing the seizure of the bay and the province of East Shantung. Tirpitz told Hohenlohe that a war with China was probably inevitable if such a programme were carried out.[14] The High Command began to get nervous about the possibility of intervention by other powers, especially Japan, and started work on a plan for war with that power, while the Minister of War told Hohenlohe that he was "alarmed by the very serious character of the Kiaochow question."[15] Ironically, the civilians of the Foreign Ministry showed more pluck than either defence minister. True to what had mistakenly come to be accepted as Bismarck's basic axiom of diplomacy, they refused to consider the prospect of retreat. As Holstein put it, the real danger was that "the English as soon as they perceive that we will retreat from Kiaochow in the face of the Russian uproar, will for their part summon up the courage to keep us out of places which might be uncomfortable for England . . ."[16] The eventual Russian acquiescence in the

[11] GP, Vol. XIV, 1, No. 3686, p. 67.

[12] GP, Vol. XIV, 1, No. 3693, pp. 73 f.

[13] Tirpitz to Hohenlohe, cipher telegram, Berlin, November 10, 1897, Hohenlohe, *op. cit.*, p. 412. Tirpitz mentions neither the decisive report of Admiral Diederichs nor his own hesitation in his memoirs. Instead he pretends to have been for Kiaochow all the time and to have regarded the Russian threat as "legendary". (Tirpitz, *op. cit.*, p. 65.)

[14] Holstein to Hatzfeldt, November 13, 1897, *The Holstein Papers*, IV, No. 630, p. 51.

[15] "Zusammenstellung zum Immediatvortrag am 13 Dezember 1897" and "Denkschrift betreffend Vorbereitung zum Krieg gegen Japan", December 18, 1897, MGFA-DZ: 2024. PG 65990a, ADMC I 3-8; diary entry, November 29, 1897, Hohenlohe, *op. cit.*, pp. 419 f.

[16] Holstein to Hatzfeldt, cf. Footnote 14.

German move failed to obliterate the bad impression which the Kaiser's haste had created in St. Petersburg.[17]

Foreign political alarms and excursions could only temporarily divert Tirpitz from his preoccupation with the main issue. Throughout the turbulent weeks of excitement over Kiaochow, he and his staff continued to assemble every single scrap of evidence which might be used in the Reichstag. Inquiries were sent to the naval attachés in London and Rome requesting information about the "Naval Defence Act" of 1889 and the Italian Naval Law of 1877.[18] Statistics were collected with painstaking thoroughness to show how far behind Germany had fallen in naval construction. A special folder was compiled of "Material for use in argument for the draft of the law concerning the German Fleet".[19] Many of the tables were based on figures collected by a retired Kapitän-Leutnant, Bruno Weger, who had written a pamphlet entitled "The Decline of German and the Rise of Foreign Sea Power". It is a striking confirmation of the growing intimacy between the Naval Office and rabid nationalism that this particular study had been paid for, and published by, the extremist Pan-German League.[20] At the same time work continued on a solider, far less explosive, White Paper entitled "The Sea Interests of the German Empire", which was published together with the Navy Law draft in November of 1897.[21] This impressive, printed volume offered the Reichstag deputies nine lengthy chapters of statistics on population, emigration, foreign trade, shipping, ship and harbour construction, the develop-

[17] Radolin to Holstein, St. Petersburg, December 28, 1897, *The Holstein Papers*, IV, No. 639, p. 60: "I am convinced, as I already said at the time in Berlin, that Tsar Nicholas will bear a grudge against us for this affair. He feels that he has been taken by surprise and will hold it against us despite all the telegrams and greetings."

[18] Tirpitz to Naval Attaché (London), October 26, 1897, and cable to Attaché (Rome), November 26, 1897, and replies of November 2 and 26, 1897, RMA III. 1.5.3., Vols. 2 and 3. The Italian Navy Law was published in full in the *Norddeutsche Allgemeine Zeitung* in answer to the argument in the *Freisinnige Zeitung* that "nowhere, not even in the absolutist states, is the strength of a navy determined by a law".

[19] Order No. A 6720, Berlin, November 10, 1897, "Material zur Vertretung des Gesetzentwurfs betreffend die deutsche Flotte im Reichstage", RMA III. 1.5.3., Vol. 2.

[20] Bruno Weger, Kapitänleutnant a.D., "Der Niedergang deutscher, der Aufschwung fremder Seemacht", herausgegeben vom Alldeutschen Verbande,—Heft. No. 6; in RMA III. 1.5.3., Vol. 2.

[21] Das Reichs-Marine-Amt, *Die Seeinteressen des Deutschen Reichs*, Berlin, 1897.

ment of German deep sea fishing, German colonies, German overseas investments and comparisons between the battle fleets of England, France, Russia, Italy, the United States of America, Japan and Germany during the years between 1883 and 1897.

Not even the bitterest opponent of Germany's Navy could fail to be impressed by the thoroughness and weight of evidence which Tirpitz and his men had collected. Page after page of facts and figures pointed to the same set of circumstances. Germany's population, foreign trade, fishing, commerce, merchant fleet and heavy industry had grown fantastically since 1871. Even the depressing flow of emigration, which reached 221,000 per annum in 1881, had dwindled in the six years between 1891 and 1897 from 116,339 a year to a mere 33,824.[22] Imports had risen from an average of M 1,900,000,000 in the decade 1861-1871 to M 4,558,000,000 and exports from M 1,360,000,000 to M 3,753,000,000, despite the fact that the period was one of falling prices.[23] The growth of Germany's merchant navy had been spectacular. From a total tonnage of 82,000 in 1872, it had grown to 10,392,000 tons by 1897; in numbers of ships from 147 to 1127.[24] Population had expanded by thirty per cent over the period, growing at a rate of one per cent per annum despite the loss of more than 2,400,000 Germans to other countries.[25] No matter how one measured it, Germany was literally bursting with growth.

Chapter Nine told a different story. Here were the figures on the growth of the Imperial Navy between the year 1883, when Stosch left the Admiralty, and 1897, when Tirpitz took over the Naval Office. While the rest of society was experiencing a tremendous upsurge, Germany's Navy had sunk from fourth in the world in number of battleships over 5,000 tons to fifth in the world in number of ships, or sixth if total tonnage was the measure.[26] England had sixty-two to Germany's twelve, France's thirty-six and Russia's eighteen. In tonnage of cruisers (over 1,000 ton displacement), Germany had sunk from fifth to last among the great powers, and in terms of relative strength in both types of ship, she had lost ground to

[22] *Ibid.*, Ch. 1, p. 2.
[23] *Ibid.*, Ch. 2, p. 24.
[24] *Ibid.*, Ch. 4, p. 10.
[25] *Ibid.*, Ch. 1, p. 2.
[26] *Ibid.*, Ch. 9, p. 3

every single power.[27] Of course, this comparison was made to look artificially unfavourable to Germany, because it excluded German ships in commission but not yet on duty, and in the English totals included ships built back in the days of sail. If the Naval Defence Act of 1889 were used as a starting point, by 1897 Britain had built twenty-four new battleships to Germany's six, to France's ten and Russia's eight.[28] Whatever the basis of comparison used, there was no question that Germany's naval growth had simply not kept pace with her growth in all other fields. To demonstrate this point from every possible angle, Tirpitz wrote to the Hamburg-Amerika Line and the North German Lloyd for figures on the average age of their transatlantic passenger and freight ships, and found that the average age of the two fleets was 9·3 and 8 years respectively.[29] This compared unfavourably with an average age of 10·3 years for the battleships of the German Home Fleet. Again the Navy was lagging behind the rest of the society.

The News Section (M II) was humming with activity. Von Heeringen and his staff scoured the daily papers throughout the whole country for articles for and against naval expansion. Absolutely every hostile comment was answered in detail and at once. The files of M II are full of drafts for articles to be planted with the friendly or semi-official Press. The tone of many of these 'plants' was unusually, and I think, genuinely, liberal. Von Heeringen and his bright young men played variations on the theme that only decisive, legal action by the Reichstag could put an end to the era of naval confusion, uncertainty and sloth. When the *Freisinnige Zeitung* attacked the Naval Office's programme as "merely the hazy outline of a naval bay, the shore-line of which disappears in the limitless distance", von Heeringen drafted a reply that there was "only one tool against limitlessness: the parliamentary organs, Bundesrath and Reichstag, must build dams and limits

[27] *Ibid.*, Ch. 9, p. 4.

[28] Cf. "Aufzeichnung der Konstruktionsabteilung", May 18 and July 2, 1897, RMA III. 1.5.3., and for the comparative building, Hans Hallmann, *Krügerdepesche und Flottenfrage*, Stuttgart, 1927, Appendix, pp. 68 ff.

[29] Tirpitz to North German Lloyd, November 18, 1897, and to Hamburg-Amerika Line, October 13, 1897, and replies of November 22 and October 19, 1897, RMA III. 1.5.3., Vol. 2.

as solid as possible; *i.e.*, the size and effective strength of the Navy must be fixed by a law."[30]

When the figures were bandied about by opposition papers, von Heeringen pounced on every inaccuracy.[31] Popular Berlin daily papers, like the *Berliner Neueste Nachrichten*, were liberally fed with statistics and information on naval matters,[32] but important papers in the federal capitals were not ignored. The *Münchener Allgemeine Zeitung* ran a series of articles in mid-November, 1897, called "The Navy in Parliament", for which M II supplied the raw material. These articles skilfully told the story of the initial attempts to found a Navy in 1848 and reminded readers of the long association of the Navy with the liberal tradition.[33] "In general," von Kusserow, a prominent member of the Colonial Society, wrote to von Heeringen on November 24th, "you can be well pleased with the Navy propaganda carried out by you and your friends, although the language of the opposition papers does not permit any feeling of security for the coming Reichstag."[34]

By the middle of the month of November, 1897, the Bundesrath had approved the draft of the Navy Bill with only minor alterations. The Grand Ducal Plenipotentiary of Mecklenburg, as representative of the Bundesrath, wrote to Capelle to say that he saw no reason why the draft could not be printed in its present form.[35] With the way clear, Tirpitz arranged for the text of the law to be printed in full in an extra edition of the *Norddeutsche Allgemeine Zeitung*, to appear on Saturday

[30] See Footnote 62, Chapter Four, p. 142, for the original article, and "Antwort auf die Polemik der Freisinnigen Zeitung", original draft in von Heeringen's hand, October 1897, RMA III. 1.5.3., Vol. 4.

[31] "To B—*Immediate.* The opposition papers are constantly using the assertion in their agitation that since the coronation of Kaiser Wilhelm II in nine years 91 warships for 310 million have been built or are still under construction. To get this assertion back into its proper proportions, I urgently need an accurate survey of all the ships built since 1888, including torpedo-boats.—M II, von Heeringen", RMA III. 1.5.3., Vol. 2. In fact, only 79 ships had been built at a total cost of M 254,280,000. (B to M II, November 29, 1897, RMA III 1.5.3., Vol. 2.)

[32] Cf. article, "Frankreichs Ausgaben für Heer und Flotte", *Berliner Neueste Nachrichten*, Morning edition, November 14, 1897, in Newspaper File, RMA III. 1.5.3., Vol. 3.

[33] *Münchener Allgemeine Zeitung*, November 15, 1897 ff, in Newspaper File, RMA III. 1.5.3., Vol. 2.

[34] Kusserow to von Heeringen, November 24, 1897, quoted in E. Kehr, *op. cit.*, p. 120.

[35] Grossherzöglich Mecklenburgischer Gesandte von Oertzen to Capelle, Berlin, November 14, 1897, RMA III. 1.5.3., Vol. 3.

afternoon, November 27th. This meant, in effect, that the opposition Press would be unable to comment on it for thirty-six hours at least, and Tirpitz intended to exploit that advantage no matter how slight it might be. The opposition Press responded in their Monday morning editions, and the response was less than enthusiastic. Their main objections were directed at the provision that the Navy Law was to run for seven years. The Reichstag's right to control the annual budget would be severely limited by such a long-term, inflexible commitment. "If the popular assembly allows itself to be bargained out of a part of its annual budget rights," warned the *Berliner Tageblatt*, "it will be sawing off the branch on which it sits." The *Frankfurter Zeitung* agreed: "The present Reichstag is actually expected to rob its successors of a part of their rights."[36] The *Kölnische Volkszeitung* reminded its readers of past events: "What would have happened if the memorandum of Admiral Hollmann had been accepted as law? . . . It is just impossible to put any confidence in experts who change their minds all the time and come forward with ever more costly plans."[37] On the other side, the list of papers which came out strongly in favour of the programme was extremely long.[38] Von Heeringen's careful groundwork had begun to pay off.

On November 30th, the Kaiser opened the fifth and last session of the 9th Reichstag with the Speech from the Throne. "The development of our battle fleet," he declared, "has not kept up with the tasks which Germany is compelled to present to its maritime force. Our fleet is not sufficiently strong to secure our home ports and waters in the event of hostilities and to prevent a blockade or extensive operations by the enemy. It has not kept up with the lively growth of our overseas interests." The Kaiser categorically denied that "it can be our aim to compete with sea powers of the first rank". The fleet was

[36] Quoted in "Zeitungsschau", a review of the press in the *Norddeutsche Allgemeine Zeitung*, November 30, 1897, p. 5.

[37] *Norddeutsche Allgemeine Zeitung*, "Zum Flottengesetz; Entgegnungen der N.A.Z. auf die gegen die Marinevorlage gerichteten Angriffe", Berlin, December 1898, Heft 2, p. 11.

[38] The *Norddeutsche Allgemeine Zeitung* listed in its "Zeitungsschau" of November 30th the *Hamburgische Correspondent*, *Der Reichsbote*, *Kölnische Zeitung*, *Tägliche Rundschau*, *Conservative Correspondenz*, *Münchener Neueste Nachrichten* and the *Magdeburgische Zeitung*, in addition to the score of other papers friendly to the fleet already mentioned.

merely intended to "assert German prestige in the eyes of the people of the world." There was "vigorous applause" when the Kaiser, referring to the events in Kiaochow, demanded "full reparation and security against a recurrence of similar deplorable incidents."[39] The evening edition of the *Norddeutsche Allgemeine* on the day of the parliamentary opening ceremonies devoted itself mainly to the Navy. In addition to the Speech from the Throne, the paper printed a vigorous leading article, "A Strong Navy—A Necessity of Life for Germany", and surveyed the arguments in the Press for and against the proposed Navy Law. The campaign was on and nobody could doubt it.

About this time, Tirpitz began to suspect that certain members of the government were not quite in step. Rumours reached him that members of the Reichstag had been talking to high officials about a compromise on the Navy Bill. In order to disarm the objection that the Navy Law encroached on the Reichstag's right of annual review of appropriations, they suggested that Tirpitz's law be demoted to a mere statement of intent. The Reichstag would then happily do its share by voting the first instalments for the building programme as outlined in the White Paper. Should this occur, the whole programme, in Tirpitz's eyes, would be threatened. The concealed purpose of the plan would be frustrated if the *lex imperfecta*, the open-ended legal commitment, were not adopted. The naval lever against England might well fall from the nerveless fingers of later Reichstags or the Kaiser's whim might jerk it from its fulcrum in the North Sea. His whole strategy depended on the fixed Navy Law and he had to have it no matter what the cost. On December 1st, he went to see Hohenlohe to complain. "Tirpitz is extremely angry about this," the old Chancellor recorded in his diary. "He says that the government cannot possibly accept it. In such a case, it must dissolve the Reichstag. He thinks that elections on the naval programme issue would come off very well. I told him that I would have to think about it."[40]

Dissolution was strong stuff, and Tirpitz knew it. His confidence in the success of his propaganda campaign could easily

[39] Full text in *Norddeutsche Allgemeine Zeitung*, Abend-Ausgabe, November 30, 1897.
[40] Diary entry, December 1, 1897, Hohenlohe, *op. cit.*, pp. 422 ff.

be misplaced, and elections fought on the naval issue could be absolutely calamitous. His position was not yet secure enough to survive a defeat arising from his own tactical miscalculation, and, in any case, provoking a dissolution, a method which Bismarck had often used and more frequently threatened, was wholly out of character. There was not a trace of Bismarck's sardonic and Olympian contempt for the opinion of other men in Tirpitz's make-up. He did not share Bismarck's malicious delight in irritating the Reichstag, nor the notorious Bismarckian belligerence. Dissolution of the Reichstag would certainly enrage the Centre Party without whom the Navy Law was lost. Besides, Tirpitz had too much confidence in his own powers of persuasion to need to use threats in his manipulation of the Reichstag. It was, probably, Hohenlohe whom he had to threaten. If the feeble old gentleman collapsed in a heap or allowed himself to be wheedled into some sort of wretched compromise, Tirpitz could well find the battle lost by default, before he had opened fire.

Pounding the table apparently did the trick, and no more was heard of the compromise in government circles. Having propped up Hohenlohe, Tirpitz was free to return to his favourite technique of intensive private negotiations with Reichstag deputies. In the heavily curtained privacy of his spacious office on Leipzigerplatz, he met a series of prominent deputies. Seated around the big table next to his desk, they could chat confidentially and exchange frank opinions. His soundings were not entirely encouraging. The conservatives struck him as "luke-warm", but Dr. Lieber "proved himself to be objectively very well suited although personally extremely sensitive".[41] He knew that, as Hohenlohe said, "Lieber's relationship to the government flatters his self-esteem".[42] By courting Lieber he might win not only the leader of the Centre Party, but also the Reichstag's acknowledged naval spokesman and an influential committee member. In the week between the opening of the session and the first reading of the Navy Law, he accomplished a great deal in private negotiation.

The Kaiser's speech and the introduction of a major piece of naval legislation had, in the meantime, provoked unfavourable

[41] Tirpitz, *op. cit.*, p. 100.
[42] Diary entry, October 28, 1897, Hohenlohe, *op. cit.*, p. 397.

reactions in London. Hatzfeldt, the German Ambassador, reported that *The Spectator* was adopting a menacing posture. "Germany should not forget," it reminded its readers, "that other nations were well in advance of her in the occupation of overseas territory and that the world had already been divided up." "Unfortunately!" the Kaiser scribbled on the margin of Hatzfeldt's report. "That's why we are trying to catch up with all our might." When *The Spectator* warned Germany not to add a fleet of the first rank to its already enormous army, the Kaiser wrote, "there is not a word of that in my speech", and in reply to the paper's prediction that Germany would collapse under the burden of its arms expenditure before Britain, he observed: "England is like Nero, who always imagined that whenever any two people laughed, spoke or did anything together, it was about, against or because of, him."[43]

The Kaiser's moral indignation has a curious quality of sincerity to it, although he knew perfectly well that a fleet of the first rank was exactly what he intended to create. This is just one of the scores of examples of that strange ambivalence toward England which the Kaiser and most of his close associates shared. That Wilhelm II, himself half-English and virtually bilingual, and Tirpitz, who read English novels for recreation and whose children went to English schools, should have destroyed the amiable Anglo-German ties cultivated by the reactionary Prussian Junker Bismarck is one of the great ironies of modern history.[44]

B. The First Reading of the Navy Law

When the Reichstag convened on December 6, 1897, to hear the first reading of the *Gesetz betreffend die deutsche Flotte*, it could look back on twenty-six years of mounting controversy over naval development. Never had more been struck from the naval

[43] Hatzfeldt to Hohenlohe, London, December 4, 1897, RMA III. 1.5.3., Vol. 3, with Kaiser's marginal comments.

[44] "Even contemporaries were struck by the fact that this bitter rival of England (Tirpitz) was not only a good student but also an honest admirer of English manners and institutions. His free hours were devoted to the study of English and his children were sent to English schools." (R. Stadelmann, *op. cit.*, p. 98.) "At a dinner in Berlin in 1911, in honour of a British general, the guest of honour was astonished to find that all forty German guests, including Bethmann-Hollweg and Admiral Tirpitz, spoke English fluently." (B. Tuchmann, *op. cit.*, p. 77.)

estimates than in the most recent past.[45] Only nine months earlier it had cut the colossal sum of M 12,000,000 from an estimate of M 70,000,000. Now it was being asked to authorize a law involving expenditure on construction alone of more than M 400,000,000. Both the size of the sum demanded and the technique of a fixed Navy Law were clearly meant to challenge the Reichstag directly. If some deputies doubted that the Bill before them had the highest priority, the unwonted appearance of the aged Chancellor of the Reich, whose dislike of public speaking was well known, would have dispelled their misapprehensions. Prince Hohenlohe's speech was vigorous and unusually well delivered.[46] Its central thesis was the modesty of the proposed programme. "This measure shows you that we are not thinking of competing with the great sea powers and for those with eyes to see it demonstrates that a policy of adventure is far from our minds. Precisely because we want to carry out a peaceful policy, we must make an effort to build our fleet into a power factor which carries the necessary weight in the eyes of friend and foe alike . . . In maritime questions, Germany must be able to speak a modest but, above all, a wholly German word."[47]

Tirpitz was the next to rise from his place at the Bundesrath table to address the deputies in the name of the Associated Governments of the German Empire. His maiden speech began with an assertion of the pacific and harmless nature of the proposed expansion. "Our fleet has the function of a protective fleet. It changes its character not one bit as a result of this law." Its object was merely to give Germany "a chance against a superior enemy" by providing "a sea force which will compel even a sea power of the first rank to think twice before

[45] Over the twenty-six years, an average of 12 per cent of the sums demanded had been cut by the Reichstag, but during the reign of Wilhelm II this had risen to over seventeen per cent. In the nine years since the Kaiser had mounted the throne, more had been demanded than in the previous eighteen. "Ubersicht über die in den Jahren 1872-97/98 für Schiffsbauten geforderten und bewilligten Geldmittel", RMA III. 1.5.3., Vol. 4.

[46] His old friend, Freiherr von Völderndorff, wrote to him shortly afterwards, "My warmest congratulations on the fine, long speech. I read that Serene Highness read it very freely and that your voice was extraordinarily clear and strong throughout . . ." Letter of December 12, 1897, in Hohenlohe, *op. cit.*, p. 423.

[47] *Stenographischer Bericht*, der Reichstag, 9. Legisl.-Periode, V. Session, 4. Sitzung, December 6, 1897, pp. 41 f.

attacking our coasts . . . (Hear! Hear!)"[48] Next he turned his attention to questions rarely discussed by his predecessors, and gradually even the most grumpy and restive opposition deputy began to recognize that this was no Hollmann before them. The old hesitancy and bumbling were gone, and the Reichstag was treated to a brisk and business-like discussion of administrative efficiency, accuracy in cost accounting in naval construction and the proper criteria for a rational distribution of orders to private and public shipyards. Serenely confident, Tirpitz spoke as if the passage of the law were a mere technical detail which reasonable men could fix up in an afternoon. Obviously any sensible man could see that if the Reichstag set the effective fighting strength of the Navy by a law, there would be no more talk of limitless fleet plans. How much more satisfactory a fixed law would be was plain. There would be an end to the tiresome annual spectacle of disunion and conflict over each ship. Finally, he declared that since no changes in ship types were being considered, the deputies could be certain that the programme would cost no more than the government proposed to spend.

It was an impressive and persuasive performance, but Herr Schoenlank of the Social Democrats was having none of it. With evident glee, he read in full the government statement of September 12, 1896, in which Admiral Tirpitz's connection with a programme of naval expansion was officially denied.[49] "The government of the Reich at whose head, then as now, Prince Hohenlohe stands, has simply hauled down the flag in the face of this 'flag officer in an irresponsible position' . . . This very draft of a Naval Law, and I quote, 'which could become worthless through unforeseeable future developments in the shortest possible time' lies before us now dated November 30, 1897 . . ."[50] Here, Schoenlank cried, was just another example of the uselessness of governmental promises. He reminded the Reichstag of promises about the law forbidding coalitions and about the reform of the military penal code. Finally, there was the Kaiser's telegram with its reference to "unpatriotic rascals". "Now Herr Tirpitz comes and does obeisance before the same 'unpatriotic rascals'. (Laughter on the Left) . . . We know that a small but powerful group has

[48] *Ibid.*, p. 43. [49] Cf. Chapter Three, p. 102. [50] *Stenographischer Bericht*, pp. 46 f.

purposefully agitated against the authority of parliament for years (Very true! Left) . . . we know that very prominent persons are trying to degrade the Reichstag in the eyes of the public by a stream of pamphlets, fly-sheets, dispatches, addresses and speeches . . . (It is) the duty of self-preservation of parliament . . . to resist."[51] There was little doubt that the Navy's past record was the best source for the opposition's polemics. Not only had the Associated Governments formally disavowed Admiral Tirpitz little more than a year earlier, but they had repeatedly made speeches in which the attempt to predict weapons development for years in advance had been called impractical or impossible. On March 18th of that very year, Admiral Hollmann had stated: "To bind ourselves by a formal memorandum for years ahead . . . is simply impossible . . . It is just not possible for a naval administration to tell you today what we shall need in ten years." "Now," Schoenlank gestured toward the Bundesrath table, "a *homo novus* suddenly appears and in a flash the new man can tell us how it is to be done."[52] Equally astounding was the new attitude toward industrialism. "What enthusiastic defenders of modern industrialism and the modern industrial state the same government has suddenly become which recently presented us with the Margarine Law, the Guild Law and the Stock Exchange Law."[53] He was not impressed by the wave of artificial propaganda agitation, nor the ponderous pronouncements recently made by the professors. "That," he observed disdainfully "is only to be expected from German professors . . . Really all that is missing now . . . is a Navy theatre and a Navy opera."[54] The agitation was mere froth on the surface of public life. The real current in the depths was the "personal regime". "This personal regime brings us a Christmas present, a Navy Law, which at the same time conceals the first blow of the personal regime against the budget rights of the German parliament . . . Sudden change has become the rule. The whole political and social organism sickens and languishes because of this absolutely neurasthenic government of cross purposes."[55]

[51] *Ibid.*, p. 48.
[52] *Ibid.*, p. 49.
[53] *Ibid.*, p. 50.
[54] *Ibid.*, pp. 50 f.
[55] *Ibid.*, p. 52.

After Schoenlank returned to his seat, Tirpitz, who had little choice, rose to reply on a point of personal privilege. It was not easy to rebut charges read from the text of an official government statement, which in any case were entirely accurate. His reply would have to turn the point in such a way that only the Kaiser or Senden could have revealed the true circumstances. "What the *Reichsanzeiger* stated in the previous year," he began, "was absolutely right. In the previous year, Admiral Tirpitz was not an officer responsible to this high house and did not submit a fleet plan. That the said Admiral, in his position as Chief of Staff, worked on the military development of the Navy can hardly be held against him. I have nothing further to say."[56] This statement was greeted with a hefty "Bravo" on the right side of the house and satisfied his critics for the moment. It was a slick and deceptive evasion. Its literal meaning was perfectly true. In September of 1896 Tirpitz had indeed not been responsible to the Reichstag, nor had he submitted a fleet plan. In substance it was, of course, false as well informed deputies like Richter had reason to suspect. There were enough rumours that Tirpitz as Chief of Staff, although equally irresponsible, had submitted a plan not to the Reichstag but to the Kaiser.

The debate continued and each of the parties took its turn to express its preliminary position on the Bill. Count Limburg-Stirum of the extreme right-wing Conservatives admitted that a minority of his party opposed the Bill but the majority would accept it in the interests of industry and commerce provided that "this solidarity of interests is appreciated and supported by the other side".[57] In other words, the agrarians wanted a *quid pro quo*. Dr. Barth of the Radical Union cited the White Paper, "The Sea Interests of the German Empire", which in his view destroyed "the main argument for the far-reaching pretensions of the Agrarian Party" that Germany was still an agricultural nation. His party was favourable.[58] Dr. von Jazdzewski of the Polish Party opposed the Bill and pointed out how inconsistent it was to protect German missionaries in China "while the same missionaries, who belong to the same

[56] *Ibid.*, p. 53.
[57] *Ibid.*, pp. 55 f.
[58] *Ibid.*, p. 61.

orders, who pursue the same religious and cultural objectives in the homeland, are, strangely enough, not granted the same protection in their own fatherland, indeed are not even tolerated. (Lively applause in the Centre and among the Poles.)"[59]

The debate resumed on the following day with a thunderous attack on the government, the Navy and Tirpitz, delivered by that implacable old warrior, Eugen Richter. With all the bite of his brilliant sarcasm, he took up Admiral Tirpitz's denial of previous responsibility and reminded his audience that the official statement had contained the phrase "Rear-Admiral Tirpitz . . . has never found himself in a position in which an order to work out such a plan could have been given to him". To vigorous shouts of "Hear! Hear!" from the Left, Richter continued, "in other words the qualifications of Herr Tirpitz to prepare fleet plans are denied on the basis of his previous career in the service, the same Herr Tirpitz whom we are now to regard as the greatest authority on fleet plans. So the Herr Reich Chancellor assures us of one thing in the *Reichsanzeiger* fourteen months ago and yesterday he says the opposite . . . Well, gentlemen, you will surely agree with me that it is high time to ask whether Herr Tirpitz himself has always been of a constant mind in recent times . . ."[60] Richter's opposition, although embarrassing, was not serious because his Radical People's Party had dwindled to a mere twenty-four deputies. The moderately conservative *Reichspartei* with its twenty-five members could expect to cancel out the Radicals. Its spokesman, Count von Arnim, attacked Richter for always opposing government bills. There had been a change of roles: "we are the progressives and you, gentlemen, are the reactionaries." Amid laughter and hooting from the Left, Arnim promised that the great majority of his party would support the law "despite the depressed condition of agriculture".[61]

The next speaker was the key man in Tirpitz's calculations, Dr. Ernst Lieber, Deputy from Montabaur near Koblenz. Lieber's speech was a masterly demonstration of political tightrope walking. The Centre Party could not yet reach "a

[59] *Ibid.*, pp. 65 f.
[60] *Ibid.*, 5 Sitzung, December 7, 1897, p. 72.
[61] *Ibid.*, pp. 82 f.

final decision"; it would be unworthy to expect such a commitment of a party, "which bears the burden of knowing that the number and strength of its members in this house give it the power of ultimate decision."[62] After all, the political situation domestically was not a happy one. The government had shown little "spirit of compromise" on reform of the penal code, on the coalition Bill and on the Jesuit Law. It was not, of course, his party's intention to pursue a "policy of revenge", but the warning to those sitting at the Bundesrath table was unmistakable. The substance of the law was good. It would turn the fleet "from a mechanism into an organism", but was it, perhaps, not a little too clear "for certain circles in the know, who can read between the lines, outside of the German Empire?"[63] Lieber had put his finger on one of the vital issues at stake, and although he did not press the point, he was clearly aware of the hostage to fortune which arose from a commitment to build a fleet of a certain size at a publicly stated rate by an equally clearly stated time in the future. For the moment he was content to hint at the dangers involved in laying all Germany's cards on the international table. In essence, he shared Tirpitz's view that "weapons decide things in this world and not the superiority of culture. Fighting spirit and unity of purpose maintain the peoples . . ."[64]

The cost of the programme was another central theme in Lieber's speech. He demanded a "maximum limit for expenditure . . . There is no deal to be made by offering increases in indirect taxation to the Centre Party . . . Even the most implacable federalist will have to wipe the tears from his eyes and get used to the idea that a source of direct Reich income must be tapped."[65] When Lieber sat down, Tirpitz again took the floor and in tones of amazement stated that "the idea of limiting the amount of expenditure . . . is absolutely new to me . . . I have estimated the sums needed as well as I could and as well as they can be really predicted . . . personally, I should consider such a limitation with sympathy, provided naturally that . . . the main purpose can be achieved . . ."[66] Such a

[62] *Ibid.*, p. 83.
[63] *Ibid.*, p. 87.
[64] *Ibid.*, p. 89.
[65] *Ibid.*, pp. 88 f.
[66] *Ibid.*, p. 90.

demonstration of sweet reason and parliamentary deference was as impressive as it was unexpected. It put Tirpitz in a particularly favourable bargaining position and may well have been cooked up in one of those private sessions at the Leipzigerplatz. Lieber's cue fits Tirpitz's rejoinder too well to have been an impulse of the moment.

The Hanoverian deputy, Count Bernstorff, closed the afternoon session with a warning which few of his listeners took seriously. He was afraid of the "battle of armaments among the nations" and saw in the Navy Law "yet another turn of the screw".[67] That an arms race might result from Tirpitz's programme was a perfectly justified fear, but it apparently affected members of the small parties and the representatives of the dissatisfied groups in the Reich more than it worried members of the large parties. During the first two days of debate, only the spokesman of the Polish Party had touched on the same theme. Even the Social Democrats ignored the obvious implications of a large and inflexible naval expansion.[68] Almost as strange as this general blindness to the greatest single objection to the Navy Law was the fact that Dr. Lieber and his followers apparently believed that if the Navy accepted an upper limit on expenditure, its growth could be controlled. Lieber evidently failed to see that Tirpitz had laid a trap for them by fixing the effective strength of the fleet without binding the Naval Office to build specific ship designs. The effective strength of two full squadrons could be composed of anything from sail-boats to dreadnoughts, which would make a great deal of difference to the cost of the programme. But the parties were so busy assessing its effect on their interests that they ignored the loop-hole in the law. Lieber and his colleagues had not yet grasped the nature of modern technology. They had the word of the State Secretary of the Imperial Naval Office that the limit on expenditure for the fleet was acceptable and they felt safe. Tirpitz knew how rapidly marine engineering advanced, and also that no Reichstag would dare to go back on

[67] *Ibid.*, p. 90.

[68] August Bebel objected to naval expansion not because of its international ramifications, but because of its superfluity. "I am not usually in agreement with Prince Bismarck," he told the Reichstag on December 8th, "but on one point he is undoubtedly correct . . . the ultimate outcome of any future war will be decided by the land army and not by the fleet." (*Ibid.*, p. 160.)

a commitment to build two squadrons if Germany's foes began to construct larger and more expensive ships.

All things considered, the first two days of public debate on the Navy Law had been remarkably pleasant for the Associated Governments. After the session, Hermann von Lucanus, the Kaiser's Civil Cabinet chief, who had watched the proceedings closely from the gallery, sent a telegram to Wilhelm II in which he predicted that "unless unforeseen difficulties arise, the passage of the Navy Law can be assumed to be certain. The Centre has made the difference... On the substance of the Law, Lieber spoke more favourably than almost any other speaker and seemed almost to be making himself the father of the proposal on the grounds that he was the first to demand a legal foundation for the organization of the fleet... Otherwise what he had to say was mere decoration designed to glorify the Centre."[69]

Tirpitz, too, had cause for satisfaction in the course of the debates. His parliamentary début, if not brilliant, had been competent. He evaded humiliation on the question of his past associations with the agitation for a big naval programme and had even drawn a laugh from his arch-enemy, Eugen Richter, to whom he gallantly offered the services of the Naval Office's news bureau. None of the opposition speakers had been able to nail him down on the inconsistency of the Navy's demands in the past nor to manoeuvre him into a public disavowal of his predecessor's policies. He had displayed flexibility and reasonableness, deference to parliament and no inconsiderable talent as an orator. The embarassing question raised by Prince Bismarck's tacit hostility to the fleet was another threat which Tirpitz neatly parried. Unknown to the opposition, Prince Bismarck had been sent an advance copy of the Navy Law, and in his letter of thanks, the former Chancellor had written: "I find the totals demanded reasonable for our needs, although I should have preferred more attention to cruisers. This view would not restrain me, if I were a Reichstag deputy, from voting for the Bill..."[70] It could hardly be said that Bismarck's attitude was wildly enthusiastic, and Tirpitz was careful not

[69] Lucanus to Kaiser Wilhelm II, Berlin, December 7, 1897. 6.40 p.m., MK I.f.1.
[70] Bismarck to Tirpitz, Friedrichsruh, December 4, 1897, MGFA-DZ: 2050, PG 66105, RMA IV.

to read out the passage in favour of more cruisers. The fact of the letter was more than enough and the willingness to vote for the Bill a bonus. Tirpitz knew only too well that Bismarck's attitude to the fleet programme resembled his reaction to the news of the seizure of Kiaochow: "It is a small piece of earth but large enough to encompass very big blunders."[71]

In one important respect, Tirpitz surpassed Bismarck. He had openly acknowledged the cordial relations between the Catholic Centre Party and the government of the Reich. It was this liaison for which Tirpitz worked extremely hard that "made the difference", as Lucanus put it. If Lieber could hold his party together, the Bill was safely passed. Tirpitz continued to watch the Centre Party members closely and with good reason. When Dr. Hammacher of the National Liberals tried to claim that the support for the Navy Law was unanimous, Herr Fritzen of the Centre was at pains to point out that "the last word in this question has not by any means been spoken and will not be so quickly spoken either".[72] There were still the elections for the standing committees to get through and weeks of debate on the budget as a whole. The Navy Law had been referred to the Budget Committee for detailed consideration, and much could still happen to upset the fragile amity between the Associated Governments and the Centre in the coming weeks. Tirpitz knew that the greatest threat to his programme lay in the financial question. Unless a means of paying for the fleet could be worked out, which was neither too centralist nor too federalist, neither too radical nor too conservative, the Centre would go into one of its characteristic spins, whirling off all its various loosely associated groups in reaction to unhappily chosen solutions. The centrifugal forces in the Reich were too strong for a party like the Centre attempting to bridge the regions and classes by slender threads of religious loyalty. The disintegration of the Liberals into three parties was an unpleasant warning. Lieber and Tirpitz were not allowed to forget the precarious quality of the alliance contracted between them.

When the Reichstag adjourned for the Christmas recess, Tirpitz redoubled his efforts in the propaganda field. He had

[71] Werner Richter, *Bismarck*, p. 625 (German edition).
[72] *Stenographischer Bericht*, 8 Sitzung, December 11, 1897, p. 143.

made useful contacts with many Hanseatic businessmen during his trips to Hamburg and Bremen in the autumn of 1897. Now he began to cash in on them. On December 19th, a committee headed by Adolf Woermann and supported by the Central Committee of the Association of German Industrialists issued an invitation to a mass meeting at the Kaiserhof in Berlin, to be held on January 13, 1898. The invitation was signed by 251 individuals and groups including the presidents of seventy-eight Chambers of Commerce.[73] The meeting was a huge success. In an article called "Businessmen at the Kaiserhof", the *Grenzboten* reported that the sense of the meeting had been that something effective must be done. "It becomes an urgent obligation of sheer self-preservation that representatives of economic and political wisdom and business experience stir themselves from their almost irresponsible passivity and wag their fingers unmistakably at the deputies from other social classes as a sign of the way the affairs of the business community, that is, trade policy and the fleet, are to be treated in the future."[74]

Although demonstrations of support by well-heeled businessmen had certain advantages for Tirpitz in his parliamentary struggles, their real significance is to be found outside parliament. Any deputy likely to be influenced by the Kaiserhof meeting could only come from the National Liberal Party or the Radical Union, both of which were behind him anyway. But the noise and excitement generated by such mass meetings had a value of their own. It came close to a government by decibels. While Richter continued to thunder that the fleet bill was "born of mistrust of the people's representatives and of the people itself",[75] more and more his voice was lost in the din raised by supporters of the fleet. Although very few people in Germany realized what Tirpitz was up to, the editor of the *Neue Zürcher Zeitung* saw it clearly: "On all sides interest groups are being called upon to participate in political life. Their votes are beginning to achieve a significance in support of the government which parallels the real, legal parliaments equipped with proper constitutional rights by the Prussian and German

[73] E. Kehr, *op. cit.*, p. 116.

[74] Quoted in E. Kehr, *op. cit.*, p. 118.

[75] "Frivoles Treiben", a leading article in the *Freisinnige Zeitung*, January 1, 1897, in the newspaper files of the I.N.O., RMA III. 1.5.3., Vol. 4.

constitutions. This necessarily reduces the importance of these parliaments, and since in any case the Prussian Landtag has become merely a governmental institution, it must work out chiefly to the detriment of the Reichstag."[76] The Swiss journalist had spotted an ominous trend first exploited by Tirpitz's news bureau and later to be a favourite device of the National Socialist Party. By creating a deafening uproar outside, the parliamentarians inside could be frightened and bullied into approving anything. It was this, rather than vote-getting in the normal sense, which lay behind the Kaiserhof mass meeting and, indeed, behind Tirpitz's entire propaganda campaign.

C. The Navy Law in the Committee Stage

There was still a long way to go before the street replaced the vote in German domestic politics. In 1898 beating the drum and agitation alone were not enough, and Tirpitz knew it. His office continued to turn out highly sophisticated analyses of financial and technical questions for use in persuading the members of the Budget Committee of his reasonable approach.[77] He himself followed every reference in the Press which might be used against him in the Committee. When the British Admiral Colomb, in a lecture in London on the future of the torpedo, expressed doubts about the long-term value of the great battleship as a weapon, Tirpitz immediately ordered the naval attaché in London to produce "any sort of evidence that the views of Admiral C. are not shared in influential circles in England. I should imagine that the best evidence on this question would be if we could find out that the British Admiralty intend to include armoured battleships in the

[76] *Die Neue Zürcher*, January 19, 1898, quoted in E. Kehr, *op. cit.*, p. 118.

[77] "Aktennotiz", immediate, A to B, January 13, 1898, RMA III. 1.5.3., Vol. 2, containing calculations about the amount of the capital investment in the fleet to be charged to ordinary revenue and to loans. Cf. also von Heeringen, "Denkschrift zur finanzstatistischen Drucksache für den Reichstag", RMA III. 1.5.3., Vol. 4, January 22, 1898. This study had three objectives: To counter the arguments: "(1) That our expenditure for national defence is proportionately high and oppressive, and the fear that with a further increase (2) our expenditure for cultural purposes will be reduced in an unacceptable manner or (3) that our capacity to bear the taxation will be impaired."

estimates for the coming year."[78] Tirpitz was evidently resolved to leave nothing to chance in his preparations for the Budget Committee hearings.

Whether or not the Navy Law impaired the parliamentary rights of the Reichstag was another crucial question in his mind. Since the German Reichstag had less than its share of the customary powers of constitutionally established parliaments in other western countries, many of its eminent members viewed the slightest infringement of its few remaining powers with the gravest concern. Parliamentary touchiness weakened, in turn, the effect of the evidence drawn from British naval experience. If, for example, Tirpitz cited the Naval Defence Act of 1889 to support his demand for a fixed Navy Law, he was certain to be greeted by cries from the liberals for responsible ministries and greater parliamentary authority. He had to parry the argument that the Navy Law meant yet another attack on the authority of parliament, before he could win over the Centre Party. To help him in this endeavour, he approached Johannes von Miquel, the crafty Prussian Finance Minister, and asked him to prepare a memorandum on this question. The twenty-six page document which Miquel composed discussed the legal and political arguments for adoption of the *Flottengesetz* and treated the constitutional objections in detail. In Miquel's opinion, the idea that "the legal obligation" involved in the Navy Law was an impairment of the powers of the Reichstag "rests . . . in the main on an incomplete and erroneous conception of the task and position of the finance-appropriating bodies within the constitution".[79] Since most expenditures by the state arose "from continuous appropriations . . . which could not be unilaterally revoked by the Reichstag", it followed that the Reichstag had no right to claim an annual power of review. By what Miquel called an "*ipso jure*" argument, it was equally clear that the Reichstag's parliamentary powers extended only to the appropriation of the estimate for each year and not to the validity of an appropriation as such. "The appropriation of an annual instalment, say, for the completion of the Reichstag building on the basis

[78] Tirpitz to Naval Attaché (London), Berlin, January 18, 1898, original draft with corrections in Tirpitz's hand, RMA III. 1.5.3., Vol. 2.

[79] J. von Miquel, "Denkschrift", February 1898, RMA III. 1.5.3., Vol. 4, p. 4.

of a certain plan of construction does not depend on legal compulsion. The annual instalment must be approved because one stage in a building plan necessarily leads to the next."[80] The parallel with the fleet, Miquel argued, was apparent here. "Without a legal basis for the building plan, a firm guarantee cannot be given to the builder of the fleet; individual appropriations for individual ships is nonsense. The only sensible choice is that between a large public loan for the entire amount or the method suggested here, a legal basis for the building plan."[81]

Tirpitz's first reaction to this argument was to try to convince Miquel to deliver it in person. In his note of acknowledgement, he expressed the hope that "Your Excellency would feel free to speak in a similar vein, either before the Committee or during the Second Reading of the Navy Law. Such utilization of the great authority enjoyed by Your Excellency would in my opinion be of essential importance in the promotion of the Navy Law."[82] As a Prussian Minister, Miquel was not directly involved in the Reich, nor obliged to assist Tirpitz by appearing before the Reichstag. Only Prince Hohenlohe, who held the offices of Reich Chancellor and Prussian Minister-President in personal union, had the right to make such a request, which at best was of questionable propriety. Tirpitz's motives in going behind the back of the responsible official, Reich Secretary of the Treasury, Freiherr von Thielmann, were very likely political rather than administrative. He knew that Miquel, whose reputation as an intriguer was notorious but whose influence among conservatives was considerable, would make a dangerous enemy. It was safer to placate Miquel, even at the cost of affronting his colleague, than to run the risk of falling into one of Miquel's complicated webs. After all, von Thielmann was a mere diplomat and of no great importance, whereas Miquel was reputed to be a king-maker. As it turned out, Miquel chose not to appear in person, but, Tirpitz explained to Capelle, there had been that possibility from the start. "Excellency von Miquel placed the document at my disposal," he wrote, "with

[80] *Ibid.*, p. 10.
[81] *Ibid.*, p. 16.
[82] Tirpitz to Miquel, Berlin, February 14, 1898, RMA III. 1.5.3., Vol. 4.

the intention that it should be delivered either by him in person at the Budget Committee or exploited by me."[83] Its value was not impaired.

Shortly before the Budget Committee began its hearings on the Navy Law, the Imperial Naval Office drew up a list of all the members. Deputies on the Committee were grouped by party affiliation, occupation, constituency and connection with the military or government, if any.[84] This document, a kind of political geography of the German Reich in miniature, gave Tirpitz the necessary information to refine his approach and to adjust his appeal to suit individual tastes. Each party in the Reichstag with more than ten members was represented on the Committee relative to its strength in the house as a whole; Hanoverians, Danes and Alsatians were accordingly excluded from the Committee, but the Polish Party with its twenty deputies was not. The largest group on the Committee, the Centre Party, had nine members and the four smallest (the German Social Reform Party (anti-Semites), Polish Party, German People's Party and the Radical Union) had one member each.

That all these parties, with the exception of the Centre, were little more than class or regional pressure groups is obvious from the occupation and constituency columns. Both conservative parties, the German Conservative and the less radical Reichspartei, were, with one exception (Count Limburg-Stirum, a former diplomat), represented by large landowners elected exclusively from districts east of the Elbe. All but one bore sonorous titles of ancient Prussian renown; five held army commissions in the reserves or high office in local government or the diplomatic service. The anti-Semites and the German People's parties were drawn from the lower middle classes in the large towns of the west and south of Germany, the Radical Union from the Hanseatic trading community and Eugen Richter's Radical People's Party from the professional, clerical and administrative middle classes. The National Liberals were either professors, lawyers or big industrialists from urban constituencies, and the three Social Democrats, listed as "writer",

[83] Tirpitz to Capelle, February 12, 1897, "Aktennotiz", RMA III. 1.5.3., Vol. 4.
[84] Reichstag Budget-Kommissionsmitglieder, February 14, 1897, RMA III. 1.5.3., Vol. 4.

"cigar worker" and "private individual", were drawn from the large, urban, working class districts.

This brief glance at the make-up of the Budget Committee of the German Reichstag in the year 1898 demonstrates the peculiar interdependence of the Navy and the nation. How was the Navy to find its majority among the twenty-nine members of the Committee, a committee splintered by party, class and regional divisions? The old Bismarckian "Cartel" of right-wing parties was no more. The Conservatives and National Liberals together could only provide eleven of the fifteen votes needed. The Radical Union would add another vote and the anti-Semites, whose crude racist prejudices were expressed in violent nationalism, would probably support the Bill as well. In other words, the nationalist parties could not even provide half of the votes needed to pass the Bill out of committee. All the rest of the parties might easily vote against the Navy and Tirpitz would go the way of all failed Reich ministers, as Eugen Richter put it, "like flowers in the field. When the wind from above blows over them, their scent is soon blown away and after a few weeks nobody speaks of them any more."[85]

The nine Centre Party deputies on the Budget Committee were again, as in the full session, the key to the situation. Here was a party which seemed to cut across class lines and to spread over broad areas of the Empire. It might with some justice be called a national party, and with the collapse of the Liberals, it was the only major party which could come near to such breadth. Perhaps it might yet be transformed into the dominant, solid, responsible party of Lieber's dreams—in effect become what Adenauer's Christian Democratic Union later became. To make the Centre into a Wilhelmine C.D.U., would involve a break with its traditions and a rejection of its origins as the catch-all for every opponent of Bismarck's Reich. The Centre would have to grow out of its rabid antipathy to strong, central government and shed its past subservience to the powerful Roman prelates. If it were to expand to its new tasks, Lieber's ambitions were within his reach. Yet the facts were not so pretty. The Centre was only broadly based because there

[85] *Stenographischer Bericht*, der Reichstag, 9. Legisl.-Periode, V. Session, 5. Sitzung, December 7, 1897, p. 79.

were a great many Roman Catholics within the Reich. The irony of the Centre's position of power was inescapable. The great German fleet, the only absolutely national institution Bismarck's Reich ever produced, had to depend principally on what was still, despite Lieber's efforts, an anti-national, Roman Catholic pressure group. Which of the Liberals of 1848 would have believed it possible? A generation after the unification of Germany, there was so little national cohesion that the anti-nationalist Catholic, clerical party, because of its size alone, fell heir to all their aspirations.

The precariousness of the Centre's claim to hold the balance meant that Tirpitz had to walk the razor's edge. A sizable defection within the fragile coalition of Catholic politicians would break the Centre and doom the Navy Law. Tirpitz turned his propaganda engines towards the south. Separatist and Catholic Bavaria was treated to a crude sort of public opinion poll conducted by the *Münchener Allgemeine Zeitung*. Dozens of distinguished lawyers, doctors, university professors, artists, pastors and writers received a long questionnaire with a selection of loaded questions such as "Do you consider a strong German fleet to be a necessary power factor for German policy, especially in Europe?"[86] Favourable responses were printed in the newspaper on the last three days of January 1898, and many great names of German intellectual and artistic life were to be found among the supporters of the fleet: Lujo Brentano, Hans Delbrück, Otto Gierke, Adolf Wagner, Dietrich Schäfer, Max Weber and Ulrich von Wilamowitz-Moellendorff. Some of the responses were particularly flagrant examples of the aggressive ideology of German *Kultur*. The Munich architect, von Schmaedel, wrote that "the will to power must never be allowed to languish, if we want to be and remain a great '*Kulturvolk*'".[87] Next, the big Bavarian daily treated its readers to an even more enthusiastic expression of naval convictions culled from industrialists and businessmen. It was not surprising that Friedrich Krupp and Albert Ballin were friends of the fleet. Any Bavarian knew how much such men stood to gain by the passage of the Navy Law, but the appearance of

[86] "Flottenumfrage der *Münchener Allgemeine Zeitung*" reproduced in *Norddeutsche Allgemeine Zeitung*, "Zum Flottengesetz", Heft No. 3, Berlin, 1898, p. 7.
[87] *Ibid.*, p. 13.

many South German business leaders, "men whose names have the very best ring to them," was more impressive. Their arguments followed the lines laid down by the intellectuals and high priests of German *Kultur*. "All peoples, which have played a leading and creative role in the development of humanity," wrote Arthur Gwinner of the Deutsche Bank, "have been mighty sea powers."[88] The union of power and *Kultur* seemed self-evident to a generation of business leaders trained in the schools of Treitschke and Schmoller. Adolf Woermann suggested that Germany might attain a position as arbiter in Europe if she had a fleet. "With a strong fleet it could be the decisive factor in a conflict between Russia and Great Britain, whether Germany decided for the one or the other."[89]

This agitation and the successful progress of the Navy Bill in its first reading had begun to disturb officials in Whitehall. Woermann's argument that Germany might eventually hold the naval balance of power had already occured to many people in Britain. As long as British superiority in naval power over the forces of the Dual Alliance was so narrow, an impressive expansion of Germany's fleet would tilt the balance decisively against Britain. Admiral Sir Frederick Richards, First Sea Lord, made this point without any reservations in a memorandum of February 4, 1898, addressed to Mr. Goschen, the First Lord:

"We all know that the present accepted basis of mere equality with two Powers is not a sufficient margin for the Navy which occupies the inferior strategical position. The present time would be very inopportune for pulling up (in battleship construction), in view of what is being done by Powers other than France and Russia. For a nation which claims for herself supremacy upon the high seas, the margin which England allows herself for securing her dominion is decidedly small."[90]

The Times had already begun to lecture the Reichstag on this same theme. In a leading article in December the newspaper pointed out that the real issue before the German parliament was "whether it is prudent for a Power which 'does not wish to rival the naval Powers of the first rank' to

[88] *Ibid.*, Heft 6, February 3, 1898, p. 25.
[89] *Ibid.*, p. 27.
[90] Quoted in A. J. Marder, *op. cit.*, p. 297.

embark on a career of naval ambition, when it is certain that such a policy must, by disturbing what Mr. Goschen has called 'the balance of power in the navies of Europe', entirely upset the ingenious theory invented by the German Government to give a semblance of finality to a programme which cannot in the nature of things be final, and is probably not seriously intended to be final by its authors."[91] The warning behind the involved syntax was certainly visible. Other less circumspect journals in Britain took stronger lines. *The Morning Post* and *The Spectator* were particularly violent.

Nothing could have been more useful to Tirpitz than these rumbles of protest in the British Press. They helped to demonstrate how right the alarmists had been to warn the country of "perfidious Albion". Even extreme conservatives within the Navy, men like Admiral Seckendorff, Adjutant to Prince Heinrich, began to feel more sympathy with the popular agitation. In February 1898, Seckendorff wrote to his old friend Senden and described the Kaiser's birthday celebrations which had been put on by a local naval association in Kiel. He was moved by the enthusiasm and fervour of the volunteers and friends of the Navy who made up such groups. "While there," he wrote, "I was struck most forcibly by the thought that these naval clubs, which are fairly well distributed all over Germany, must become the true and proper bearers of the great 'Reich idea' in all the federal states . . . Navy clubs have sprung up like mushrooms everywhere in German cities and towns . . . The Army organizations stand beneath the protecting hand of the Prussian Ministry of War and the Ministry of the Interior; Navy associations must also enjoy the moral support of the Imperial Naval Office and the Imperial Ministry of the Interior. I regard the matter as absolutely essential to the interests of the Navy and the Reich, and it seems to me that our attention must be directed to internal as well as external matters."[92] It had apparently escaped Seckendorff's notice that the "mushrooms" were hot-house plants, forced fungi, of the Naval Office's cultivation, and that the great "Reich idea" had occurred to the energetic young men on Leipzigerplatz months earlier. None the less, the Admiral's excitement

[91] *The Times*, December 3, 1897.
[92] Seckendorff to Senden, February 11, 1898, BA K 08-7, "Senden Nachlass".

testifies to the strength of the naval ground swell now lifting the nation.

The Prussian Ministry of State was less sanguine about the immediate prospects. At a meeting on February 23rd, 1898, the Prussian Ministers considered the worrying question of the fixed life of the law. What would happen if the Reichstag refused to accept the principle of a long-term programme? "It would be very hard to hold His Majesty back from demanding a dissolution," Bülow said, "if the fixed duration of the law is not accepted."[93] He believed that it would be prudent to concentrate governmental strategy on getting the budget itself passed before forcing action on the Navy Law. Hohenlohe was also pessimistic. If the Reichstag were to be dissolved, Hohenlohe "could not perceive any favourable influence for the elections arising from the fleet Bill. Everything which the nationally-minded gentlemen like to cite in this connection carries no weight with the great mass of voters. The great mass voted Social Democrat, Radical and Centre."[94]

Tirpitz, who was not a member of the Prussian cabinet, was more cheerful. He was certain that his two-fold campaign, propaganda and negotiation, would certainly succeed. When the Budget Committee of the Reichstag began its hearing on February 24th, the vast propaganda campaign had reached deafening proportions. The effect of the agitation had nearly accomplished its purpose. Many deputies were being hustled into the view that there was no longer any doubt that the Navy Law would be adopted. Public support for the principle of a fixed naval establishment embodied in formal legislation seemed overwhelming. The Budget Committee alone had received 165 petitions from all over Germany and from overseas. Only two of the petitions opposed the Bill. Admittedly, many of the messages from Germans abroad, as Dr. Lieber put it in his opening remarks, "tasted absolutely as if they were 'made in Germany' (Laughter) . . . lacked in the most naive manner the slightest hint that the Germans overseas were inclined to con-

[93] "Protocol of the Prussian Ministry of State", February 23, 1898, Central Archive, Merseburg, Rep. 90 A, Abteilung B III 2B, No. 6. This document was kindly made available to me by Mr. J. C. G. Röhl of the University of Sussex.
[94] *Ibid.*

tribute to the burdens."[95] It was also true that other petitions, such as the one from Kiel Imperial Dockyards, were obviously "made in the Leipzigerplatz". Yet even if all the favourable petitions had been cooked up by officials, the fact that there was so little opposition remained an impressive testimony to the vigour of Tirpitz's campaign.

Tirpitz himself attended the opening session of the Committee accompanied by his brains trust: nine senior officers and section chiefs in all. Count Posadowsky-Wehner and Freiherr von Thielmann represented the Reich Ministries of the Interior and Treasury respectively. It was, all things considered, a distinguished gathering. Three Reich Secretaries faced twenty-nine deputies, among whom could be numbered the most famous names in parliamentary life. There was Eugen Richter, veteran of more than thirty years in opposition; there was August Bebel, perhaps the greatest of the German Social Democrats; the moderately conservative *Reichspartei* had sent its biggest names, Wilhelm von Kardorff and Count von Arnim, and the National Liberals had chosen a powerful delegation, including Bassermann and Hammacher, led by the party's chief, von Bennigsen. In a way the Budget Committee was the Reichstag in miniature, very much more than would have been the case if the Reichstag had enjoyed more power. Since its only indisputable privilege was the appropriation of funds, the Budget Committee assumed an importance which justified the presence of the highest party luminaries.

Dr. Lieber, as official reporter of the Committee, opened the discussion by suggesting that the draft of the law be considered in three stages: first, the contents of the Bill; second, its form; third, its financial basis. This procedure was quickly approved. Lieber began the debate on the first stage, the contents of the law. "How and why did the naval administration arrive at this clear plan?" he asked, "and with what right can the Navy assert that this Bill was not developed in three months but is the result of many years of experiment?"[96] Tirpitz requested that his reply be heard off the record. After this portentous beginning, his answer came as a considerable anticlimax. Instead of denying the allegation that the draft was only three

[95] *Kommission für den Reichshaushalts-Etat,* der Reichstag, 9. Legisl.-Periode, V. Session, February 24, 1898, p. 2. [96] *Ibid.*, p. 4.

months old (which he could hardly have done), he launched into a discussion of the danger to trade and shipping arising from Germany's geographical circumstances. In the view of the Navy's most gifted strategists, he continued, any power at war with Germany would need a fleet at least twice as large as Germany's proposed fleet in order to force open German coastal defences. England would need roughly twenty-eight battleships and fifty cruisers to do the job, and France would require her full Mediterranean fleet. Why Tirpitz insisted that his remarks be regarded as secret is not clear. There was scarcely anything in them which could not be read in any daily newspaper. Eugen Richter objected strenuously to secret sessions. Despite the noisy agreement of the Social Democrats, the objection was over-ruled. Lieber declared that the explanation given by Admiral Tirpitz was satisfactory and called for an end of discussion on the contents of the bill. A motion to that effect was passed over the protests of the Left, and the meeting was adjourned.[97]

On Saturday morning, February 26th, discussion resumed in committee on the second stage of the agenda: the proposed form of the law. Lieber again began the debate by arguing that the nature of the organism of the Navy required a legal foundation. No one could deny that certain long-term programmes extended beyond the life of a given Reichstag. It had certainly not been the intention of the drafters of the constitution of the Reich to prevent such "normal" budgets for the Army or Navy, and the draft law before them was in fact no more than a modest variation of the concept of "normal estimates". Was the government sufficiently clear that it too would be bound by the legal obligations of the Navy Law? "The government must for its part agree to an undertaking that it will not demand higher sums of money than the law provides within the next seven years."[98] Perhaps a fixed upper limit of expenditure could be adopted.

Tirpitz had the formal text of his answer ready, no doubt as a result of a private agreement with Lieber. "With permission of the Chancellor, I declare that in my opinion the Navy Law

[97] *Ibid.*, pp. 5 ff.
[98] Official Transcript, reproduced in *Norddeutsche Allgemeine Zeitung*, Evening Edition, Saturday, February 26, 1898.

would be unacceptable to the Associated Governments, if it were not to provide legal certainty that: (1) the fleet will be completed within the time specified by the Associated Governments and within the proportions which those governments regard as necessary; and (2) the fleet held to be necessary can be maintained in combat readiness."[99]

Although Tirpitz's prepared statement evaded the direct question put by Dr. Lieber, he was clearly prepared, if necessary, to accept some limit on governmental expenditure. He would not himself name a figure, so that future opponents of further naval expansion would be unable to accuse him of breaking a promise. He knew better than the civilians how likely future demands would be and, by avoiding the slightest suggestion of a sum, he could always claim that an upper limit had been forced on him. Once he had been seen to meet Lieber halfway, the question of the form of the law itself was no longer in doubt. The Committee moved rapidly through the second phase of the debate.

The smooth passage of the Bill in the Budget Committee did not go unnoticed. In a leader on February 27th, the *Freisinnige Zeitung* declared, "The Navy Law is finished." Its success, the paper complained, was a foregone conclusion. Lieber and von Massow (Conservative) had been negotiating secretly with the Imperial Naval Office, and the result was "a deal". "A law is adopted which until the beginning of the year not one party had desired and the usefulness of which even the government had emphatically denied. But there must be punishment! The Reichstag had committed the terrible crime of rejecting two cruisers and, as a result, must have its hands tied so that such a terrible thing can never happen again . . ."[100] The Socialist *Vorwärts* agreed. In an article called "Tirpitz, Lieber and Co." the newspaper denounced the Centre Party. "The deal between the government and the Centre is fixed. In this deal the *quid pro quo* will not take place all at once. By the deal the Centre has proved itself ripe for the role of government party and its reward will be forthcoming in every way . . . Now the Centre has become national-liberal. Now it is Herr

[99] *Ibid.*
[100] *Freisinnige Zeitung*, Sunday, February 27, 1898, in newspaper files, RMA III. 1.5.3.

Lieber who commands the floor and Herr von Bennigsen stands aside. Now Tirpitz and Lieber form the trading company and the National Liberals and Conservatives are the silent partners of this excellent firm."[101]

Both papers drew a line under their estimates of the situation too quickly. The third phase of the discussion of the Budget Committee, the provision of funds for the naval building programme, was far from concluded. Disagreements over principles were beginning to threaten the existence of the deal between Tirpitz and Lieber. The difficulty about providing money was two-fold. On the one hand, there were the demands of social justice which called for a progressive income tax or, as the Radical People's Party suggested, a Reich capital tax.[102] On the other hand, there were the demands of the supporters of states' rights. Any form of direct taxation by the Reich would upset the traditional financial independence of the individual German states and would also mark a big step forward in the process of consolidation and centralization of the Reich. Lieber's party contained advocates of social justice and of states' rights. Lieber had to be careful to play off one against the other. Too little democracy or too much centralism might rapidly cost him the leadership of the party. Once again the struggle to expand the Navy became hopelessly entangled in the struggle to create a German nation-state.

Lieber's solution was to introduce a series of amendments to Section Four of the Navy Law, and to add a Section Five entitled "Costs". In these amendments, he incorporated both the principle of an upper limit to expenditure and the principle of states' rights. Instead of a direct Reich tax, Lieber proposed to retain the traditional system of proportionate quota contributions to the Imperial Exchequer from the individual states, but he added the proviso that "federal states which employ a general income tax shall not contribute according to their quota in paragraph one, but shall add an extra charge on all taxable incomes of M 10,000 or more."

[101] *Vorwärts: Berliner Volksblatt,* Sunday, February 27, 1898, *ibid.*

[102] "The Radical People's Party at a joint parliamentary meeting with the German People's Party voted to introduce an amendment to the Navy Law, which provides that additional costs be covered by a Reich capital tax since the present tax structure will not yield sufficient funds. The capital tax is to be set at half of one per cent on all fortunes above M 100,000." (*Freisinnige Zeitung,* March 3, 1898.)

This extra charge was to be applied on a graduated scale and to be so collected that the sum of the additional charge equalled the amount of the quota normally payable by the state.[103] There was no doubt that this was an extremely shrewd compromise, but it was not long before cries of outrage were heard. Von Kardorff (*Reichspartei*) feared that the amendments "would place the whole Navy Law in jeopardy". Dr. Hammacher (Nat.-Lib.) believed that "an intervention in this sense in the affairs of the federal states was not feasible . . ." and von Bennigsen (Nat. Lib.) called the Lieber amendments "the greatest conceivable alteration to the constitution that there ever was; we are being asked for the first time to meddle directly in the affairs of the individual states".[104] Freiherr von Thielmann, State Secretary of the Treasury, argued that the amendments "had no hope of passing the Bundesrath . . . It was both a break with a tradition and a violation of Article 58 of the Constitution which forbids preferential treatment for individual states or classes."[105] Lieber defended his amendment with great energy. "Nine-tenths of the opposition to the Navy Law would disappear if the law made it clear that only financially sturdy shoulders and the groups most interested would bear the probable burdens."[106] He rejected any additional public loans, any new indirect taxes or increases in existing taxes.

The deadlock seemed to be complete. On March 5th, von Bennigsen attempted to find a compromise solution. Surely a more practical arrangement could be found, he argued, that would satisfy the demands of social justice without raising awkward constitutional questions. Since it seemed to be the sense of the meeting that some sort of protection for the lower

[103] "Abänderungsanträge (Hauptantrag)", *Drucksache Nr. III der Kommission*, Berlin, Wednesday, March 2, 1898. The scale of progressive taxation was as follows: for each M 100 of annual income between

		Taü
M 10,000 to	M 50,000	M 0.25
50,000 to	100,000	0.50
100,000 to	200,000	0.75
200,000 and above		1.00

[104] *Kommission fur den Reichshaushalts-Etat*, 4. Sitzung, March 3, 1898, Copy No. 14, pp. 71 ff.

[105] *Ibid.*, "Drucksache ad Nr. 193".

[106] *Ibid.*, pp. 68 f., and 5. Sitzung, March 5, 1898, pp. 92 f.

income groups be provided, he proposed the following formula:

> "Whenever the sum of ordinary and extraordinary expenditure in any year exceeds the amount of M 117,525,494 (*i.e.* the naval estimates of 1897–98) and the normal sources of Reich income are insufficient to cover the deficit, additional appropriations may not be voted which would raise the present level of indirect taxation or increase the number of indirect taxes in the Reich."[107]

Although the von Bennigsen formula offered no more than negative guarantees, as Lieber was quick to point out, it might provide the Centre Party with a face-saving camouflage. It was clear that without some recognition, however perfunctory, of the "social question", there would be no Navy Law. Even August Bebel was forced to admit that the concern for the welfare of the poor expressed on all sides of the committee was "a very important achievement". How long it would last was another question. In any event it was "remarkable that of all parties the Centre should be the one to abandon the federal principle".[108]

Bebel's satisfaction was not shared in the Prussian Ministry of State. That evening, Herr Brefeld, Prussian Minister of Trade, entertained his cabinet colleagues at an informal gathering in his home. Naturally, the main topic of conversation was the deadlock in the Budget Committee and the implications of Lieber's proposals. The conservative Minister of Culture, Herr Bosse, was extremely unhappy about the threat to the traditional relationship between the Reich and the federal states, and so were most of his colleagues. The consensus in the cabinet, as Bosse summarized it in his diary, was that "Lieber's leadership of the Centre, as Lieber himself admits, has no appeal to the individual German states. It fosters the movement for a unified, centralized state in the Reich in complete disregard of the spirit of the constitution and endangers the federalistic character of the Reich. The Bavarian Centre deputies are simply too stupid to see that on their own. As a result we must be much more friendly to the individual states. For this reason a South German newspaper is to be founded by the government, which will be set up here

[107] *Ibid.*, p. 91. [108] *Ibid.*, p. 95.

but appear nominally in Karlsruhe. One can only be astonished at the confusion of thought."[109] How far Bosse's objections were constitutional and how far they were really a form of concealed anti-Catholicism is not clear. The prospect of the Catholic Centre posing as champion of Bismarck's Reich was certainly unattractive to Prussian Protestants under any circumstances, but it was positively dangerous if that role were granted to the Centre Party at the expense of the Prussian state's inviolable rights.

Tirpitz, who was neither a member of the Ministry of State nor an advocate of Prussian particularism, had less cause for alarm. There was, to be sure, a deadlock in the committee, but if it could be solved by concession on the social questions, he was more than ready to meet the Centre half-way. In any case, there was still time to negotiate. The next hearings of the Budget Committee were scheduled for March 16th and Tirpitz proposed to use the time wisely. In the second place, the general attitude of the Centre Party had been far more sympathetic to the Navy Law than Tirpitz could have expected. Herr Müller (Centre) had even gone so far as to introduce an amendment shortening the length of the law from seven to six years.[110] The result of Herr Müller's industriousness was to increase the building tempo once again and, in effect, to accelerate the arms race treadmill. This could not have been more welcome to Tirpitz in military and political terms. He got his fleet a year earlier without having to bear the onus of suggesting it. Again the Centre Party had shown itself to be more nationally minded than the nationalists and that, too, was all to the good.[111] For the rest of the activity of the committee, Tirpitz could be truly grateful. The other amendments proposed in committee were either editorial in nature or only

[109] Diary entry, Berlin, March 5, 1898, BA "Nachlass Bosse"—Tagebücher, Vol. 9.
[110] Abänderungs-Anträge—Müller (Fulda), "Flottenbauplan mit Erreichung des Sollbestandes in 6 Jahren", Drucksache Nr. III, *Kommission für den Reichshaushalts-Etat*, Berlin, March 2, 1898.
[111] Tirpitz to Kaiser, Telegram, Berlin, March 5, 1898, 11.50 a.m., MK I.f.1. "On a motion of the Centre Deputy Müller (Fulda) the Budget Committee has just voted over the opposition of Radicals, Poles and Social Democrats to complete the new construction required to meet the effective strength demanded within six instead of seven years and to postpone the construction of the replacement for a heavy cruiser for one year. The amendment was warmly supported by the Chancellor and myself."

seemingly important. Tirpitz could happily accept the fixed upper limit to total expenditure on naval construction, knowing full well that the Reichstag would never be able to default on its obligation to build a fleet of the desired size, no matter how much the individual units might cost.

So far Tirpitz had been able to lead the Centre Party by the nose, but it was an unpredictable beast. If it bolted, he and his programme were finished. If it lay down for a snooze, he was unable to go on without it. No wonder he kept gingerly reaching out to pat its scruffy pelt. He was as dependent on the good will of the Centre as if that party had created him, as subservient to its every whim as no other Reich minister had ever been before. To take one example: on March 8th, a caucus of the party was held at the Reichstag and an angry disagreement bubbled to the surface. The feeling that somehow in some way they had been duped gave vent to rebellious murmurs and threatening gestures. The controversy soon centred on the provisions of the Navy Law which governed the machinery for replacement of obsolete ships. In the text of the draft, the approval of both Bundesrath and Reichstag were to be required for any alteration of the tempo by which obsolete ships were replaced. Tirpitz depended on this apparently innocent stipulation. Through it, he could prevent any tampering with the rate and number of replacement vessels built, because he could always use the Bundesrath's veto to quash a Reichstag amendment. This ensured the wholly automatic, unalterable modernization of the fleet. Herr Fritzen, one of the leading Centre deputies, led the revolt and demanded that the Bundesrath's right of intervention be deleted from the draft. Tirpitz was horrified. This amendment struck at the very heart of his entire conception. Unless the replacement of obsolete ships was absolutely automatic and beyond the annual interference of the Reichstag, Tirpitz's plans could not be carried out. Any chance improvement in Anglo-German relations might tempt the Reichstag to postpone the replacement of older vessels and thus slow down the tempo of the programme. If that were permitted, the whole significance of the deterrent as a calculable and credible power factor would be destroyed and the leverage gained against England would be frittered away. Tirpitz was extremely upset. "This omission would decisively mutilate the replacement paragraph. I told the leader of the Centre Party today that the cut was not acceptable to me and that I should have to submit my resignation if the Associated Governments were to agree to it. I hope the Centre will reconsider its position."[112]

Tirpitz hoped that this threat would work. It exerted tremendous pressure on Dr. Lieber, for Lieber was as dependent on Tirpitz as Tirpitz was on the ninety-six deputies of the Centre. If Tirpitz were to resign, his departure would also mark the end of Dr. Lieber's dreams of glory. The Centre's one real ally in the administration would go, and without him the party would lapse again into that fruitless opposition which had been its lot from the beginning of the Reich. There was also an element of bluff in Tirpitz's ultimatum, because he had no right to make such a threat. From the constitutional standpoint, Tirpitz was not a free agent but merely an administrative organ of the Chancellor. He had no more right to tender his resignation over a disagreement within a parliamentary party, than Hollmann had twelve months earlier. In fact, he had less, because Hollmann was at least in possession of an order from the Kaiser. It was, moreover, unbecoming of an officer to act as if he could resign of his own volition. As Seckendorff wrote to Senden, "I can perfectly well understand that he will not allow himself to be bargained out of the essentials of the law, but I cannot understand how Tirpitz could have come to accept the idea, and to express it openly, that the failure of the Navy Law has anything to do with his remaining in or leaving office. I consider it most alarming that a State Secretary should have revealed such a confusion of thought about the constitution. We do not have a parliamentary regime and I hope that we never shall have one."[113] What Seckendorff failed to see was that it was precisely because Tirpitz behaved as if Germany had a parliamentary regime that he was so successful. It was because he took the Reichstag seriously, because he cultivated its leaders, entertained and flattered its rank and file, and because he depended on it that he got what he wanted from it. For the first time, a State Secretary of the Navy enjoyed the confidence of the Catholic Centre and did so precisely because a

[112] Tirpitz to Senden (handwritten), March 9, 1898, MK I f.1.
[113] Seckendorff to Senden, Kiel, March 12, 1898, BA K 08-7, "Senden Nachlass".

parliamentary regime held no terrors for him. His very vulnerability to a parliamentary defeat was paradoxically one of his greatest strengths.

The threat to resign was enough. Fritzen dropped his motion and Tirpitz and Capelle picked up the thread where it had broken. On March 16th, Dr. Lieber and Herr Müller called at the Leipzigerplatz on their way to the sixth session of the Budget Committee. Tirpitz and Capelle received them by pointing out that although they were prepared to accept either a majority or a unanimous decision of the Centre Party, they had to have "a guarantee of fifty votes". "A dissolution in the event of a refusal" would be unavoidable, Tirpitz warned, and the government would be compelled "to agitate against the Centre, even if the party (were) indispensable in the new Reichstag".[114] Lieber and Müller had no real choice. Either they continued to insist that their amendments, the compulsory income tax levied by the states, be adopted, with the consequent risk of becoming the scapegoat in a general election and also losing their best friend in the government, or they gave up the fight in the hope of future rewards. Once again, Tirpitz's threat carried the day. Later that morning, when the Budget Committee hearings began, it was a very different Dr. Lieber who took the floor. Wearily, he told the deputies that "he must reckon with the fact that a great majority opposed his amendment and that for this reason he had no choice but to vote for the Bennigsen amendment instead". In order to save face, he moved that instead of the phrase "indirect taxes" the words "taxes which burden mass consumption" be substituted.[115] Lieber's collapse made it clear, according to Bebel, that "the newly found egg of Columbus . . . was just wind", and that the Centre had sold out on the social question. Richter angrily denounced the compromise and pointed out "how little the Bennigsen amendment and the government's declarations actually mean . . . The Prussian House of Lords is more than sufficient to render all such promises absolutely worthless."[116] The loophole was the tariff. It could be raised at any

[114] Rough draft of a minute (in pencil) in Tirpitz's and Capelle's handwriting, March 16, 1898, RMA III. 1.5.3., Vol. 4.

[115] *Kommission für den Reichshaushalts-Etat*, 6. Sitzung, Wednesday, March 16, 1898, p. 104.

[116] *Ibid.*, p. 107.

time and produce the same result as any number of indirect taxes. Once again the Associated Governments had evaded the "social question". The following morning, after another tactical withdrawal by the Centre, the amended draft of the Navy Law was passed in committee by nineteen votes to eight. Only Herr Müller deserted the Centre in the end and joined the three Social Democrats, two Radicals, the one Pole and the lonely Herr Galler of the German's People's Party in opposition.[117]

D. The Passage of the Navy Law

The final debate on the Bill in full session began on the following Wednesday. By now it was clear to every member of the house that the Navy Law would pass, and any lingering doubts were dispelled by Count von Hompesch (Centre). Amidst vigorous shouts of "Bravo!" from the right side of the house, he declared, "the majority of my political associates will vote in favour of the Bill."[118] The band-wagon was trundling ahead. Herr von Levetzow (Conservative) delighted the house by beginning his speech: "Gentlemen, patriotic landowners gladly offer their contributions to the well-being of other classes in society ... (Laughter, on the Left; Very True! on the Right) ... We landowners are only too willing to share in the costs of the fleet, which is designed to benefit industry and trade, export and import ... (Cries of protest, Left)."[119] It remained for Herr Schoenlank of the Social Democrats to spoil the fun. The present debate, he said, was "merely the epilogue to decisions already made . . . What Herr Doctor Lieber says today stands the previous policy and tactics of the Centre Party on its head. Herr Lieber had 'out-heroded' Herod. He is more governmental than Herr Admiral Tirpitz ... (Laughter) ... A year ago Herr Lieber was the 'embarrassed European', now he is the insider who saw it all coming."[120] Dr. Schaedler,

[117] *Ibid.*, 7. Sitzung, Thursday, March 17, 1898, p. 114.

[118] *Stenographischer Bericht*, der Reichstag, 9. Legisl.-Periode, V. Session, 68. Sitzung, Wednesday, March 23, 1898, p. 1703.

[119] *Ibid.*, p. 1705.

[120] *Ibid.*, pp. 1708 ff.

representing the dissenting members of the Centre Party, also had his doubts that between March 18 and November 30, 1897, "everything could have been so completely smoothed out."[121] Lieber had an answer for that argument. "I can hardly blame the prophets of the Old Testament," he replied suavely, "that they are not prophets of the New . . . (Laughter) . . . so I do not accuse the State Secretaries from Stosch to Hollmann for not having been Tirpitz."[122]

Richter resumed his futile attack on the Bill on the second day of the debate. "If it is true that imperial power is sea power and that sea power conditions imperial power . . . and if Neptune's trident belongs in our fist, then for the great Reich with its great big fist a little fleet is not enough . . . We shall have to have more and more battleships . . . coaling stations are essential for the battleships, the docks too, in short, everything which a Navy of the first rank requires, and that is the goal toward which we are steering with this law . . . We can be absolutely certain of one thing: 'Full speed ahead' will soon be the cry in this direction."[123] For the last time Tirpitz took the floor to reply to Richter. He began by accusing Richter of refusing every government request on principle and calling it moderation. A fleet is necessary, Tirpitz argued, not only for economic reasons but "for general purposes as well. Gentlemen, a state which has actively taken up trade, and has thereby become a considerable competitor in world markets, cannot exist without a certain measure of naval power or else it must go under. If the battle fleet is to prevent an acute illness in case of war, that is, death by strangulation for Germany, it must equally prevent a chronic feebleness of our economic life in peace-time."[124] If world trade was a jungle, Tirpitz urged Germany to sharpen its claws.

All the parties save one had now been heard and, as the afternoon lengthened, old August Bebel rose to make the final speech on the Navy Law. After a brilliant analysis of the emptiness of parliamentary forms in Germany and a scathing attack on the treacherous deputies of the Centre, Bebel turned to face the seats on the right wing of the house. "There is,

[121] *Ibid.*, p. 1717.
[122] *Ibid.*, p. 1718.
[123] *Ibid.*, 69. Sitzung, Thursday, March 24, 1898, p. 1730.
[124] *Ibid.*, p. 1732.

especially on the right side of this house, a large group of fanatical anglophobes made up of men who want to pick a fight with England and who would rather fight today than tomorrow. But to believe that with our fleet, yes, even if it is finished to the very last ship demanded in this law, we could take up the cudgels against England, is to approach the realm of insanity. Those who demand it belong not in the Reichstag but in the madhouse . . . (Prolonged Laughter)."[125]

From the retrospect of more than sixty years, there is something tragic in the laughter which greeted Bebel's warning. A kind of madness had indeed begun to afflict the men of Wilhelmine Germany, and out of that madness came the laughter which punctuated Bebel's words. For the first time in all the debates on the Navy Law of 1898, a Reichstag deputy had told the whole truth about the motives behind that law, and his listeners laughed. Perhaps Tirpitz had been too cautious in his approach to parliament, too circumspect in unveiling his full strategic conception. He had chosen to conceal his real strategy, because he was afraid of popular reaction to his "Fleet against England". But would the result have been different if he had told the truth? Was not the laughter with which the deputies howled down Bebel a sign that Tirpitz's prudence was unnecessary? No one can say with any certainty how far the acceptance of the Navy Law rested on Tirpitz's agitation, skilful though it was, or even on the ambitions of an aspiring Catholic politician. The response to Bebel's warning reflected a change in attitude so profound that it had yet to come to the surface. What had been the closely guarded plan of an inner cabal in January of 1896 had become the wish of a substantial majority of the Reichstag by March 1898. The transformation of German attitudes to the outside world was complete.

When Bebel returned to his seat, the voting on the Navy Law draft began. Each paragraph of the Bill had to be voted separately in order to incorporate the amendments proposed in committee. Throughout the afternoons of March 24th and 26th, the monotonous procedure went on. There was some fluctuation in the voting on each paragraph, but Tirpitz's

[125] *Ibid.*, p. 1746.

coalition never fell below 198 votes and at no time were more than thirty Centre deputies in opposition. At 5.10 p.m., on the 26th, Tirpitz informed the Kaiser by telegram that "all paragraphs of the Navy Law in the version approved by the Budget Committee have been passed by the full house in second reading."[126] Bülow, not to be outdone, sent a similar message twenty minutes later, adding only the words "Long Live the Kaiser!"[127]

The impossible had been achieved. The Navy Law had had passed. Telegrams of congratulations began to pour into the palace. Prince Heinrich's was very much to the point: "German Emperor, Berlin. Hurrah! Heinrich."[128] The sycophants and intriguers joined the chorus. General Waldersee hoped "that the nation will become aware that it owes the attainment of great power status on the sea to the initiative and resolute will of Your Majesty".[129] "Phili" Eulenburg responded to the news rhapsodically, "On this day of honour for Your Majesty, I recall all the struggles and suffering out of which, like a phoenix, today's success has emerged. I thank God with overflowing heart for having granted us this Kaiser! How much effort and resoluteness of purpose have gone into today's triumph, I know better than most. My entire house is celebrating this glorious holiday with a joyful cheer for the Kaiser."[130] Even the Tsar had been impressed, Prince Radolin, German Ambassador at St. Petersburg, reported, by the "tact with which our most gracious Lord prepared and carried through the Naval Bill . . ."[131]

Comment in Great Britain was restrained. Most British observers regarded the expansion of the German fleet not as a threat in itself but as a new factor in what the First Lord called "the balance of power in the navies of Europe". *The Times* summed up the position in a leader on the Navy Law and

[126] Admiral Tirpitz to Kaiser Wilhelm II, Special Train, Uelzen, 5.10 p.m., Berlin, March 26, 1898, MK I.f.1.

[127] Bernhard von Bülow to Kaiser Wilhelm II, *ibid.*, 5.35 p.m.

[128] Prince Heinrich of Prussia, Hong Kong, to Kaiser Wilhelm II, Berlin, March 28, 1898, MK I.f.1.

[129] Waldersee to Kaiser Wilhelm II, March 28, 1898, MK I.f.1.

[130] Count Philipp Eulenburg to Kaiser Wilhelm II, Vienna, March 28, 1898, MK I.f.1.

[131] Radolin to Foreign Ministry, Dispatch No. 69, St. Petersburg, March 20, 1898, MK I.f.1. Note in Senden's hand: "H.M. has read this to Admiral Tirpitz."

Germany's naval aspirations: "Every reasonable man must admit that in these circumstances she does well to consider her naval position. Foreign critics may or may not think that she is doing so in rather too ambitious a spirit . . . but the government has propounded a programme which the Reichstag has accepted. In these circumstances, whatever we may think of the policy involved, there is not much that can profitably be said . . ." The difficulty as *The Times* saw it lay in the effect of German naval expansion on the fleet plans of France and Russia and thus on the maintenance of the two-power standard. Its conclusion was clear: "The country must be prepared for the change which is now inevitable, and resolve to face it before it is effected."[132] Nobody in Britain had noticed the implicit challenge behind the design of Tirpitz's fleet, save a few naval extremists, and their cries of alarm were dismissed as pure fantasy. Not until the turn of the century was the Admiralty or the British public awakened to the startling change which Tirpitz had brought about. Germany had been granted an invaluable period of immunity.

For all his pride in "his" work, the Kaiser did not forget the man who had really given him the Navy Law, and in a letter to Prince Hohenlohe he urged that in recognition of Tirpitz's extraordinary services, he be granted an extraordinary reward: membership in the Prussian Ministry of State, "not only the rank and title, but a seat and a vote as well". The Kaiser would not hear of constitutional objections. "To be sure," he continued, "the Navy does not belong among the Prussian ministries, but it is under the command of the Prussian King, who is German Emperor. Besides, it is like the Army a fully equal partner and component in our national defence. This may perhaps encourage it to dare to claim a place in the illustrious assemblage of the Ministers of State . . . Moreover there is the Admiral himself. No sooner was he home from China, a man with a weakened constitution, than cheerfully and alone, he took up the awesome task of orientating an entire people, fifty million truculent, short-sighted and foul-tempered Germans, and of bringing them round to an opposite view. He accomplished this seemingly impossible feat in eight months.

[132] *The Times*, London, March 28, 1898.

Truly a powerful man! A man who so gloriously accomplishes such a gigantic work against the opinions of the majority of the ministers must be a full-fledged member of My administration! It can only redound to the credit of that most learned body to count such a man one of its own. Perhaps he will give it fresh initiative and new incentive to energetic work . . ."[133]

The frail old Prince had neither the heart nor the force to resist Wilhelm II in an impetuous mood. The solid men in the frock-coats grumbled, but no one resigned in protest. Admiral Alfred Tirpitz became a member of the Prussian Ministry of State, an appointment which placed him in a position of power shared only by the Chancellor, Bernhard von Bülow at the Foreign Ministry and Posadowsky-Wehner at the Ministry of Interior. In his person Tirpitz now enjoyed the prerogatives of a minister of the Reich and of Prussia, a union which Bismarck had initially designed for himself alone. His triumph meant more than personal elevation. It was the sign that the Imperial Navy had at last come of age. Now it enjoyed equality of status with the incomparably more senior service, the Prussian Army. The constitutional barriers to its participation in the deliberations of the Ministry of State of the largest and most important Federal German State had been removed. The Navy's acknowledged spokesman now had a voice and a vote in Prussia.

The imperial signature which elevated Rear-Admiral Tirpitz to the rank of Prussian Minister of State was the consummation of another, more ominous development. It marked the final disintegration of the Prussian cabinet as a separate, stable factor in Germany's affairs. By its very separation from world politics in the past, Prussia's cabinet acted as a brake on imperial adventurousness. Now Tirpitz, the embodiment of the new international aggressiveness, joined that body, and Hohenlohe could no longer retreat behind its conservative suspiciousness. Although the Prussian cabinet's reactionary tendencies repeatedly frustrated Hohenlohe, they also helped to prop him up. He might get nothing through, but he could at least be confident of Prussian conservatives' distaste for imperial flamboyance and transatlantic speculations.

[133] Kaiser Wilhelm II to Prince Hohenlohe, Berlin, March 27, 1898, Hohenlohe, *op. cit.*, pp. 436 f.

Dull, plodding, narrow-minded and stuffy its members certainly were, but they acted as a ponderous brake on impetuous policies. The Prussian Ministers of War regarded every change in the *status quo* as somehow an advance for democracy. They had no use, nor did most of their frock-coated colleagues, for imperialism, world politics, colonial involvements and public opinion. Men like Tirpitz inevitably diluted the cabinet's composition and loosened its unyielding grip. Tirpitz's elevation to the Ministry of State tipped that balance further in the direction of world politics. He and Bülow brought the new generation into prominence in Prussia.

They were truly Wilhelm's men and Wilhelmine creations. No longer "saturated", no longer obsessed by Bismarckian nightmares and no longer troubled by uncertain allegiance to a ramshackle Reich, they looked forward to an ever expanding future, to limitless possibilities and to a dawn of the *pax germanica*. When they were cautious or timid, and Bülow and Tirpitz could be both, they were cautious in a new way. They lacked the most prominent traits of the old Prussian mentality. They had no loathing of outward pomp and splendid ceremonies. They were, consequently, capable of the grand gesture and the terrified rout, types of behaviour alien to the terse Prussian style. What Holstein in his grizzled Prussian soul dismissed as Tirpitz's "lack of stomach for a fight" and Bülow's lack of nerve was in reality the every essence of the spirit of the new generation. It was not accidental that the Kaiser's fateful tendency to insubstantial bombast and hollow posturing was faithfully reflected in different ways in his new advisers.

The old age was passing away. Men like Tirpitz, who had been young men during the Franco-Prussian war, were taking over. Bismarck, the old giant, had withdrawn to the solitude of his wooded estate to await the coming of death. He was not to wait long. One by one his contemporaries, the ancient field marshals, captains and kings, the men of the old society, were disappearing. The new world, which Bismarck watched rising around him, was not his any longer. Its aspirations and alliances were no more of his making. *Weltpolitik*, which for him had not been worth the bones of a single Pomeranian grenadier, had become the illusion for which many were to die. The hopeless defence of Kiaochow and the colonies was to cost a great deal in human life and yet to contribute not a jot to Germany's strength or the ultimate outcome of the world war. The age of Bismarck was giving way to the "Tirpitz Era", and the passage of the Navy Law in the Reichstag was the symbol of that transformation. When the Royal Assent was given to the Bill on April 10, 1898, the first, but in some ways the most significant, phase of the "Tirpitz Era" was already over, a little more than nine months after it had begun.

Conclusion

The Navy Law of 1898 was no ordinary piece of military legislation. It began a new era. The emphasis in German military affairs shifted dramatically from the land to the sea. From April 1898 to August 1914, the fleet, which the *Flottengesetz* of 1898 called into being, dominated Germany's international relations. After centuries of preoccupation with her land forces, Germany altered her defence priorities and now committed herself to a supreme effort to attain "standing" at sea with the dominant naval power of the day. That this new effort led to new tensions in her international relations could hardly be avoided. That the ultimate aim of this programme was more than mere defence can no longer be denied. Tirpitz's memorandum of June 15, 1897, the testimony of Senden and the Kaiser, remove the last shreds of doubt about the resolution and stubborn determination of the three most influential men of the Imperial Navy to wrest from Great Britain her exclusive hegemony over the world's oceans.

This determination was behind the agitation for a big fleet from its beginning in 1895. It was the prime mover behind the intrigue which put Tirpitz into office, and it was the implicit strategy on which the Navy Law was drawn up. In the past this truth has been overlooked or denied. Now that a full account of the day-to-day struggle to develop and to implement that programme exists, it is clear that the first Navy Law, and not any of its later alterations, is the real turning point in this period. The commonly accepted version of the origins of the great German battle fleet must be abandoned. It was not a response to the failure of Anglo-German relations to improve after 1899 which led to the formulation of the "risk theory" in the preamble to the second Navy Law of 1900. That theory was fully developed by June of 1897. The increasing anglophobia in Germany after the Boer War broke out merely removed the need to conceal it.

Kaiser Wilhelm II, Tirpitz, Senden and the bright young men of the Imperial Naval Office shared with many members of the German middle classes a peculiar ambivalence toward England. When the Navy Law was passed in 1898, Germany adopted an impressively conceived and logically developed naval strategy, but the roots of that strategy ran deep into the substrata of emotion and unreason. The superstructure of the risk theory may have been rational but much of the force behind it was not. It is not chance that what the anglophobic Bismarck carefully fostered was destroyed by anglophiles such as Wilhelm II and Tirpitz. Nor is it a coincidence that the Imperial Navy, the darling of the German middle classes, received its anti-English direction during the 1890s. These were the years in which the commercial and industrial middle classes finally merged with the Prussian conservatives in effective economic and social power. The union of bourgeois capitalism with Prussian aristocratic conservatism was the hallmark of the first post-Bismarckian decade. In that union the natural Prussian distrust of English commercialism and liberalism was swamped by the much more dangerous ambivalence of the middle classes. "My feelings toward England," Tirpitz recalled after the First World War, "were determined by family and profession . . . My father, who in domestic affairs inclined to liberal views, shared the antagonism toward selfish England common in reformist circles . . ."[1] This ill-will was a kind of disappointed infatuation, an emotional and thoroughly irrational sentiment.

The sources of this "undeniable England-complex"[2] spring from psychological and historical elements in the education and experience of men of the German liberal middle classes which are much too complicated to fit into this study. Its symptoms can be seen in the behaviour of "that class of Germans, who spoke English and copied English manners, sport and dress, in a strenuous endeavour to become the very pattern of an English gentleman",[3] in the hysterical reaction to

[1] Tirpitz, *op. cit.*, p. 8.
[2] Walther Hubatsch, *Die Ära Tirpitz*, p. 13.
[3] Barbara Tuchman, *op. cit.*, p. 77.

English criticism and, not least, in Tirpitz's naval strategy. As Professor Stadelmann points out, "this inner competition with the British way of life was inconceivable to the self-contained old Prussian mentality of the generation of Bismarck".[4] The adoption of the Navy Law of 1898 can be seen as the final triumph of the new ambivalent attitude to England over the older, continental and conservative outlook.

Close examination of the evolution of the Navy Law highlights another complex phenomenon of this period: the fragility of the German nation-state. By focusing our attention on the Navy in German domestic politics, certain aspects of that fragility have sprung into sharp relief. The Reichstag with its shifting coalitions of class, religious, ethnic and regional groupings stands out as the immediate manifestation of Germany's dynamic disunity. Its inherently centrifugal tendencies forced Tirpitz into an uneasy dependence on the one party which had withstood them, the Catholic Centre Party. The motives which moved Dr. Lieber of the Centre to co-operate with Tirpitz, the vision of the Centre as the government party, arose from his desire to strengthen the heart of the Reich at the cost of the federal states. Lieber's ambitions contradicted the nature of his party as a coalition bound only by religion and by opposition to the Reich. What Lieber hoped to accomplish remained a dream until after the Second World War when Adenauer made the old Centre Party into the modern Christian Democratic Union, but the price was high. Adenauer had to pay for his power by the loss of German unity.

Tirpitz's alliance with the Centre suggests the need to correct the inaccurate, but all too widespread, image of Wilhelmine Germany as a kind of impregnable fortress growing ever more menacing and powerful. Although Germany grew rapidly in strength and influence after 1871, her internal disunity and centrifugal dynamics continued to plague her political leadership until the Empire disintegrated. Part of the explanation of the erratic course of German policy after 1890 lies in the political instability of the nation-state and the desperate attempt to shore it up. The fleet programme, the Austro-Hungarian alliance and the growth of rabid nationalism, all

[4] Rudolf Stadelmann, *op. cit.*, p. 98.

express in different ways the pressures of life in an Empire in search of itself.

The alliance of the Centre Party and the Navy also underlines Tirpitz's political liberalism. It was his liberal attitude to parliament and his fundamental acceptance of its forms which made him the most successful German politician between Bismarck and Stresemann. He broke with Prussian conservative, protestant tradition in approaching the Centre, and horrified his older colleagues by his methods. His use of the threat to resign and his open-minded willingness to negotiate were equally foreign to the minds of men like Admiral Seckendorff and Prussian ministers like Bosse. Their intense rejection of parliamentary government and all its works was wholly alien to his nature, and when he let himself become so dependent on the Centre that internal disputes within the parliamentary party could force him to submit his resignation, he showed far greater wisdom than his critics. It was, paradoxically, his weakness which was his strength. Because he depended on them, the Centre deputies were willing to trust him, and to vote for his Navy Law without demanding or achieving their pound of flesh.

The murky story of Tirpitz's accession to power recalls from obscurity the figure of Admiral Senden. His important position was perfectly described in the contemporary cartoon which showed him lowering a hook from the rafters above a stage and supporting Hohenlohe and Tirpitz in their parliamentary weight-lifting act. His emergence from the shadows revises the story of this period which Tirpitz wrote and, at the same time, emphasizes the difficulties of conducting a unified and consistent policy in Wilhelmine Germany. Senden's seat in the rafters rested on the peculiar constitutional position of his imperial master and that, in turn, affected the conduct of affairs by those who nominally held the power of decision. The Kaiser's role in German politics may be likened to a flywheel or mechanical governor which has somehow been disconnected from the machine, whose even and regular motion it is meant to ensure. The forces within the machine act on it erratically and cannot be controlled or contained. Its eccentric spinning responds to the play of energies streaming from all angles, and as the pressure within the machine mounts dangerously, it is lifted further from its proper socket. Under Wilhelm I, Bismarck's heavy hand held the loose part in its place. When the aged Emperor gave way to his impetuous grandson, not even Bismarck's weight was enough.

The consequences of this vertical instability are as apparent in the history of the first Navy Law as are the horizontal and centrifugal forces. An energetic and ambitious man such as Tirpitz could, by playing the right vertical vector, accomplish an enormous amount very quickly. His assiduous cultivation of Senden between 1892 and 1897 shows how much could be done this way. But he could never really gain control of the whole apparatus. Only the man on top could do that and by the nature of the Prussian-German monarchy that man had to be the monarch. Tirpitz found that, once in power, he could never quite reach a position in which he could manipulate all the forces necessary to the success of his strategy. His own rise to the top called forth countervailing pressures within the governmental structure and the naval hierarchy, and increasingly often he found himself locked in an internal war of all against all. Full control of the political leverage generated by the expanding fleet eluded him, and he had to watch with mounting frustration how other branches of the government lurched into adventures and calamities which crushed the premises on which the risk theory depended. "A general weakness of the politics of our time," he observed, "was the consumption, piece by piece, of the great, but not quite adequate, substance of power which Bismarck left us. We engaged in repeated demonstrations where our peaceful intentions but our nervousness also shone through. These were generally followed by sudden collapses . . . We threw ourselves into the arms of others, then unexpectedly fell upon them and never missed an occasion to remind them how magnificently far we had come . . . I fought against our self-destruction without possessing the necessary power."[5] Tirpitz became a kind of Frankenstein whose monster he could no longer control.

Those who, like Professor Hubatsch,[6] defend Tirpitz and

[5] Tirpitz., *op. cit.*, p. 164.

[6] "The mechanically unfolding Navy Law with its ramifications over time never became an instrument of the political leadership, nor indeed was ever sufficiently

Continued on page 206

exonerate him from all blame fail to see that the risk theory was a dangerous and daring political device in the steadiest of hands. In Wilhelmine Germany, under a regime almost out of control, it was simply calamitous. That Tirpitz knew this by 1905 is clear from his desperate reactions to the Kaiser's demands for ever larger and faster battleships. His attempt to grasp all the levers had disastrously miscarried, but he refused to alter his fundamental direction. He saw the erratic, irregular course of German foreign policy successively flatten every condition of success for his theory. It frightened away the smaller European powers, nullified the possibility of an anti-British continental league and gradually drove Britain to abandon her isolation by joining anti-German coalitions. Yet he would not slow the tempo of the building programme, the one lever of power which he firmly controlled. If historical guilt for subsequent catastrophes can be apportioned, this is Tirpitz's.

It has been Tirpitz's fate at the hands of historians to be studied for his failures and to be neglected for his success. Admittedly the risk theory, the great fleet and his foreign policies must be considered as failures, but the passage of the Navy Law of 1898 and its successors was not. Tirpitz's skill as a domestic politician was remarkable. In the turbulent and uneasy climate of Wilhelmine society, there was no one to equal him as a manager of men, a manipulator of public opinion, an administrator and a negotiator. He had a sureness of touch and depth of insight into the tangled lines of force in the community which led him to success after success. He made the impossible look easy, which is the indelible mark of the champion at any game. In his way he had genuine greatness. It may be that he applied his immense talents to an unworthy end, but as long as men live in political society, there will always be something to admire in the consideration of those singular men who can make it work and who understand its needs. Tirpitz was one of those men whom Emerson called

Continued from page 205
subordinated to the general interests of foreign policy. That cannot be blamed on Tirpitz." Thus Professor Hubatsch (*Die Ära Tirpitz*, p. 18). The Admiral himself knew better. The fact was that there was no one to make either the fleet plan subordinate to foreign policy or foreign policy to the fleet plan.

the "relatively great". "They are such, in whom, at the moment of success, a quality is ripe which is then in request. Other days will demand other qualities . . . The men who exhibit them have now more, now less, and pass away; the qualities remain on another brow."

"Never seen before! Miraculous performance of the acrobatic pair. This performance must have a hook in it." (*The caption is a pun on the German equivalent to the English "a fly in the ointment."*) *Cartoon of 1899, illustrating the way in which Hohenlohe's and Tirpitz's legislative programme depends on the invisible support of Admiral von Senden Bibran in the rafters*

APPENDIX

The Tirpitz Memorandum of June 1897

Geheim Sache Juni 1897

Allgemeine Gesichtspunkte bei der Feststellung unserer Flotte nach Schiffsklassen und Schiffstypen

1. Der Abgrenzung der Schiffsklassen gegeneinander und der Bestimmung der Schiffstypen innerhalb der verschiedenen Schiffsklassen muss die schwierigste Kriegslage zugrunde gelegt werden, in die unsere Flotte kommen kann. Denn diejenige Zusammensetzung, die der schwierigsten Situation entspricht, wird auch für alle übrigen Situationen als ausreichend angenommen werden müssen. Jeder denkbaren Situation für sich auf das vollkommenste Rechnung zu tragen gestattet die Beschränktheit unserer Mittel nicht.
2. Für Deutschland ist zur Zeit der gefährlichste Gegner zur See England. Es ist auch der Gegner, gegen den wir am dringendsten ein gewisses Mass an Flottenmacht als politischer Machtfaktor haben müssen.
3. Kreuzerkrieg und transozeanischer Krieg gegen England ist wegen Mangels an Stützpünkten unsererseits und des Ueberflusses Englands an solchen so aussichtslos, dass planmässig von dieser Kriegsart gegen England bei Feststellung unserer Flottenart abgesehen werden muss.
4. Unsere Flotte muss demnach so eingerichtet werden, dass sie ihre höchste Kriegsleistung zwischen Helgoland und der Themse entfalten kann.
5. Eine auf dieser Grundlage geschaffene Flotte entspricht auch unseren Bedürfnissen gegen Frankreich bis Brest oder Cherbourg und gegen Russland bis Kronstadt in so guter Weise, dass wir fürs Erste eine besondere Rücksicht auf diese Gegner bei der Abgrenzung der Arten und Bestimmung der Typen nicht zu nehmen haben. Voraussetzung hierbei ist, dass der Kohlenvorrath der einzelnen Schiffstypen hoch

APPENDIX

The Tirpitz Memorandum of June 1897

Very Secret June 1897

General Considerations on the Constitution of our Fleet according to Ship Classes and Designs

1. In the distinctions between one class of ship and another, and in the choice among ship designs within the various classes, the most difficult situation in war into which our fleet can come must be used as a basis. For that constitution of our naval force which meets the most difficult situation will be seen to be sufficient for all other situations. The limits of our resources prevent any attempt to meet every conceivable eventuality on its own in an ideal manner.
2. For Germany the most dangerous naval enemy at the present time is England. It is also the enemy against which we most urgently require a certain measure of naval force as a political power factor.
3. Commerce raiding and transatlantic war against England is so hopeless, because of the shortage of bases on our side and the superfluity on England's side, that we must ignore this type of war against England in our plans for the constitution of our fleet.
4. Our fleet must be so constructed that it can unfold its greatest military potential between Heligoland and the Thames.
5. A fleet constructed on this basis corresponds so well to our requirements, both against France as far as Brest or Cherbourg and against Russia as far as Kronstadt, that for the moment we need not pay particular attention to those enemies in the determination of our ship classes and in the selection of designs. The precondition here is that the coal capacity of the individual ship designs should be sufficiently large to permit a radius of action as far as Brest or Cherbourg.
6. The military situation against England demands battle-

genug für die Kriegsführung bis Brest oder Cherbourg bemessen ist.

6. Die militärische Situation gegen England erfordert Linienschiffe in so hoher Zahl wie möglich. Nach Massgabe unserer Entwicklungskraft, die beschränkt ist durch die Leistungsfähigkeit unserer Schiffsbau-, Panzerplatten-, und Waffenindustrie, durch die Ausdehnung unserer Kriegshäfen und Werften, durch die Möglichkeit, das erforderliche Personal auszubilden und die benöthigten Geldmittel flüssig zu machen, sowie auch nach unserer in den letzten Jahren durchgearbeiteten und erprobten Organisation, können wir bis auf Weiteres, d.h. etwa bis 1905, nicht mehr wie zwei volle Geschwader von je 8 Linienschiffen schaffen. Um auf diese Geschwader in voller Stärke im Mobilmachungsfall rechnen zu können ist Reservematerial unerlässlich. Das geringste Mass hierfür ist ein Schiff für jedes Geschwader, also zwei Schiffe für die Flotte. Es kann späterer Erfahrung überlassen bleiben, ob diese Zahl an Reserveschiffen ausreichend ist, um zwei Geschwader ununterbrochen verwendungsbereit zu halten.

7. Mit dem bestehenden Küstengeschwader (Siegfriedklasse) muss vorläufig als einer vorhandenen Grösse gerechnet werden.

8. Die Linienschiffe unserer Geschwader müssen für den Kampf in der Linie geeignet sein, dazu gehört vor allem gute Drehfähigkeit,[1] schwere Artillerie und ein so starker Panzer, dass das Durchsieben verhindert wird. In der Grösse der Linienschiffe werden wir wegen der Kosten und wegen der Tiefenverhältnisse unserer Gewässer zweckmässig nicht weiter gehen, als eine "gute"Geeignetheit für den Kampf in der Linie gerade bedingt.

9. Torpedostreitkräfte werden nach der alten Berechnungsweise zu 12 Divisionen auch fernerhin als eine für die Linienstreitkräfte entsprechende Zahl angesehen werden können.

10. Ueber Werth und Verwendungsweise von Aufklärungskräften (Kreuzern) in Verbindung mit der Entscheidungsflotte besitzen wir eine sehr viel geringere Kenntnis und Sicherheit als über Streitkräfte der Kampflinie. Gegen England sowie überhaupt gegen jede in unsere Gewässer eindringende Flotte tritt die Bedeutung der Aufklärungskräfte sehr zurück.

[1] Admiral Senden (pencilled comment): "Hohe Geschwindigkeit".

ships in as great a number as possible. Given the measure of our powers of development, which are limited by the capacity of our shipbuilding, armour and armament industries, by the expansion of our military harbours and shipyards, by the possibility of training the necessary personnel and making available the necessary funds, and by our organisation which has been developed and tested in the last few years, we cannot create in the near future, that is, roughly up to 1905, more than two full squadrons of eight battleships each. Reserve material is vital in order to be able to count on these squadrons at full strength in case of mobilisation. The minimum here is one ship for each squadron, *i.e.*, two ships for the fleet. It can be left to later experience to say whether this number of reserve vessels is sufficient to maintain two squadrons in uninterrupted operational readiness.

7. The present coastal squadron ("Siegfried" Class) must temporarily be considered as an existing quantity.

8. The battleships for our squadrons must be designed for actions in the line. This demands above all flexibility of the line,[1] heavy guns and armour thick enough to prevent hits from penetrating. Because of the cost and also because of the depth of our home waters, we shall be prudent if we go no further in the displacement of our battleships than a "good" capability for action in the line makes absolutely necessary.

9. Torpedo boat forces can still reasonably be estimated, by using the established calculations, at twelve divisions. This number should be quite adequate for the forces we plan to have in the line.

10. We possess much less experience and certainty about the value and means of using scouting groups in association with the main body of the fleet than we do about the forces in the fighting line. Against England, indeed against any fleet penetrating our home waters, the value of scouting vessels is much reduced. In principal therefore we shall be wise not to make the relationship between reconnaissance vessels and the fleet larger than absolutely necessary; such vessels represent in a sense a reduction from the forces needed for the ultimate outcome.

11. In the case of reconnaissance vessels, we have to remember

[1] Admiral Senden (pencil comment): "High speed."

Wir werden daher grundsätzlich die Aufklärungskräfte im Verhältnis zur Flotte nicht grösser machen als durchaus erforderlich; dieselben stellen gewissermassen einen Abzug von der für die Entscheidung dienenden Kraft dar.

11. Bei der Aufklärungskräften haben wir zu berücksichtigen, dass sie "detachiert" verwendet werden. Dies erfordert einmal gewisse strategische Eigenschaften, die ich als genügend studiert hier annehmen will. Diesen strategischen Erfordernissen müssen sämtliche Arten von Aufklärungsschiffen ausreichend gerecht werden.

Es gibt zwei Arten von Detachierungen auf See. Bei der einen muss man taktisch stark sein, bei der anderen kommt es weniger oder gar nicht hierauf an, sondern hauptsächlich auf das Vorhandensein eines Schiffsindividuums. Dieser Umstand führt naturgemäss zu einem grossen und einem kleinen Kreuzer. Bei der zur Zeit noch nicht genügend geklärten Erfahrung über Werth und Verwendungsweise der Aufklärungskräfte, zumal in einem Kriege gegen England, wird es sich empfehlen, in die grossen Kreuzer nicht allzuviel Kapital und Personal hineinzustecken, vielmehr den Schiffstyp thunlichst klein zu wählen. Der grosse Kreuzer muss aber doch Kraft zum Stehen und daher einen gewissen Grad von Linienqualität besitzen. Damit ist nicht gemeint, dass der grosse Kreuzer auch geeignet sein soll, in die Linien unserer heimischen Schlachtflotte einrangiert zu werden.

Den anderen Kreuzer darf man nur so gross machen, als nothwendig ist, um ausreichende Geschwindigkeit auch bei schlechterem Wetter zu bewahren. 3,000 Tonnen müssen also für die Hauptzwecke des kleinen Kreuzers als ausreichend angesehen werden. Dass es trotzdem einzelne Fälle gibt, wo ein 3,000 Tonnen Kreuzer in der Nordsee bei schwerem Sturm und Dampfen recht gegenan an Leistung nicht unerheblich nachlässt, kann und darf nicht bestimmend sein.

12. Die taktische Stärke einer Aufklärung muss durch die Gruppierung oder durch den Zusammenschluss mehrerer Gruppen den Bedürfnissen nach geregelt werden. Es ist daher eine falsche Richtung, wenn sich die Aufklärungsgruppe planmässig und reglementarisch zu einer Gefechtsdivision entwickelt. Damit soll natürlich nicht bezweifelt werden, dass sie im gegebenen Fall sich zu einer ihrer Zusammensetzung

that they can be used "detached". This requires, in the first place, certain strategic characteristics which here I shall assume to be sufficiently studied. All types of reconnaissance vessels must take account of these strategic requirements.

There are two types of detachment at sea. In the first, one must be tactically strong, while in the second it is less a question of strength than of the presence of an individual vessel. These facts lead naturally to a large and a small cruiser. Since we do not at present have sufficient experience about the value and operations of scouting vessels, especially in a war with England, it would be wise not to stick too much capital and personnel into the large cruiser, but rather to choose the smallest possible ship design. The large cruiser must, of course, have the force to resist and must thus possess a certain measure of the quality of vessels of the line. This does not mean that the heavy cruiser should be designed to lie in the line of our home battle fleet.

The other cruiser should be made only as large as is necessary to preserve sufficient speed even in rather bad weather. 3,000 tons must thus be considered appropriate for the main purposes of a small cruiser. That there are nevertheless individual cases where a 3,000 ton cruiser in the North Sea in heavy weather and under full steam loses a great deal of its usefulness can and must not be decisive.

12. The tactical strength of reconnaissance vessels must be controlled by grouping or by combinations of several groups depending on the requirements. To try to design, develop and organize scout vessels into fixed fighting units would be the wrong thing to do. Naturally one cannot doubt that in certain cases reconnaissance vessels must combine to form a unit corresponding to their composition. There are, for example, individual groups of:

2 large and 2 small cruisers
1 ,, ,, 2 ,, ,,
1 ,, ,, 3 ,, ,, possibly also strengthened
1 ,, ,, 4 ,, ,, by battleships;

or also some composed of two or three small cruisers without large ones. It would not be wise to try to seek the tactical strength of a group (apart from coastal waters) in the small cruisers. In the interests of the fleet as a whole, these latter

entsprechenden Gefechtsformation zusammenschliessen muss. Es gibt Einzelgruppen, z.B.

von 2 grossen und 2 kleinen Kreuzer
„ 1 „ „ 2 „ „
„ 1 „ „ 3 „ „
eventl. noch verstärkt
„ 1 „ „ 4 „ „ durch Linienschiffe;

ferner solche von 2 oder 3 kleinen Kreuzer ohne grosse Kreuzer. Es wäre nicht zweckmässig die taktische Stärke einer Gruppe (Küstengewässer abgesehen) in den kleinen Kreuzern suchen zu wollen. Letztere sind der Gesamtflotte wegen möglichst billig gehalten, nur dadurch ist es möglich, eine grosse Zahl der Aufklärungsschiffe bereit halten zu können, ohne unverhältnismässig Geld und Kraft in dieselben hineinzustecken. Die kleinen Kreuzer werden besonders dann verwendet werden, wenn die Detachierung die Entfernung von dem voraussichtlichen Kampfplatz und demzufolge das Nicht-zur-Stelle-sein beim Kampfe in sich schliesst. Das gilt sowohl für den Gruppen-als auch für den Geschwaderkampf. Eine Flotte, die planmässig keine gefechtsschwachen Kreuzer zum Detachieren besitzt, wäre unrichtig zusammengesetzt.

13. Obwohl wahrscheinlich über das Erfordernis (freilich gewiss nicht über den Wunsch des Befehlshabers) gehend, ist bei der deutschen Flotte, die gegen England aufgebaut ist, die früher geschätzte Zahl von 6 Gruppen zu 6 grossen und 18 kleinen Kreuzern festgehalten worden. In der Zahl der kleinen Kreuzer liegen die Wiederholer.

14. Das gibt im Ganzen eine Flotte von

1 Flottenflaggschiff
2 Geschwadern zu je 8 Linienschiffen } = 19 Linienschiffe
2 Schiffen als Reservematerial

Es kann der Erfahrung bis 1905 überlassen bleiben, ob das vorstehend angesetzte Reservematerial auf die Dauer genügt.

1 Geschwader zu 8 Küstenpanzerschiffen
6 grossen Kreuzern
18 kleinen Kreuzern

Reservematerial ist bei den Kreuzern nicht vorgesehen. Dasselbe liegt in der Reserve für das Ausland.

must be kept as cheap as possible. Only in this way is it possible to keep ready a large number of scouting vessels without investing inappropriate sums of money and energy in them. The small cruisers are especially suitable for operations where the detachment involves distance from the probable place of battle and therefore their absence from the spot during the battle. This holds true both for the group and squadron engagements. A fleet which possessed no lightly armoured cruisers for planned detachment would not be correctly composed.

13. Although probably more than necessary (to be sure, less than a commander might wish) for a German fleet to be built against England, we have accepted the number estimated earlier of six reconnaissance groups composed of six large and 18 small cruisers. In the number of small cruisers, the older types are included.

14. That makes in total a Home Fleet of

1 fleet flagship
2 squadrons of 8 battleships } = 19 battleships
2 ships as reserve material

We can leave it to our experience up to 1905 to decide whether the number of reserve ships stated above will be sufficient in the long run.

1 squadron of 8 coastal armoured ships
6 large cruisers
18 small cruisers

Reserve material has not been provided for the cruisers. It is contained in the reserve for overseas service.

15. The ships of the overseas service may be regarded as detached from the home fleet, mainly because we do not possess wholly adequate bases for operations (fortified shipyards with dry docks). This state of affairs suggests that for the time being we should employ naval vessels which correspond to the characteristics of the scouting vessels at home. This basic principle of design is supported by the requirement that all vessels on duty abroad be able to combine as perfectly as possible with any support vessels from the home fleet and, accordingly, be able to form groups with them. At the same time, vessels withdrawn from overseas duty must fit into the home fleet.

15. Die Schiffe des Auslandsdienstes sind als detachiert von der Heimath aufzufassen, insbesondere weil wir vollständig ausreichende Operationsbasen (befestigte Werft mit Dock) nicht besitzen. Dieser Umstand spricht dafür, dass wir bis auf Weiteres Seestreitkräfte verwenden, die den Eigenschaften der Aufklärungskräfte unserer Heimath entsprechen. Diese Typengrundlage wird bestärkt durch das Erfordernis, dass die im Ausland befindlichen Schiffe möglichst vollkommen an etwaigen Nachschub aus der Heimathsflotte anpassen, und entsprechend in dieselben eingliedern können, und umgekehrt die zurückgezogene Auslandsschiffe in die Heimathsflotte hineinpassen.

16. Es muss daher als Grundsatz festgehalten werden, dass dies für das Ausland planmässig vorgesehenen Schiffe so lange gemäss den Typengrundsätzender Heimath konstruiert werden, als eine Nothwendigkeit davon abzuweichen nicht durch die Erfahrung bewiesen ist. Das ist bisher nicht der Fall gewesen. Nur bei strenger Festhaltung dieses Grundsatzes und des Gesichtspunktes, dass der Typ der einzelnen Schiffsgattung sich dem Bedürfnis und der Höchstleistung der Gesamtflotte unterzuordnen hat, werden wir in der Typenentwicklung folgerichtig vorwärts kommen. Würden als Masstab für die Typenbestimmung einer Schiffart vorhandene Schiffe gegnerischer Nationen genommen mit dem Gedanken, dass wir ein Schiff bauen wollten, das diesem fremden Schiff gewachsen sei, so würden wir gedrängt in unseren eigenen Typen beständig zu wechseln. Wir werden nie eine folgerichtige, der Tageströmung entzogene Entwicklung unserer Typen erreichen und werden die Höchstleistung unserer Flotte schädigen.

Wir müssen uns durchaus die stolze Initiative sowohl für die Gruppierung der Schiffsarten zur Flotte wie zur militärischen und hoffentlich auch zur technischen Entwicklung unserer Typen bewahren. Eine gewisse Sparsamkeit, wenn man will Einseitigkeit, in der Zahl der Typen ist wichtiger als das Gegenteil. Der Umstand, dass gelegentlich ein einzelner im Ausland befindlicher Kreuzer hierdurch in Nachteil versetzt werden könnte, darf nicht bestimmend sein, denn nur der Hauptkriegsschauplatz ist entscheidend. In diesem Sinne ist die Typenbestimmung im Frieden ausgeübte Seestrategie. Im übrigen wird in der Wirklichkeit nie verhindert werden

16. We must therefore establish as our basic principle that vessels provided for overseas service must be constructed according to the design specifications of the home fleet, as long as the necessity to depart from them is not demonstrated by experience. So far that has not been the case. Only if we hold firmly to this principle and to the view that the design of each individual class of vessel must be subordinate to the requirements and overall performance of the entire fleet, shall we be able to make the development of our designs logical. If we were to take existing ships of foreign nations as the standard for the design of our own and to try always to match their performance, we should be compelled constantly to change our own designs. We should never arrive at a development of consistent designs, uninfluenced by the fashion of the day, and we should impair the maximum performance of our fleet.

We must maintain for ourselves a certain proud initiative, both in the grouping of classes of ships within the fleet and in the military, and hopefully also in the technical, development of our designs. A measure of economy, perhaps even of one-sidedness, in the number of designs is more important than its opposite. The fact that occasionally an individual cruiser overseas may be weaker than its opponent must never be considered important. Only the main theatre of war will be decisive. In this sense the selection of a ship design in peace-time is applied naval strategy. It will never be possible, in any event, to prevent a German ship occasionally confronting a stronger adversary. It is a delusion to imagine that it is possible to meet such an eventuality by the appropriate choice of ship types.

17. In all those situations abroad where we want to have available the weight of real sea power, we shall have to revert to ships with the quality of vessels of the line. In view of the detached position of our ships overseas, the large cruiser at present meets this need better than the battleship. This cruiser is the appropriate vessel of the line in encounters with small transatlantic nations. Wherever larger forces are necessary, these ships can be formed into divisions and possibly into squadrons (the cruiser division). In such encounters, and also for the command of weakly fortified coastal positions, a situation often likely to confront our transatlantic naval forces, vessels without armour would be totally inadequate.

können, dass ein deutsches Schiff gelegentlich auf einen stärkeren Gegner stösst. Es ist ein Trugschluss, wenn man hofft, einer solchen Möglichkeit durch geeignete Typenbestimmung begegnen zu können.

17. Da, wo wir im Ausland das Gewicht wirklicher Seestreitkraft zur Verfügung haben wollen, werden wir auf Schiffe mit Linienqualität zurückgreifen müssen. Mit Rücksicht auf die detachierte Lage unserer Auslandsschiffe entsprechen die grossen Kreuzer diesem Bedürfnis zur Zeit besser als die Linienschiffe. Dieser Kreuzer ist das planmässige Linienschiff bei Differenzen mit transatlantischen kleinen Nationen. Dort, wo grössere Kräfte erforderlich sind, werden sich diese Schiffe zur Division und eventl. zum Geschwader formieren müssen (Kreuzer-Division). Sowohl hierfür als auch für die Bekämpftung von schwächeren Küstenstellungen, was besonders häufig für unsere transatlantischen Seestreitkräfte in Erwägung kommt würden ungepanzerte Schiffe gänzlich unzureichend sein.

Andererseits bestimmt das Bedürfnis den Suez-Kanal passieren zu können, die oberste Grössengrenze für die Streitkräfte, die zwischen der Ostküste Afrikas und der Westküste Amerikas stehen, und damit um der Einheitlichkeit willen für unsere grossen Kreuzer überhaupt. Ausländische Hafen- und Dockverhältnisse, sowie der Kostenpunkt machen es sogar wünschenswerth, mit der Grösse noch weiter hierunterzugehen als der Suez-Kanal unbedingt erfordern würde. Unter diesen Umständen scheinen 8,000 Tonnen schon eine hoch gewählte Grössengrenze für die grossen Kreuzer zu sein. Der Ehrgeiz, diesen Schiffen vollgültige Linienqualität zu geben und sie gleichzeitig geeignet machen zu wollen, in die heimische Schlachtflotte einrangiert werden zu können, würde zu unrichtiger Typenbestimmung führen; wohl aber bleibt es, z.B. für Gruppenkämpfe, dringend wünschenswerth, dass 2 grosse Kreuzer eine Chance gegen ein einzelnes Linienschiff behalten.

18. Ausser den grossen Kreuzern brauchen wir im Auslande Schiffe, bei denen mehr die Flagge wirken soll als die vorhandene Kraft oder für deren militärische Aufgabe (z.B. gegen Wilde oder unbefestigte Landstellungen) eine kleine Kraft genügt. Diese Schiffe entsprechen den kleinen Kreuzern, durch die der Abzug einer nur geringen Streitkraft ermöglicht wird.

On the other hand, the need to pass through the Suez Canal sets the upper limit on the displacement of those vessels stationed between the east coast of Africa and the west coast of America, and thus, in the interests of uniformity, on all our large cruisers. Overseas harbour and dockyard facilities as well as considerations of cost make it desirable to reduce the size of such vessels even further than the Suez Canal makes absolutely necessary. Under such circumstances, 8,000 tons seems to be almost too large a planned displacement for the heavy cruisers. The ambition to give these ships full-fledged quality as ships of the line and at the same time to make them suitable for service with the battle fleet at home must lead to an improper choice of design. Admittedly, it remains vitally necessary, for example, in encounters between small groups, that two large cruisers should have a chance against one individual battleship.
18. In addition to the large cruisers, we need vessels overseas whose effect depends more on the flag than on any existing force of their own or whose military tasks (for example, against natives or unfortified land positions) require very little force. These vessels correspond to the small cruisers. They permit the detachment of a relatively minimal fighting force.
19. For the overseas service planned for the years up to 1905, the following ships have been provided:

3 large cruisers
9 small cruisers
4 gunboats

In addition a reserve at home to strengthen the above of:

3 large cruisers
3 small cruisers

It can be left to the further development of Germany's interests at sea to decide whether an additional strengthening of our forces overseas after 1905 is needed.
20. In total, the following ships are required:

19 battleships (2 as reserve)
8 armoured coastal ships
12 large cruisers (3 overseas reserve)
30 small cruisers (3 overseas reserve)
12 torpedo boat divisions

19. Es sind bis 1905 für den planmässigen Auslandsdienst in Aussicht genommen:

3 grosse Kreuzer
9 kleine Kreuzer
4 Kanonenboote

Ausserdem eine Schiffsreserve in der Heimath zur Verstärkung von:

3 grossen Kreuzern
3 kleinen Kreuzern

Es kann der Entwicklung der Seeinteressen Deutschlands überlassen bleiben, ob nach 1905 eine weitere Verstärkung unserer Auslandsstreitkräfte erforderlich wird.

20. Im Ganzen sind erforderlich

19 Linienschiffe (2 Reservematerial)
8 Küstenpanzerschiffe
12 grosse Kreuzer (3 Auslandsreserve)
30 kleine Kreuzer (3 Auslandsreserve)
12 Torpedobootsdivisionen

Diese Flotte lässt sich in ihrer Hauptsache bereits bis 1905 fertigstellen. Die Ausgaben für Schiffsbau einschl. Artillerie und Torpedoarmierung betragen 408 Millionen Mark oder jährlich 58 Millionen Mark, ausserdem über 1904-5 hinausreichende Restraten von 72 Millionen Mark. Das Ordinarium wird durch Schaffung einer derartigen Flotte jährlich um etwa 4 Millionen Mark steigen, mithin im Jahre 1904-05 86 Millionen betragen.

21. In die planmässige Flotte sind Kanonenboote und Schiffe zu besonderen Zwecke nicht aufgenommen, weil man die erforderliche Zahl nicht in ähnlicher Weise vorhersehen kann, sie ausserdem für die politische Bedeutung unserer Flotte ohne Belang sind.

22. In der anliegenden Tabelle sind einige Vergleichsmomente zwischen der zuerst und der jetzt geplanten Flotte zusammengestellt.

This fleet can be largely completed by 1905. The expenditure for shipbuilding, including guns and torpedo armaments, will amount to M 408 million or 58 million per annum, plus final payments after 1905 of 72 million. The ordinary estimates will be increased by 4 million per annum as well, thus reaching 86 million by the fiscal year 1904/5.

21. Gunboats and vessels of other description have not been included in the estimates for the fleet, because we cannot predict precisely the numbers we shall need. In any case such vessels are without importance for the political significance of our fleet.

22. In the attached table, a few points of comparison have been set out between the fleet as it was initially planned and as now amended.

VERGLEICH

zwischen der zuerst und der jetzt in Aussicht genommenen Flotte

zu vergleichen	ZUERST	JETZT	ERLÄUTERUNGEN
1) Planmässige Zusammensetzung	4 Typen: 17 Linienschiffe 8 grosse Kreuzer (10.000 Tonnen) 30 Mittelkreuzer (6.600 Tonnen) 16 kleine Kreuzer (2–3.000 Tonnen) bis 1910	3 Typen: 19 Linienschiffe 12 grosse Kreuzer (8.500 Tonnen) 30 kleine Kreuzer (3.000 Tonnen) bis 1905	VORLÄUFIG bis 1905 bereits mehr: 2 Linienschiffe 4 Panzerkreuzer Ausserdem noch 5 Jahre zum weiteren Ausbau
2) Deplacement der Schiffe *mit* Seitenpanzer (in tausend Tonnen)	250 (bis 1910)	292 (bis 1905)	
3) Deplacement der Schiffe *ohne* Seitenpanzer (in tausend Tonnen)	238	81	
4) Prozentsatz des ungepanzerten Deplacements	48% (etwa die Hälfte)	22% (etwa ein Fünftel)	
5) Gesamt Schiffsbaukosten in Millionen Mark (nach Ersatz sämtlicher vorhandenen Schiffe)	848	708	Einheitssätze: Linienschiffe 20 Mill. Mark 10.000 ton Kreuzer 18 Mill. Mark 8.500 ton Kreuzer 15 Mill. Mark 6.600 ton Kreuzer 10 Mill. Mark 3.000 ton Kreuzer 5.5 Mill. Mark 2.500 ton Kreuzer 4 Mill. Mark
6) Nach dem Gesetzentwurf sind für Schiffsbau (einschl. Artillerie und Torpedoarmierung) aufzuwenden:	bis 1910 nicht ermittelt	bis 1905 408 Millionen Mark	Die Differenz mit der vorhergehenden Reihe erklärt sich aus der bis 1905 noch vorhandenen älteren Schiffe deren Altersgrenze noch nicht erreicht ist.
7) Steigerung der laufenden Ausgaben:	bis 1910: (nicht durchgearbeitet) Steigerung geschätzt auf etwa 90 Mill. Mark Jetzt: 58 „ „ 1910: 150 „ „	bis 1905: Steigerung: 28 Mill. Mark Jetzt: 58 „ „ 1905: 86 „ „	
8) Personalvermehrung	20.558 jährlich 1.722 (bis 1910)	7.973 jährlich 1.139 (bis 1905)	
9) Jährliche Schiffsbauquote	nicht berechnet	Durchschnittlich bis 1905 58.4 Mill. Mark	1897/98 bewilligt: 49.1 Mill. Mark

COMPARISON

between the Fleet as first planned and as it is now projected

To compare	First	Now	Comments
1) Planned establishment	4 Types: 17 battleships 8 large cruisers (10,000 tons) 30 medium cruisers (6,600 tons) 16 small cruisers (2–3,000 tons) To 1910	3 Types: 19 battleships 12 large cruisers (8,500 tons) 30 small cruisers (3,000 tons) To 1905	Provisionally to 1905: Already achieved 2 battleships, 4 large armoured cruisers, plus 5 additional years for further construction
2) Displacement of ships WITH armoured sides (in thousand tons)	250 (to 1910)	292 (to 1905)	
3) Displacement of ships WITHOUT armoured sides (in thousand tons)	238	81	
4) Percentage of total displacement without armour	48% (approx ½)	22% (approx ⅕)	
5) Total cost of shipbuilding (in million Marks) after replacement of all existing vessels	848	708	Uniform rates: battleships 20 Mill. Mks 10,000 ton cruiser 18 Mill. Mks 8,500 ton cruiser 15 Mill. Mks 6,600 ton cruiser 10 Mill. Mks 3,000 ton cruiser 5·5 Mill. Mks 2,500 ton cruiser 4 Mill. Mks
6) According to the draft Bill it is expected to spend on shipbuilding including artillery and torpedo armaments	To 1910 NOT CALCULATED	To 1905 408 Million Marks	The difference with the row above arises from the number of ships which will not have reached replacement age by 1905
7) Increase in the ordinary expenditure	To 1910 (not calculated) estimated at approx.: 90 Mill. Mks Now: 58 Mill. Mks 1910: 150 Mill. Mks	To 1905 Increase: 28 Mill. Mks Now: 58 Mill. Mks 1905: 86 Mill. Mks	
8) Increase in personnel	20,558 per annum: 1,722 (to 1910)	7,973 per annum: 1,139 (to 1905)	
9) Annual rate of expenditure on shipbuilding	Not calculated	On average to 1905 58·4 Mill. Mks	In 1897/98 estimates as passed: 49·1 Mill. Mks

Bibliography

Berlau, A. J., *The German Social Democratic Party* (Columbia University, 1949).

Bismarck, Otto von, *Mensch und Staat: Aus den Briefen, Reden und Schriften* (Munich, 1956).

Brandenburg, Erich, *Vom Bismarck zum Weltkriege* (Berlin, 1924).

Bruck, W. F., *Social and Economic History of Germany, 1888–1938* (Cardiff, 1938).

Bülow, B. v., *Memoirs, 1897–1903* (English trans., 4 vols., London, 1931).

Conze, Werner, "Friedrich Naumann—Grundlagen und Ansatz seiner Politik in der nationalsozialen Zeit", *Schicksalswege deutscher Vergangenheit*, Festschrift für S. Kaehler (Dusseldorf, 1950).

Craig, Gordon A., *The Politics of the Prussian Army* (Oxford, 1955).

Demeter, Karl, *Das deutsche Heer und seine Offiziere* (Berlin, 1930).

Donner, Herman, *Die Vorgeschichte des Weltkrieges, eine Sammlung aller wichtigsten Daten, 1870–1914* (Berlin, 1932).

Einem, K. von, "Fürst Bülow und das deutsche Heer", in Thimme, Friedrich, *Front wider Bülow, Staatsmänner, Diplomaten und Forscher zu seinen Denkwürdigkeiten* (Munich, 1931).

Eyck, Erich, *Das persönliche Regiment Wilhelms II* (Erlangen/Zurich, 1948).

Görlitz, Walter, "Einleitung", *Kriegstagebücher, Aufzeichnungen und Briefe des Chefs des Marine-Kabinetts Admiral Georg Alexander von Müller, 1914–1918* (Göttingen, 1959). *The Kaiser and His Court* (Macdonald, London, 1961).

Haller, J., *Aus dem Leben des Fürsten Philipp zu Eulenburg-Hertefeldt* (Berlin, 1924).

Hallmann, Hans, *Der Weg zum deutschen Schlachtflottenbau* (Stuttgart, 1933).

Hallmann, Hans, *Krügerdepesche und Flottenfrage* (Stuttgart, 1927).

Hassell, Ulrich von, *Tirpitz* (Stuttgart, 1920).

Heer, Friedrich, *Europäische Geistesgeschichte* (Stuttgart, 1953.)

Hinsley, F. H., *Power and the Pursuit of Peace* (Cambridge, 1963).

Hohenlohe-Schillingsfürst, Chlodwig Fürst zu, *Denkwürdigkeiten der Reichskanzlerzeit*, ed. K. A. von Müller (Stuttgart/Berlin, 1931).

Hollyday, F. B. M., *Bismarck's Rival, A Political Biography of Albrecht von Stosch* (Durham, North Carolina, 1960).

The Holstein Papers, *The Memoirs, Diaries and Correspondence of Friedrich von Holstein*, ed., by Norman Rich and M. H. Fisher (4 vols., Cambridge, 1955–1963).

Howe, Günter, "Gedanken zur deutschen Wehrpolitik zwischen 1871 und 1914", *Weltmachtstreben und Flottenbau*, ed. W. Schüssler (Witten/Ruhr, 1956).

Hubatsch, Walther, *Die Ära Tirpitz* (Göttingen, 1955); *Der Admiralstab und die obersten Marinebehörden in Deutschland, 1849–1945* (Frankfurt/Main, 1958).

Hurd, Archibald S., "The Kaiser's Dream of Sea Power", *Nineteenth Century and After* (August, 1906, London).

Kehr, Eckart, "Schlachtflottenbau und Parteipolitik", *Historische Studien*, cxcvii (Berlin, 1930).

Kohn, Hans, *The Mind of Germany* (New York, 1960).

Kruck, Alfred, *Geschichte des Alldeutschen Verbands* (Wiesbaden, 1954).

Langer, William L., *The Diplomacy of Imperialism* (New York, 1935).

Marder, A. J., *British Naval Policy 1880–1905. The Anatomy of British Sea Power* (London, 1940).

Marienfeld, Wolfgang, "Wissenschaft und Schlachtflottenbau in Deutschland, 1897-1906", *Marine Rundschau*, Beiheft 2 (April, 1957).

Marriott, J. A. R., and Robertson, C. G., *The Evolution of Prussia* (Oxford, 1937).

Moltke, Generaloberst Helmuth von, *Erinnerungen, Briefe, Dokumente* (Stuttgart, 1922).

Monts, Anton Graf v., *Erinnerungen und Gedanken*, ed. by K. Nowak and F. Thimme (Berlin, 1932).

Nichols, J. Alden, *Germany After Bismarck* (Cambridge, Mass., 1958).

Nowak, Karl Friedrich, *Das dritte deutsche Kaiserreich* (2 vols., Berlin, 1929 and 1931).
Rathenau, Walther, *Autonome Wirtschaft* (Jena, 1919).
Reventlow, Ernst zu, *Deutschlands auswärtige Politik* (3. Aufl., Berlin, 1916).
Richter, Werner, *Bismarck* (Frankfurt/Main, 1962; Macdonald, London, 1964).
Ritter, Gerhard, *Staatskunst und Kriegshandwerk: Das Problem des 'Militarismus' in Deutschland* (2 vols., Munich, 1954 and 1960).
Rogge, H., *Holstein und Harden* (Munich, 1959).
Roskill, Captain S. W., *The Strategy of Sea Power* (London, 1962).
Schieder, Theodor, *Das Deutsche Kaiserreich von 1871 als Nationalstaat* (Cologne/Opladen, 1961).
Schröder, E., "Albrecht von Stosch", *Historische Studien*, cccliii (Berlin, 1939).
Schulze-Hinrichs, A., *Tirpitz* (Göttingen, 1958).
Schüssler, Wilhelm, "Deutsche Weltpolitik 1890 bis 1914", *Weltmachtstreben und Flottenbau*, ed. by W. Schüssler (Witten/Ruhr, 1956).
Stadelmann, Rudolf, "Die Epoche der deutsch-englischen Flottenrivalität", *Deutschland und Westeuropa* (Schloss-Laupheim, 1948).
Steinberg, Jonathan, "A German Plan for the Invasion of Holland and Belgium: 1897", *The Historical Journal* (Cambridge, March, 1963).
Tirpitz, Alfred von, *Erinnerungen* (Leipzig, 1920).
Tuchman, Barbara W., *The Guns of August* (New York, 1962).
Wilson, C. H., "Economic Conditions", *The New Cambridge Modern History*, xi (Cambridge, 1962).
Zedlitz-Trützschler, Graf Robert, *Zwölf Jahre am deutschene Kaiserhof* (Berlin, 1924).

Index

Note: "Navy Law" refers to the Navy Law of 1898, unless otherwise specified.

Adalbert (Wilhelm Adalbert), Prince of Prussia (1811–1873): creation of German Navy (1848), 37
Adenauer, Konrad (1876–): 178, 203
Albrecht, King of Saxony (1828–1902): 114
Anglo-German Naval Arms Race: *see* Naval Arms Race
Anglo-German relations: *see* Great Britain, *and* German Empire of 1871
Anti-Semitism: 34, 177, 178
Arnim-Muskau, Count Hermann von (1839–1919): 168, 183
Associated Governments of the German Empire: 76, 164, 172, 191, 193; constitutional basis, 48
Association of German Industrialists: 173
Auer, Ignaz (1846–1907): 59
Austro-Hungarian Alliance: 203

Baden, Grand Duke of: *see* Friedrich I
Badische Landeszeitung: 141
Ballin, Albert (1857–1918): 179; on Bülow's character, 152
Barth, Dr. Theodor (1849–1909): 35, 153, 167
Bassermann, Ernst (1854–1917): 183
Battleships: active life of, 146; advocated by Stosch, 66, by Tirpitz, 19, 83–4, 127, by Wilhelm II, 117; "Baden" class, 122; effect of Krüger Telegram, 85; favoured by High Command, 72, 81, 121–2; neglected by Hollmann, 19, and by Caprivi, 66–7; number constructed under Navy Law, 134–5, 146; in Royal Navy, 174–5; "Sachsen" class, replacement of, 146
Bauernbund: 47, 115
Bavaria: constitutional position in Empire, 32, 46–7; and Navy Law, 179; and reform of courts-martial, 77, 153; separatism, 34, 93, 188–9
Bavaria, Prince Regent of: *see* Luitpold
Bebel, August (1840–1913): 59, 183, 192; on financing of Navy Law, 188; mocks National Liberals, 45; speech on Navy Law, 194–5
Bennigsen, Rudolf von (1824–1902): 45, 95, 183, 186, 187; amendment, 192; compromise on financing of Navy Law, 187–8; and naval expansion, 86
Berliner Neuesten Nachrichten: 116, 159
Berliner Tageblatt: 160
Bernstorff, Count Andreas von (1844–1907): 170
Bismarck-Schönhausen, Prince Otto von (1815–1898): 110, 115, 151, 153, 189, 199, 200, 204, 205; and Britain, 163; death of, 199; and German Empire (of 1871), 32, 33, 44; on Kiaochow, 172; and naval expansion, 63, 67, 171–2; and office of Reich Chancellor, 49, 98; and Reinsurance Treaty, 105–6; relations with Reichstag, 34, 46, 162, 178; and Tirpitz, 140–1, 171–2; on violations of neutrality, 23; and Wilhelm II, 49, 105–6
Boer Republic: German policy towards, 72, 76, 82–3, 116; Jameson Raid on, 82–3
Boer War: 202
Boetticher, Karl Heinrich von (1833–1907): dismissal, 120, 125
Borckenhagen, Kapt. z. S. Ludwig: 106

Bosse, Julius Robert (1832–1901): 188–9, 204
Brandenburg, Professor Erich (1868–1946): *Vom Bismarck zum Weltkriege*, 26
Brandenburg Provincial Diet: 110
Braun, Kapt.-Lt. Otto (? –1896): 103–4
Brefeld, Ludwig (1837–1907): 188
Bremen: 41, 173
Brentano, Professor Lujo (1844–1931): 41, 179
Bronsart von Schellendorf, General Walter von (1833–1914): alarmed at seizure of Kiaochow, 155; and Wilhelm II, 82–3
Büchsel, Rear-Adm. Wilhelm (1848–1920): 116, 122, 130, 132, 134, 137, 139; on financial objections to fixed Navy Law, 139
Bülow, Prince Bernhard von (1849–1929): 59, 73, 109, 196, 198; character, 151–2, 199; appointed State Secretary of Foreign Ministry, 125; influence on Wilhelm II, 152; and Navy Law, 147, 182; role in Wilhelm II's Italian trip (1904) questioned, 54–5; "Place in the Sun" speech, 59–60; on Senden, 102; on Tirpitz, 116
Bülow, Bernhard Ernst von (1815–1879): 151–2
Bundesrath: 91, 113, 147, 148, 151, 158, 164, 169, 187, 190; function and position, 48; and naval expansion, 86, 141; Navy Law, 159
Bündnisfähigkeit("Alliance-worthiness"): 84, 206; concept developed by Stosch, 66

Capelle, Korv.-Kapt. Eduard (1855–1931): 131, 134, 139, 141, 144, 159, 176, 192; Tirpitz's opinion of, 132
Caprivi, Count Georg Leo von (1831–1899): as Chief of Admiralty, 39; development of strategic plans under, 67–8; dismissed (1888), 62–3, 67, 86; as Reich Chancellor, domestic crises and resignation, 72; foreign policy of, 35, 72, 105; inter-departmental and naval disputes, 111
Carnot, President Sadi (1837–1894): 72
Cassini, Count A. P.: 104
Centre Party: attitude to naval expansion and Navy Law, 36, 86, 114, 115, 153, 168–70, 175, 177–8, 185–6, 188, 189–90, 192, 193–4, 195–6; attitude to reform of courts-martial, 47, 115, 153; as government party, 34, 60, 172, 178, 179, 191, 203; opposition to Law of Association Amendment Bill, 119; relations with Tirpitz, 162, 189–90, 203–4; threatened by federalist pressures, 47, 115, 153, 169, 172, 178–9, 186–7, 188–9, 203; and Wilhelm II, 114, 117, 118
Chancellor, Reich: *see* Constitution of the German Empire, Bismarck, Caprivi, Hohenlohe *and* Bülow, Bernhard von
Chartered Company: 82
China: German interest in, 74–5, 104–5, 154–5; *see also* Kiaochow
Christian Democratic Union: 178, 203
Coerper, Korv.-Kapt. Carl (1854– ?): 132
Colomb, Vice-Adm. Philip Howard (1831–1899): 174
Committee for the Further Development of the German Fleet: 84; disagreements on, 94
Congress of Vienna (1815): 29
Conservative Party: 177, 178; attitude to Navy Law, 153, 167, 186, 193; and naval expansion, 86; in Reichstag, 34
Conservative *Reichspartei:* 34, 168, 177, 183
Constitution of German Empire: federal structure of, 46–7, 188–9; Kaiser's position under, 48, 49, 56, 110, 204, 205; Kaiser's powers of command over Army and Navy, 70, 76–7, 197; position of Reich Chancellor, 48–9, 51, 98, 110, 119–20; position of State Secretary of Imperial Naval Office, 113–14, 191; relations between Reich and Prussia, 44, 46–7, 112, 176, 198
Conze, Professor Werner: 38
"Copenhagen" complex: relation to Risk Theory, 21
Courts-martial: reform of procedures, 76–7, 97, 117, 153
Cowes: Wilhelm II's visit to (1895): 76
Cruisers: 19, 37, 73–4, 80, 83–5, 87–8, 93–4, 96, 106, 112, 121–2, 127–8, 133, 138, 144, 157, 184, 213, 215, 217, 219; *see also* German Navy, ships

Dahlmann, Friedrich Christoph (1785–1860): 37–8
Dähnhardt, Kapt.-Lt. Harald (1863–1944): 132
"Danger Zone": and naval arms race, 21
Delagoa Bay Crisis (1896): 87–8
Delbrück, Professor Hans (1848–1929): 41, 179
Diederichs, Adm. Otto von (1843–1918): 154–6

Emerson, Ralph Waldo (1803–1882): 206
England: *see* Great Britain
Eulenburg, Count August Ludwig zu (1838–1921): preparation of Wilhelm II's cruises, 54
Eulenburg-Hertefeldt, Count Philipp zu (1847–1921): 89, 92, 115, 196; and Senden, 102, 109; as unofficial govt. spokesman with Wilhelm II, 109
Eyck, Professor Erich (1878–1964): 26

Federalism: importance in German Empire, 33, 46 7, 203; Holstein on dangers of, 47–8; Reich *v.* Prussia, 33, 44, 48, 72, 112, 199; relations of German Princes with Wilhelm II, 93, 109, 117; rights of Bavaria, Saxony and Würtemberg, 32n., 46–7, 47–8, 153; as threat to Centre Party, 46–7, 169, 172, 178–9, 186–7
First World War: 29, 42, 55, 132
Fischel, Kapt. z. S. Max (1850– ?): 39, 122, 132, 134, 137
Flottengesetz: see German Navy Law of 1898
France: Germany policy towards, 75–6, *see also* German Navy, strategy; strength of fleet, 78, 117, 122, 131, 158, 184, 197
Franco-Prussian War: 199
Frankfurt Parliament: and creation of German Navy, 37
Frankfurter Zeitung: 160
Fränkische Morgenzeitung: 141
Freisinnige Zeitung: 133, 146, 158, 185; critical of fixed Navy Law, 142
Friedrich I, Grand Duke of Baden (1856–1907): on problems of federalism, 47; and Tirpitz, 141
Friedrich III, Emperor (1831–1888): 61
Fritzen, Dr. Alois (1840–1916): 172, 190; amendment to Navy Law, 190–2; and naval expansion, 86

Galler (Reichstag Deputy): 193
German Admiralty: dissolution of, 52–3, 62–3; under Caprivi, 39, 67–8; under Stosch, 65, 112–13
German Colonial Society: 159; propaganda for Navy Law, 142–3; and university professors, 41
German Empire of 1871: federal struc ture of, 32, 46, 110, 188–9; foreign policy of, 72, 74–6, 82–4, 154–6, 199, 203–4, 205; and German Navy as symbol of, 28–9, 46, 50, 60, 181; inner weaknesses of, 32, 119–20, 179, 203–5; Ministry of Interior, 90, 181, 183, 198; new leadership of, 199; and Prussian rights in, 33, 44, 48, 72, 112, 199; relations with Great Britain, 82–4, 86–7, 97, 163, 195, 196–7, 201–2, 206; religious tensions in, 153, 167–8, 169, 189; statistics on, 56–7, 156–7; taxation in, 169, 186–8; Treasury's relations with Imperial Naval Office, 126, 139–40, 144, 183, 187–8
German Foreign Policy: *see* German Empire of 1871
German Navy: coaling station in China, 75, 88, 103–4, 154–6, *see also* Kiaochow; constitutional position of, 32, 46, 50, 107–8, 197–9; cost of, 80, 83, 106, 122–3, 128–9, 130, 135, 145, 146–7, 164, 169–70; dissolution of Admiralty, 52–3, 62–3; expansion of, 65, 73–4, 77–82, 83, 84–5, 90, 95, 99–100, 106, 112–13, 116–17, 121–3, 128–9, 131, 135, 145, 146–7, 157–8, 164, 169–70; and free trade, 43; and German nationalism, 28, 31, 37–8, 45, 58–9, 90, 178–9, 181, 203; and German universities, 41–2, 142, 179; inter-departmental rivalries, 53, 55, 63, 69–71, 80–1, 93–4, 107–8, 111–12, 136–8, 205; and international relations, *see* Risk Theory; and *Kultur*, 28, 39, 59, 60, 179–80; liberal origins of, 28, 36, 37–8, 43, 45, 59, 90, 158–9; and middle classes, 28, 36, 39, 59, 202; naval estimates (1895/96), 74, (1896/97), 76–7, (1897/98), 106, 114–15, 130–1, 164; objectives

German Navy—*cont.*
in war and peace, *see* German Navy, Strategy; personnel of, 52, 65, 145, 222–3; and Polish Party, 35; relations with Foreign Ministry, 73; relationship to Reich Chancellor, 50–1, 98; relationship to Reichstag, 34–5, 65; in revolution (1848), 37–8, 45; Richter's criticism of, 45, 67, 80, 113, 142, 168, 194; size of battle fleet, 65, 74, 78–9, 116–17, 121–2, 127, 128, 144, 157–8

German Navy, Admiralty Staff: 40n., 53, 132

German Navy, High Command: coaling station in China, 75, 88, 103–4, 154–6; created (1889), 63–4, 67; Delagoa Bay crisis, 87–9; memoranda (Nov. 28, 1895), 77–81, 85, 117, (May 2, 1897), 120–1, (May 10, 1897), 121–2; opposition to Imperial Naval Office, 50, 69–71, 77, 80–1, 84–5, 93–4, 107–8, 111–12, 115, 136–8; Tirpitz as Chief of Staff, 69, 167

German Navy, Imperial Naval Cabinet: as arbiter in inter-departmental rivalries, 69–71, 94, 103, 107–8, 111–12, 136–7, 205; created (1889), 63; relations with Wilhelm II, 53, 63–4, 103; status and functions, 53–4, 63–4, 204

German Navy, Imperial Naval Office: created (1889), 63; disputes with High Command, 50, 69–71, 77, 84–5, 93–4, 107–8, 111–12, 115, 136–8; employs economic expert, 143; and naval propaganda, 71, 91, 100, 107–8, 131, 133–4, 137–8, 141, 143, 158–9, 174; News Section ("M II", later "N"), 100, 131, 133–4, 143, 158–9, 174; personnel, 132; position of State Secretary, 49, 55, 63, 67; preparation of Navy Law, 122–3, 128–9, *see also* German Navy Law of 1898; responsible for ship building and budget, 67, 147–8; as super-ministry of maritime affairs, 63–4, 90–1; "The Sea Interests of the German Empire", 156–8; under Tirpitz, *see* Tirpitz

German Navy, *Marine Rundschau*: 100

German Navy, *Nauticus*: 143

German Navy, Ships: *Arcona*, 2nd class cruiser, 87; "Baden" class, 122; "Brandenburg" class approved by Reichstag (1889), 67; *Bussard*, 154; *Cormoran*, cruiser 4th class, 154; *Gefion*, cruiser 4th class, 94; *Friedrich Karl*, cruiser 1st class, 53; *Hohenzollern*, royal yacht, 96; *Iltis*, 103–4, 106; *Kaiser*, cruiser 1st class, 87–8; *Kaiserin Augusta*, cruiser 2nd class, 73; *Kondor*, cruiser 3rd class, 87–8; *König Wilhelm*, 65, 118; "Sachsen" class of battleship, 65, 146; *Seeadler*, cruiser 3rd class, 87–8; "Siegfried" class, coastal armoured ships, 81, 122

German Navy, Strategy: concentration in home waters, 21, 66, 81, 83, 120–1, 127, 147; cruisers' usefulness disputed by Tirpitz, 126–7; and design of ships, 100–1, 123, 127–8; general premises, 21, 65–6, 73, 78, 81, 83, 120–1, 127, 147, 184, 202–3; under Caprivi, 66–7; war against France and Russia, 68, 78, 116–17, 120–1; war against Great Britain, 106, 121, 126–7, 184, 201; war against Japan, 155; *see also* Risk Theory

German Navy, Tactics: 62, 121, 127

German Navy Law of 1898: "Begründung zum Gesetzentwurf etc.", 144–146; Bennigsen compromise, 187–8, 192; Bismarck's attitude to, 171–2; in Budget Committee, 175, 182–93; Bülow's comments on, 147, 153–4, 182; Bundesrath's approval of, 159; and Centre Party, 153, 168–70, 171, 178–9, 186–7, 191–2; compromises in govt. on, 161–2; Conservative Party's attitude to, 153, 167, 186, 193; Conservative *Reichspartei's* attitude, 168, 177, 183; directed at Great Britain, 18, 20, 129, 160–1, 164, 190–1, 201–2; duration of, 134–5, 189; early versions, 106, 116–117, 121–3, 125–7, *see also* German Navy, High Command; Memorandum (Nov. 28, 1895); financing of, 146–7, 172, 175–6, 184–8; first reading in Reichstag, 163–72; Fritzen's amendment, 190–2; Hohenlohe's speech on, 164; as *lex imperfecta*, 24, 145, 146, 172; Lieber's amendments, 186–7, 192; Lieber's speeches on, 168–70, 183–4, 194; and Naval

Arms Race, 27–8, 135–6, 169, 180–1, 189, 196–7; opposed by Treasury, 138–40; opposition in Press, 142, 158, 160, 173, 185–6; and Pan-German League, 142–3, 156; passage of, 193–6, 200, 206; Polish Party's attitude to, 167–8; preparation of drafts, 125–7, 134–6, 143–4, 159–60; propaganda campaign for, 143, 158–9, 166, 172–4, 179–80; Prussian Ministry of State's deliberations on, 182, 188–9; Radical People's Party's attitude to, 168; Radical Union's attitude to, 153, 167; reactions in Great Britain to, 162–3, 196–7; real objectives of, 18, 20, 160–1, 164, 190–1, 201–2; and revised naval estimates (1898/99), 130–1; Richter's speeches on, 168, 194; and rights of Reichstag, 142, 145–6, 160, 161, 174–6; Schoenlank's speeches on, 165–6, 193–4; and seizure of Kiaochow, 161; Social Democratic Party's attitude to, 154, 165–6, 170, 193; text of, 144–5; *The Times* on, 143, 196–7; Tirpitz's Memorandum ("General Reflections, etc."), 125–7, 208–23; Tirpitz's speeches on, 164–5, 169–70, 194; Wilhelm II's speech on, 160–1

German Navy Law of 1900: and Risk Theory, 20, 146, 201

German Navy League: predecessors of, 101; and university professors, 41

German Social Reform Party: 177; and Pan-German League, 34

Germany as nation-state: attitude of Pan-German League, 34; and Centre Party, 60, 178–9; and Navy, 28, 31, 59, 90, 203; weaknesses of, 31–3, 44, 203

Gierke, Professor Otto (1841–1921): 41, 179

Goschen, 1st Viscount (George, Joachim Goschen, 1831–1907): 87, 180, 181

Great Britain: 43; German fleet as weapon against, 18–19, 20–2, 27, 29, 126–7, 156; invasion of discussed, 19n.; reactions to Navy Law, 180–1, 196–7; relations with Germany, 72, 75–6, 82–3, 86–7, 104, 163, 196–7, 201–2, 206

Great Britain, Foreign Policy: 75–6, 206

Great Britain, Royal Navy: 38; and battleships, 174–5; "Flying Squadron", 87–8; Naval Defence Act (1889), 156, 158, 175; ships: H.M.S. *Dreadnought*, 61; size of Navy, 131–2; "two-power standard", 180–1, 197

Grenzboten: 173

Grosses Hauptquartier: created (1888), 64

Guild Law (1897): 166

Güssfeldt, Dr. Paul (1840–1920): 41

Gutschmid, Freiherr Felix von: 76

Gwinner, Arthur von (1856–1931): 180

Hahnke, General Wilhelm von (1833–1912): 112

Halle, Dr. Ernst (Levy) von: 143

Hamburg: 41, 141, 173

Hamburg-Amerika Line: 158

Hamburger Nachrichten: 105

Hamilton, Lord George Francis (1845–1927): criticized by Wilhelm II, 61–2

Hammacher, Dr. Friedrich (1824–1904): 172, 183, 187

Handelsneid theory: 43

Hannover Courant: 133

Harden, Maximilian (1861–1927): 97

Harnack, Professor Adolph von (1851–1930): 41

Hassell, Ulrich von (1848– ?): on Tirpitz's character, 150

Hatzfeldt-Wildenburg, Count Paul von (1831–1901): 20, 86, 117, 163

Heeringen, Korv.-Kapt. August von (1855–1919): 133, 141, 142, 158–9; character, 131; and public relations, 58; Tirpitz's opinion of, 132

Heinrich, Prince of Prussia (1862–1929): 117, 125, 181, 196; "Vaterlandslose Gesellen", 118

Herff, Consul General von: on Jameson Raid, 82; support for Boers, 72

Hodenberg, Freiherr von: attack on unitary state, 33

Hoffmann, Vice-Adm.: 39

Hohenlohe-Schillingsfürst, Chlodwig Fürst zu (1819–1901): 47, 92, 97, 105, 118, 136, 140, 141, 143, 144, 148, 155, 176, 197, 198, 204; appointed Reich Chancellor, 72; attitude to Navy Law, 20, 89, 114–16, 117, 182; cabinet changes, 125–6; character, 52, 152; Delagoa Bay crisis, 87–8; defends Hollmann, 51,

Hohenlohe-Schillingsfürst—*cont.*
73, 108–9, 113–14; fears of *coup d'état,* 20, 89, 114–16; and inter-departmental naval disputes, 111–12; and Krüger Telegram, 83; and Law of Association Amendment Bill, 119, 124; on Lieber, 162; opposition to parliamentary government, 52; and Prussian Ministry of State, 198–9; and reform of courts-martial, 76–7, 117, 153; relations with Wilhelm II, 85–6, 89; resignation of, 98, 120; speeches, 113, 164; and Tirpitz, 102–3, 161–2, 165; weakening of authority, 48–9, 86, 98, 102, 112, 119–20, 124, 125–6, 152, 198–9

Hollmann, Adm. Friedrich (1842–1913): 39, 73, 75, 96, 102, 129, 136–7, 160, 165, 166, 191, 194; advocates cruisers instead of battleships, 19, 72, 74, 95, 101; attacked by High Command, 67, 69–71, 73, 93, 107–8; as chairman of committee on naval organization (1888), 63; character of, 86; and Committee for Further Development, etc., 84–5, 94; dismissal of, 108, 111, 115–16; and Krüger Telegram, 83; and Memorandum (Nov. 28, 1895), 81, 84–5; naval estimates (1896/97), 76–7, (1897/98), 106–7; ordered by Wilhelm II to resign, 51, 113–14; relations with Reichstag, 20–1, 74, 94–6, 109, 112–113; and Senden, 69, 90; speech in Budget Committee, 113; and Wilhelm II, 51, 85, 89, 110–11, 113–114

Holstein, Baron Friedrich von (1837–1909): 76, 95, 111, 118; attitude to Senden, 106, 117; attitude to Tirpitz, 116, 151, 199; on Bavarian separatism, 47–8; on coaling station in China, 154–5; and continental alliance against Great Britain, 82; and Delagoa Bay crisis, 88; and Eulenburg, 102, 109; fears of *coup d'état*, 20, 92–3, 102, 109, 117, 118; and High Command's attacks, 73; and Hohenlohe, 89, 98, 109; and Krüger Telegram, 83; opinion of Marschall, 74; submits resignation, 126; and Swaine conversations, 82; on transformation of Social Democratic leaders, 59; on Wilhelm II's agitation for naval expansion, 26, 86, 89

Holtzendorff, Kapt. z. S. Henning von (1853–1919): 154

Hompesch-Rurich, Count Alfred von (1826– ?): 193

Hubatsch, Professor Walther: analysis of Navy Laws, 23; analysis of Risk Theory, 22–3; role of technology in Navy Laws, 24

Hutten-Czapski, Count Bogdan von: on Navy Law, 140

Imperial Dockyards, Kiel and Wilhelmshaven: 41, 183

Imperial Naval Office: *see* German Navy

Ingenohl, Korv.-Kapt. Friedrich (1857–1933): 39, 132

Italy: Navy Law (1877): 156

Jameson, Dr. Leander Starr (1853–1917): raid on Boer Republic, 82–83

Japan: 157; claims to Port Arthur, 75; German attitude towards, 74–5, 155; German intervention in Peace of Shimonoseki, 75–6

Jazdzewski, Dr. Ludwig von (1838– ?): 167

Jesuit Laws: 36, 169

Kaiser, The: *see* Wilhelm II

Kaiser Wilhelm Canal: 78

Kaisherhof Meeting: 173

Kardorff, Wilhelm von (1828–1907): 183, 187

Kautzky, Karl (1854–1938): 58

Kiaochow: background to, 103–4; Bismarck's attitude to, 172; *Iltis* sinks near, 103; loss of, 199; and Navy Law, 161; seizure of, 154–6; Tirpitz opposes seizure of, 154–5

Kiderlen-Wächter, Alfred von (1852–1912): 96, 102, 118; on Wilhelm II's visit to Cowes (1895), 76

Kiel: 40, 68, 81, 109, 117, 181, 183

Klein, Geh.-Adm.-Rath.: 131

Klinckowström, Count Clemens Karl Ludwig Friedrich von (1846–1902): suspicion of Tirpitz's radicalism, 58

Knorr, Adm. Eduard von (1840–1920): 80, 116, 120–1, 149; appointed Chief of High Command, 71; and Delagoa

Bay crisis, 88; and German intervention in Peace of Shimonoseki, 75; and Krüger Telegram, 83; lack of co-operation with Tirpitz, 137–8; opposition to Hollmann, 71, 73, 77, 84, 93, 107–8, 111
Koch, Geh.-Adm.-Rath. Paul: 141
Kölnische Volkszeitung: 104, 133, 160
Kosciol-Koscielski, Joseph Theodor von (1845–1911): 35
Krüger, Paulus (1825–1904): asks for German support, 82
Krüger Telegram: 82–4; effects of, 97, 104
Krupp, Friedrich Alfred (1854–1902): 179
Kultur: as ideology, 38, 39, 44, 59; and naval expansion, 179–80; relationship to German Navy, 28; Tirpitz's understanding of, 38
Kusserow, Heinrich von (1836–1900): 159

Laband, Professor Paul (1838–1918): 41
Lans, Kapt.-Lt. Wilhelm (1861–1947): 94
Lanza di Busca, Count Carlo (1837–1918): 105
Lascelles, Sir Frank Cavendish (1841–1920): 105
Lasker, Eduard (1829–1884): opposes naval construction programme (1872), 65
Law of Association Amendment Bill (1896): 119, 124, 165
Lehr, Dr. A.: 143
Lenz, Professor Max (1850–1932): 41
"Leverage": against Britain, 129; effect on alignment on powers, 21; political control of, 205
Levetzow, Albrecht Erdmann Karl von (1827–1903): 86, 193
Liberalism in Germany: and free-trade, 43; inner divisions of, 44, 172; and origins of Navy, *see* German Navy; and the Revolution (1848), 37–8
Lieber, Dr. Ernst Maria (1838–1902): 113, 171, 172, 178–9, 182, 185, 188; amendment to Navy Law, 186–7, 192; attacked by Schoenlank, 193; attitude to reform of courts-martial, 153; and Hohenlohe, 118, 162; and Hollmann, 95, 112–13; as leader of Centre, 153, 188, 195; speeches on Navy and Navy Law, 92, 168–70, 183–4, 194; and Tirpitz, 162, 170, 185–6, 191, 203; and Wilhelm II, 115
Liebknecht, Wilhelm (1826–1900): 59
Lilienthal, Professor Reinhard von: 41
Limburg-Stirum, Count Friedrich Wilhelm zu (1835–1912): 167, 177
Lindenau, Karl von: 98
Lobanov-Rostovski, Prince Alexei (1824–1896): and German intervention in Peace of Shimonoseki, 75
Low, Sir Sidney James Mark (1857–1932): 26–7
Lucanus, Friedrich Karl Hermann von (1831–1908): 90–1, 111–12, 171
Luitpold, Prince Regent of Bavaria (1821–1912): and Tirpitz, 141

Mahan, Captain Alfred Thayer (1840–1914): *The Influence of Sea Power on History*, 142–3
Malet, Sir Edward Baldwin, 4th Bt. (1837–1908): 72, 76
Marcks, Professor Erich (1861–1938): 41
Marder, Professor A. J.: 131
Margarine Law (1897): 166
Marienfeld, Wolfgang: 41
Marschall von Bieberstein, Freiherr Adolf Hermann (1842–1912): 76, 92, 111, 117; and Boers, 72; and Delagoa Bay crisis, 87–9; and Krüger Telegram, 83; opposition to, 73, 105–6, 118; and Peace of Shimonoseki, 75; relations with Hohenlohe, 89; relations with Reichstag, 74; resignation of, 125, 152
Massmann, Geheimer Hofrath Emil (1861–?): 108
Massow, Albrecht von: 185
Mecklenburg: 159
Michaelis, Ober Lt. z. S. William (1871–?): 39
Middle Classes in Germany: attitude to England, 202; and the Navy, 28, 36, 37, 202
Miquel, Dr. Johannes von (1828–1901): 140; appointed Prussian Minister of Finance, 126; on rights of Reichstag, 175–6; and Tirpitz, 175–6
Moltke (Elder), Field Marshall Count Hellmut von (1800–1891): 110; at

Moltke (Elder)—*cont.*
dinner in Kiel (1891), 68; relation to Schlieffen Plan, 23
Moltke (Younger), Generaloberst Hellmuth Johannes Ludwig von (1848–1916): refusal to call off mobilization (1914), 23
Mommsen, Professor Theodor (1817–1903): 42, 119
Montagu, Rear-Adm. Hon. Victor Alexander (1841–1907): friendship with Wilhelm II, 62
Monts, Admiral Count Alexander von (1832–1889): 63; gains Reichstag approval of "Brandenburg" class, 67
Monts, Count Anton von (1852–1930): 93, 109
Morning Post, The: 181
Müller, Korv.-Kapt. Georg Alexander (1854–1940): 108; family background, 39
Müller, Richard: 189, 192–3
Münchener Allgemeine Zeitung: 141, 159, 179

National Liberal Party: 172, 173, 177, 178, 183; attitude to naval expansion, 35–6, 45, 86, 106, 153; decline in strength, 34, 45–6, 186; opposition to Law of Association Amendment Bill, 119.
National Social Party: aims of, 58
National Socialist (Nazi) Party: 174
National Zeitung: 104
Nationalism in Germany: and Revolution (1848), 37; *see also* Germany as nation-state
Naumann, Friedrich (1860–1919): aims of political activity, 58; imperialism and social reform, 57
Naval Arms Race: accelerated by Navy Law, 134–6, 169–70, 180–1, 189, 196–7; British comment on, 163; calculation of rates of naval expansion, 79, 158, 206; causes of, 26, 27, 28–9, 43; "danger zone", 21–2; effect on balance of power, 17, 21, 180–1, 196–7, 201; effect of Memorandum (Nov. 28, 1895) on, 79; and fixity of German Naval Laws, 23; High Command's analysis of (1895), 77–8; and "leverage" in international relations, 20, 25, 190–1, 205; and Risk Theory, 20, 190–1, 205–6
Naval Defence Act (1889): 158
Neue Zürcher Zeitung: 173–4
Nicholas II, Tsar (1868–1918): 196
Norddeutsche Allgemeine Zeitung: 161; denies existence of News Section, 143; publication of Navy Law, 159–60
North German Lloyd: 158
Nuremberg: 141

Oncken, Professor Hermann (1869–1945): 41

Pan-German League: 34; propaganda for Navy Law, 143, 156
Perels, Geh.-Adm.-Rath. Ferdinand (1836–1903): 131
Plessen, Generaloberst Hans von (1841–1929): 101
Podbielski, General Viktor von (1844–1916): appointed State Sec. of Imperial Post Office, 126
Pohl, Kapt. z. S. Hugo (1855–1916): 39, 132, 144
Polish Party: 170, 193; attitude to Navy Law, 167–8; on Budget Committee, 177; flirtations with Navy, 35; number of deputies (1897), 34
Population of Germany: growth of, 56–8, 157
Posadowsky-Wehner, Count Arthur von (1845–1932): 126, 183, 198
Pretoria: 72, 82
Prussia: 33, 119, 202; and Reich, *see* German Empire of 1871, *and* Germany as nation-state; Social Democracy in, 57
Prussia, Army: as anti-revolutionary force, 91; contrasted with Navy, 36, 39–40; courts-martial reform, 76–7, 97, 98, 117, 153; direct allegiance to King, 49; exclusiveness of officer corps, 39, 40, 76–7; Military Cabinet, 53, 77; relations with Reichstag, 25; suspicion of change, 25, 199
Prussia, House of Lords: 192
Prussia, *Landtag:* 119, 174; conflict with Reich, 72; effect of three-class voting system, 44–5
Prussia, Ministry of State: 118, 126; deliberations on Navy Law, 143–4, 182, 188–9; Tirpitz appointed to, 197–8; transformation of, 198–9

Prussia, Ministry of War: 181, 199; position of Minister, 49

Radical People's Party: 177, 193; attitude to Navy Law, 36, 168; number of deputies (1897), 34; opposition to Navy, 46; and Reich capital tax, 186
Radical Union: 173, 177, 178; attitude to Navy Law, 153, 167; number of deputies (1897), 34
Radolin-Radolinski, Prince Hugo Leszczyc von (1841–1917): 74, 95, 196
Rathenau, Walther (1867–1922): on danger to German unity, 31
Reed, Sir Edward James (1830–1906): opinion of Wilhelm II as naval expert, 62
Reich: *see* German Empire of 1871
Reichsanzeiger (Imperial Gazette): 102, 167, 168
Reichstag: 148, 167, 168, 190; budgetary rights and Navy Law, 142, 145–6, 158–9, 160–1, 165, 174–5, 185; debates Navy Law, 163–72, 193–5; election (1893), 34; and naval estimates (1895/96), 74, (1896/97), 76–7, (1897/98), 106, 114–15, 164; opposition to Law of Association Amendment Bill, 119; opposition to naval expansion, 19, 79, 86, 101, 106, 117, 153–4, 163–4; representative of German society, 25, 34–5, 203; voting on Navy Law, 195–6
Reichstag, Budget Committee: 115, 174; hearings on Navy Law, 182–92; members of, 177–8, 183; and naval estimates (1897/98), 51, 112–14
Re-insurance Treaty (1887): Bismarck's revelations, 105–6
Reventlow, Count Ernst zu (1869–1943): attitude to free trade, 43
Revolution of 1848: and Navy, 37–8, 45
Richards, Admiral Sir Frederick William (1833–1912): 180
Richter, Eugen (1838–1906): 133, 142, 146, 167, 173, 177, 178, 183, 184, 192; fears of "limitless fleet plans", 45, 67, 80, 113; on Hohenlohe's character, 152; opposition to Navy Law, 153, 168, 194; on preponderance of military over civil influence, 98–9
Rickert, Heinrich (1833–1902): 153
Risk Theory: concealed in Navy Law, 20, 129, 146, 164, 201; dangers of, 205–6; as deterrent theory, 20–1, 79, 83–4, 184, 206; and Navy Law (1900), 201; and "leverage" in international relations, 20, 25, 131, 161, 205; roots in German Society, 28; and Tirpitz's Memorandum ("General Reflections etc.", June, 1897), 126.
Ritter, Professor Gerhard: analysis of Tirpitz's character, 24–5
Rollmann, Korv.-Kapt. Max: 94
Roon, Count Albrecht von (1803–79): 116
Royal Prussian War Academy: Wilhelm II's speech to, 73–4
Russia: 141, 197; German strategy against, 120; Re-insurance Treaty with, 105–6; relations with Germany, 75–6, 104, 154–5; strength of fleet, 78, 117, 122, 157–8

St. Blasien: 130, 132, 134, 139, 150
Salisbury, 3rd Marquis (Robert Arthur Talbot Gascoigne Cecil, 1830–1903): 105; disagreement with Wilhelm II (1895), 76; receives letter from Wilhelm II on Royal Navy, 62
Saturday Review, The: 143
Saxony: constitutional position in Empire, 46–7
Saxony, King of: *see* Albrecht
Schaedler, Dr.: 193–4
Schäfer, Professor Dietrich (1845–1929): 41, 179; support for Tirpitz, 42
Scheer, Kapt.-Lt. Reinhard (1863–1928): 39, 132
Schiemann, Professor Theodor (1847–1921): 41
Schlieffen Plan: 22, 23
Schmaedel, von: 179
Schmoller, Professor Gustav (1838–1917): 41, 143, 180; imperialism and social reform, 57
Schoenlank, Bruno (1859–1901): 167; and patriotism, 58; speeches on Navy Law, 165–6, 193–4
Schröder, Korv.-Kapt. Ludwig (1854–1933): 39; invasion plan, 23
Schwäbische Merkur: 141
"Sea Interests of the German Empire": 35–6, 156, 167

Seckendorff, Kapt. z. S. Baron Albert von: 136, 181; criticizes Tirpitz's threat to resign, 191, 204
Senden Bibran, Admiral Gustav Freiherr von (1847–1909): 87, 89, 95, 114, 117, 130, 136, 148, 149, 181, 191; agitation for naval expansion, 20, 99–100, 101–2, 106, 109–10; appointed Chief of Imperial Naval Cabinet (1889), 64; character, 102; demand for coaling station in China, 154–6; and draft of Navy Law, 116–117; hostility to Great Britain, 18–19, 27, 102, 106, 201–3; influence of, 20, 69–71, 111–12, 204; as intermediary between High Command and Wilhelm II, 69–71, 111–12; on Navy's role in society, 90–1; neglects to inform Admiralty Staff about *Friedrich Karl*, 53; opposition to Hollmann, 69, 74, 86, 90, 94, 101, 107–8, 111; and Tirpitz, 69–71, 81, 85–6, 90, 93–4, 96, 150, 167, 204, 205
Shantung: *see* Kiaochow
Shimonoseki, Peace of: 75–6
Sino-Japanese War: 74–5
Social Democratic Party: 34; anti-revolutionary law, 72, 86; attitude to Navy Law, 36, 154, 165–6, 170, 193; growing strength of, 44, 57; transformation of, 58–9; under-represented in Prussia, 57
Sombart, Professor Werner (1863–1941): 41
South Africa: *see* Boer Republic, *and* Krüger Telegram
Spectator, The: 163, 181
Spithead: Naval Review at (1897): 131
Stadelmann, Professor Rudolph (1902–1949): 203
Stock Exchange Law (1897): 166
Stosch, General and Admiral Albrecht von (1818–1896): 69, 92, 95, 157, 194; aggressive attitudes towards Britain, 92; as Chief of Admiralty, 39; naval construction programme (1873), 65, 112–13; opposed by Bismarck, 53, 67; supports tripartite naval organization, 63–4, 67; and Tirpitz, 66, 81–2, 84, 136
Stresemann, Gustav (1878–1929): 204
Stumm-Halberg, Karl Ferdinand Freiherr von (1836–1901): 58, 115
Swaine, Colonel Leopold Victor (1840–1931): conversations with Wilhelm II, 82

Tausch Trial (1897): 119
Thielmann, Max Freiherr von (1846–1929): 126, 139, 140, 176, 183, 187
Times, The: leading articles on German naval expansion, 180–1, 196–7; reports from Berlin, 113, 119, 143
Tirpitz, Rear-Adm. Alfred (ennobled 1900) (1849–1930): 18, 20, 42, 101, 157, 158, 159, 160, 173, 178, 179, 181, 182, 193, 194, 200; as administrator, 64, 130–1; admiration for Treitschke, 41–2; appointed Prussian Minister of State, 197–8; appointed State Secretary, 125–6, 133; attitudes to Great Britain, 27, 92, 104, 132, 146, 163, 201–2; attitude to Social Democracy, 58, 83; and Bismarck, 140–1, 171–2; "Brains Trust", 130–1, 132; at Budget Committee hearings, 183–4; and Bülow, 151; on Caprivi's dismissal, 52–3; and Centre Party, 162, 172, 189–90, 192, 203–4; character, 23–5, 69, 116, 132–3, 149–51, 206; as Chief of Staff to High Command, 69, 167; as Commander of Cruiser Squadron, 96, 103–5; conceals real purpose of Navy Law, *see* German Navy Law of 1898; on dangers of Wilhelm II's powers of command, 50, 116; delays return to Berlin, 116; economic ideas of, 91, 194; family background, 38–9; on functions of Imperial Naval Office, 55, 70; and Grand Duke of Baden, 141; historians on, 23–5, 36, 205–6; and Hohenlohe, 102–3, 124, 161–2, 165; and Hollmann, 69–70, 86, 90, 93, 94, 95–6, 102–3, 104–5, 108, 114–15; and Kiaochow, 103–4, 154–5; and *Kultur*, 38, 42; and "leverage" in international relations, *see* Risk Theory; and the *lex imperfecta, see* German Navy Law of 1898; liberalism of, 38, 58, 91, 190, 204; and Lieber, 162, 170, 185–6, 191, 203; Memoranda: (Jan. 3, 1896), 83, "General Considerations etc." (June 15, 1897), 18, 126–9, 201, 208–23; and Miquel, 140, 175–6; and naval

arms race, 20–1, 79, 126–7, 206; on Naval Cabinet, 53; preparation of Navy Law, 126–30, 143–4; 161–2; out-manoeuvres Treasury, 138–40; and the Press, 123, 133–4, 141–2; relations with Reichstag, 19, 23, 25, 58, 80, 161–2, 165, 168, 183–4, 189–192; representative of new leadership, 23, 199; and Senden, 69–71, 81, 85, 116, 204, 205; speeches in Reichstag, 164–5, 169–70, 171–2, 184–5, 194; statement about in *Reichsanzeiger*, 102–3, 167, 168; and Stosch, 66, 81–2, 84, 136; strategic ideas of, 66, 68, 79, 81, 83, 123; struggle against High Command, 64, 136–8; threatens to resign, 55, 191, 204; and Wilhelm II, 18–19, 50, 53–4, 68, 69, 73–4, 81, 85, 96, 116, 126–9, 136, 138, 140, 148, 196, 197–8, 202

Tirpitz, Friedrich Ludwig Rudolf (1811–1905): 39

Tirpitz, Malwine Eulalia (née Hartmann) (1815–1880): 39

Tirpitz, Marie von (née Lipke) (1860–1948), 150

Torpedo-boats: 128, 147, 211, 219

Transvaal: *see* Boer Republic, *and* Krüger Telegram

Treasury, Imperial Ministry of: *see* German Empire of 1871

Treitschke, Professor Heinrich von (1834–1896): 41–2, 180

Triple Alliance, The: 82

Versailles Treaty (1870): 32–3

Victoria, Queen (1819–1901): 76, 131

Violation of neutrality: Bismarck's attitude to, 23

Virchow, Professor Rudolf (1821–1902): 119

Vollmar, Georg von (1850–1922): 59

Vossische Zeitung: 37, 133

Wagner, Professor Adolf (1835-1917): 179

Waldersee, Field Marshall Count Alfred von (1832–1904): 152, 196

Weber, Professor Max (1864–1920): 41, 57, 179

Weger, Kapt.-Lt. Bruno: 156

Weltpolitik: 28, 29, 141, 172, 199

Wilamowitz-Moellendorff, Professor Ulrich von (1848–1931): 41, 179

Wilhelm I, Emperor (1797–1888): 51, 61, 65, 110, 205

Wilhelm II, Emperor (1859–1941): 62, 143, 148, 167, 171, 196, 205; agitation for naval expansion, 19, 26, 64–5, 72, 73–4, 86, 89, 92, 99–102, 107, 110, 117, 206; appoints Tirpitz Prussian Minister of State, 197–8; as arbiter in naval disputes, 64, 80, 93, 107–8, 111–12, 138; attempts to democratize Prussian Officer Corps, 40; attitude to Great Britain, 22, 61–2, 76, 82, 87, 116, 163, 201–2; and Bismarck, 49, 105–6; and Bülow, 152; and Centre Party, 86, 114, 117–118; character, 26, 61–2, 163, 199; constitutional powers of, *see* Constitution of German Empire; conversations with Swaine, 82; creation of personal *Grosses Hauptquartier*, 64; Delagoa Bay crisis, 87–8; demand for coaling station in China, 154–6; dissolution of Admiralty, 62–3; draft of Navy Law proposed, 116–17; favours cruisers, 73, 74, 85, 96, 101; and Hohenlohe, 73, 86, 89; and Hollmann, 51, 113–14, 115–16; hostility to Marschall, 118; influenced by court entourage, 52, 109, 110–11, 114–15; influenced by Ph. Eulenburg, 109; and Krüger Telegram, 82–3; Mediterranean cruise (1904), 54–5, 96; "personal regime", 26, 110–11, 119–20, 166, 204; powers as supreme commander of armed forces, 49, 51, 62–3, 70, 93, 97–9, 107–8, 112, 197; reform of courts-martial, 76–7, 97; relations with Reichstag, 86, 114–15, 117–18, 165; and Salisbury, 62, 76; and Senden, 53, 102, 117; and Sino-Japanese War, 74–5; and Social Democracy, 59, 72; speeches, 72, 73–4, 86, 110, 160–1; strained relations with German Princes, 93, 109, 117; and Tirpitz, 18–19, 50, 53–4, 68, 69, 73–4, 81, 85, 96, 116, 126–9, 136, 138, 140, 148, 196, 197–8, 202; visit to Cowes, 76; visit to Kiel, 68; visit to Russia, 141; Wiesbaden Conference (1897), 122; *Weltpolitik*, 28, 29, 199

Wilhelmshaven: 40, 111

Woermann, Adolph (1847–1911): 141, 173, 180

Woermann, Professor Karl (1844–1933): 41
Württemberg: constitutional position in Empire of 1871, 46–7, 77
Zedlitz-Trütschler, Count Robert von (1863–?): on isolation of Prussian Officer Corps, 40
Zukunft, Die: 97